BALTIMORE TRAILS

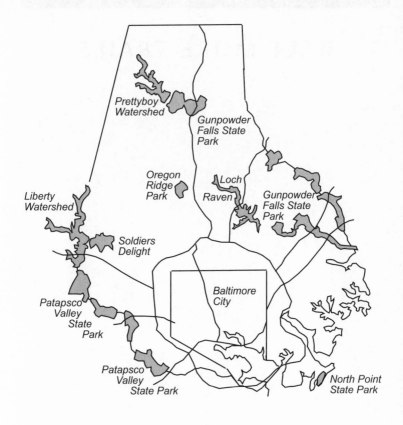

Prettyboy
Watershed

Gunpowder
Falls State
Park

Oregon
Ridge
Park

Loch
Raven

Gunpowder
Falls State
Park

Liberty
Watershed

Soldiers
Delight

Baltimore
City

Patapsco
Valley
State
Park

Patapsco
Valley
State Park

North Point
State Park

BALTIMORE TRAILS

A GUIDE FOR HIKERS AND MOUNTAIN BIKERS

BRYAN MACKAY

with illustrations by Sandra Glover

The Johns Hopkins University Press

Baltimore and London

The Johns Hopkins University Press
2715 North Charles Street
Baltimore, Maryland 21218-4363
www.press.jhu.edu

Library of Congress Cataloging-in-Publication Data
MacKay, Bryan.
  Baltimore trails : a guide for hikers and mountain bikers / Bryan
MacKay ; with illustrations by Sandra Glover.
     p.   cm.
  ISBN 0-8018-6806-8 (pbk. : alk. paper)
  1. Hiking—Maryland—Baltimore Metropolitan Area—
Guidebooks.   2. Trails—Maryland—Baltimore Metropolitan
Area—Guidebooks.   3. Baltimore Metropolitan Area (Md.)—
Guidebooks.   I. Title.
  GV199.42.M32 B344 2002
  917.52′710444—dc21

  2001001336

A catalog record for this book is available from the British Library.

CONTENTS

■■■■■■■■■■■■■■■■■■■■■■■■■■■■■■■■■■■■

MARYLAND STATE PARKS

BALTIMORE COUNTY PARKS

BALTIMORE CITY PARKS

BALTIMORE CITY WATERSHED LANDS

Liberty Watershed 159

Loch Raven Watershed 188

Prettyboy Watershed 227

■ ■

MAPS

MOUNTAIN BIKE TRAILS

On the following trails described in this book mountain biking is permitted by the managing agency. On trails marked with an asterisk, a portion of the trail may be closed to mountain bikes. For more information regarding closed sections, check the trail description or, in the case of the Baltimore City watersheds, the mountain bike maps included with the descriptions.

MARYLAND STATE PARKS

Patapsco Valley State Park

Alberton-Woodstock Trail
All Saints Trail
Buzzards Rock Trail*
Cascade Trail
Daniels Trail*
Morning Choice Trail
Old Track Loop
Ole Ranger Trail

Ridge Trail
Rockburn Branch Trail
Santee Branch Trail
Soapstone Trail
Switchback Trail
Vineyard Spring Trail
Woodstock Seminary Trails

Gunpowder Falls State Park

Barley Pond Loop
Big Gunpowder Trail
Boundary Trail
Little Gunpowder Trail
Little Gunpowder Trail
(Sweet Air area)

Lost Pond Trail
Northern Central
Railroad Trail
Pine Loop
Pleasantville Circuit

North Point State Park

Defenders Trail

BALTIMORE COUNTY PARKS

Trolley Trail / Benjamin Banneker Trail*

BALTIMORE CITY PARKS

Leakin Park

Gwynns Falls Trail

Jones Falls Trail

Lake Roland and Robert E. Lee Memorial Park

BALTIMORE CITY WATERSHED LANDS

Liberty Watershed

Coot Peninsula Trail*
Keysers Run Circuit
Middle Run Trail*
Mineral Hill Trail
Morgan Run Circuit*

Oakland Trail*
Quarry Trail
Wards Chapel / Liberty
  Dam Trail

Loch Raven Watershed

Glen Ellen Trail*
Laurel Woodlands Trail*
Loch Raven Drive

Overshot Run Trail
Warren Point Circuit

Prettyboy Watershed

C.C.C. Trail
Gunpowder Loop*

Laurel Highlands Trail*
Spook Hill Trail*

Trail Notes

PREFACE

Welcome to *Baltimore Trails: A Guide for Hikers and Mountain Bikers*! This book is a detailed guide to hiking trails on public lands in Baltimore County and Baltimore City. It includes descriptions and maps of almost eighty trails. These trails include easy paved roads free of traffic, suitable for toddlers and in-line skaters; wide dirt trails and fire roads that range greatly in hiking difficulty; and narrow, rarely used, and little-known footpaths. Given this variety, there are trails here for hikers of all levels of ability and experience. I am hopeful that even longtime hikers with many miles on their boots will find new destinations.

Although I aimed at comprehensive coverage of local hiking trails, the list of trails is not exhaustively complete. During the fieldwork for this book I explored many obscure footpaths that I have not included. Any trail that crossed private land, where access was or might become an issue, was omitted. Some shorter trails, usually less than one mile in length, were rejected. While walkers interested in a brief stroll might enjoy these trails, they are too short to be destinations for the average hiker out to get some exercise. Note that I have included almost two dozen trails between one and three miles long that might serve the purpose of a hiker with limited time. I have also purposely not included many of the short connector trails found in parks or reserves with a dense network of trails. Such connector trails are often "renegade" paths, created recently merely as a convenience, to get from one point to another. It would be better if these trails were closed, for environmental reasons. Finally, I omitted trails that were so faint that they were difficult or impossible to follow. Some such paths are described in older guidebooks; time has obviously caused such lightly used trails to fade into obscurity.

On the positive side of the trail tally, I have included some trails that, although not in Baltimore County, are within walking distance of its border. For example, trails in Patapsco Valley State Park in Howard and Carroll Counties and trails in Gunpowder Falls State Park in Harford County are described. Similarly, Carroll County trails in the Liberty watershed are reported. To have omitted such contiguous parcels of land and the trails they contain merely because of arbitrary political boundaries would have been foolish.

Each trail begins with a summary of important data. Trail distances were measured using the odometer of my mountain bike, except in state-designated Wildlands where cycling is prohibited. For those trails, mileage was supplied by the managing agency. Hiking difficulty of trails is rated in three categories: easy, moderate, and strenuous. Easy trails are generally level or nearly so. Trails of moderate difficulty typically include some hills but also stretches that are gently rolling or level. Strenuous trails are generally a continual series of hills, some of which might be quite steep. Trail length was not considered in the difficulty rating but will affect how tired you are at the conclusion of the hike. Even if you disagree with my ratings, once you walk several trails, you'll be able to calibrate my ratings to your own standards.

The bulk of the text is a description of the trail. While the trail map alone might allow you to complete a given hike, I hope that the text will clarify any trailside uncertainties. I sometimes refer to trails' being marked with blazes. Blazes are two-inch by six-inch trail markers situated at eye level, often painted on trees. A double blaze indicates a change in direction. I have tried to point out some of the scenic highlights and outstanding features of the local ecology. Here I must confess a prejudice: I am greatly interested in and moderately knowledgeable regarding wildflowers, trees, and birds but sometimes never even notice insects, fungi, and herps (reptiles and amphibians), even when they present themselves boldly. I beg your pardon for these omissions, and I hope to mend my ways in the future.

For the sake of simplicity, directions are given from the Baltimore Beltway, Interstate 695. Armed with a road map, one may approach the trailheads by other routes, of course. Once off highways, I have given mileages, taken from the odometer of my car. Although generally accurate, odometers vary from vehicle to vehicle, so be sure to read the text, so as to recognize the trailhead and nearby parking.

Interspersed among the trail descriptions are boxed short essays on aspects of Baltimore ecology. These provide more information on a topic than might be warranted within the trail descriptions. I hope you enjoy reading them as much as I enjoyed writing them.

Scattered throughout the book are pen-and-ink sketches by Sandy Glover. I have long admired Sandy's work, and when the opportunity arose to assemble this book, I never considered any other artist. I hope you agree with me that her sketches greatly enrich the book.

Each described trail is mapped. Because topographic information is of special importance to hikers, I have laid the trails over 7.5 minute U.S. Geological Survey topographic maps. These "quads" were scanned, then reduced or expanded to fit a standard size and converted to 25 percent gray scale. Trails were added to the map using a graphics program. The trails were sited on the map by dead reckoning while in the field. Although the accuracy of trail locations is not perfect, it is reasonably correct, and sufficient for most hikers. Overview maps of the three watersheds were modified from base maps supplied by the City of Baltimore Department of Public Works.

This book replaces *The Baltimore Trail Book* in the catalogue of the Johns Hopkins University Press. Last revised in 1983, *The Baltimore Trail Book* has been a valued resource for years, but many additional venues for hiking have since become available to the public. I am indebted to the author of the first edition, Suzanne Meyer Mittenthal, and the editor of the second edition, James Poultney, for their pioneering work. I used *The Baltimore Trail Book* to discover trails with which I was unfamiliar, primarily those in the Baltimore City reservoir watersheds. However, I took particular care to avoid reading the trail descriptions, so that I could view every walk with a fresh eye. Observations of the landscape and natural history are entirely my own. I hope that I have retained the factual information contained in those earlier books, while greatly expanding hiking opportunities.

Fieldwork for this book was conducted entirely in 2000. During that year, I walked or biked every mile of trail in this book, and it was great fun. I owe special thanks to Robert J. Brugger, regional books editor at the Johns Hopkins University Press, for asking me to take on this project. His support has been unwavering and enthusiastic, and I am grateful. In the field, Kathy Halle showed me the trails of Loch Raven and accompanied me on almost two dozen explorations by mountain bike. She endured mud, summer heat, innumerable cobwebs, trails that faded into obscurity, and long waits while I took notes, all with cheerfulness and good humor. Other occasional companions included Tom Donohue, Tom and Lisa Gianniccini, Art and Chris Grace, Kate Manrodt, Sarah Ewing, and Michael Beer.

A number of professionals gave me helpful information and advice. Thanks to Gene Scarpulla and Paul Barnes (Baltimore City Department of Public Works), Beth Strommen (Baltimore City Greenways coordinator), Walt Brown and Kim Lloyd (Patapsco Valley State Park), and Rob Marconi (Gunpowder Falls State Park). Tom Rabenhorst of the University of Maryland Baltimore County generously gave me a prepublication copy of his trail map of Patapsco Valley State Park between Elkridge and Ilchester. The use of the facilities of my employer, the Department of Biological Sciences, University of Maryland Baltimore County, are gratefully acknowledged.

Finally, I hope this book will stimulate you to get outside and explore these trails. If we are to create a consensus in our society about how to maintain the quality of living that open space promotes and to preserve the biological diversity associated with these public lands, every citizen must become a more fully invested stakeholder. That means getting out and experiencing our natural environment: walk over the rocky bones of the land, bicycle a recreational trail, slog through a marsh, watch the sunset from a high ridge, canoe a Piedmont river. Feel it, hear it, taste it, know it in your gut and in your heart of hearts. Advocacy requires facts, but advocates need passion.

The good news is that when you get out there, you'll find that all is not gloom and doom. The Baltimore metropolitan area still has many vital, wondrous places for recreation and re-creation. Witness the endless stretch of sea and sky across a Chesapeake marsh, listen for the flute of a wood thrush calling at dusk, taste the sweet tang of a frost-ripened persimmon, feel the tickle of tiny fish nibbling at your toes. These and other such experiences enrich the quality of our lives. They are our heritage, and it is our responsibility to ensure that our children, and their children, inherit a natural Baltimore as rich, as diverse, as resilient, as have we.

BEFORE HEADING OUT

■■■

Preparations for Hiking Trips

Every guidebook contains a litany of dangers that you might encounter on the trail, but even though such perils do exist, the overwhelming majority of outdoor excursions happen safely and without incident. Even so, you should be prepared for any conceivable problem. On a short walk with a group of experienced hikers who are friends, you may be able to get by without much planning and readiness. Anyone leading a group and any adult accompanying children needs to be more organized, however. Here are some suggestions that may help you prepare for a day hike.

Footwear. It's your feet that carry you down the trail and back again, so adequate footwear is a necessity. Athletic shoes or lightweight, low-cut hiking boots are quite suitable for day hikes on the trails in this book. They should fit well, feel comfortable, and be sufficiently broken in. Ankle-high leather hiking boots are not really necessary unless you have weak ankles or you use the boots for backpacking. Canvas or nylon uppers will admit moisture easily in wet conditions unless constructed with a breathable waterproof liner. All-leather or leather reinforced shoes resist abrasion much better than light fabrics. A well-cushioned pair of cotton socks is sufficient for day hiking, although many experienced hikers prefer a very light inner sock that wicks moisture away from the foot and a mid-weight outer sock. In case of blisters, carry some moleskin and waterproof tape in your pack.

Clothing. In cooler weather, dress in layers so that you can thermoregulate. A synthetic jersey that wicks moisture away from the skin is an ideal first layer. Almost any fabric is acceptable for the next layer(s), as long as the outer shell is waterproof. Most hikers prefer rain gear made of a breathable waterproof fabric, although a full set of parka and pants can be quite expensive. A hat helps greatly with warmth; about 40 percent of the body's heat can be lost from the head. All this being said, most hikers overheat, even in winter; take the time to remove layers before you perspire. Sweat-soaked clothing can chill you rapidly at a lunch or rest stop. Correspondingly, put on an extra layer at lunch before you get cold. In hot weather, cotton is the coolest fabric; in extreme heat, a shirt or bandanna soaked in clean water can prevent hyperthermia.

Water. Take adequate water with you on a hike and drink regularly. A four-hour hike, typical of many trails in this book, requires one to two liters (or quarts) of water per person, regardless of air temperature. Never drink from any river, stream, reservoir, or spring; consume only bottled water or tap water brought with you from home.

Food. Bring sufficient food with you on any hike. You won't starve to death on a day hike of less than ten miles, but lunch or a snack will rejuvenate you greatly when you are tired. Bring extra food in case of emergency. When hiking with children, a favorite snack doesn't just recharge their batteries but can act as an incentive to keep going.

First-aid kit. At a minimum, for day hikes, it should contain adhesive bandages in a variety of sizes, a few gauze pads, waterproof tape, a topical antihistamine, a disinfectant, an analgesic, and a first-aid manual. In addition, I recommend including (although many lists and commercial kits omit) several pairs of surgical gloves, a CPR mask, injectible epinephrine (an Epi-pen), a hemostat, forceps, scissors, and a small roll of duct tape. Know the location of the nearest hospital and how to get to it.

Emergency gear. An extra jacket and rain gear are necessities. A reflective survival blanket, a lighter, and a candle will provide a measure of comfort and safety in case of a cool-weather emergency. A multitool implement like a Swiss Army knife is often handy. A whistle, pencil and paper, extra money, a few safety pins, some cord or rope, several plastic trash bags, one or two "energy" bars, and a bandanna may all be useful, and they weigh very little. Consider bringing a cell phone for emergency communications, but be aware of its limitations. For example, no signal is available in some valleys of the Loch Raven watershed, only a few miles from the beltway.

Learn CPR. After learning cardiopulmonary resuscitation, retake the class annually to refresh your skills. Also take a good first-aid class.

Visualize what to do in an emergency. Thinking about how to handle a problem in advance is the best way to ensure that you will react properly and expeditiously if it ever does occur. For example, before you leave on a hike, think over what to do if a person becomes lost or breaks a leg.

Be familiar with your route and surroundings. It is difficult to get seriously lost on any of the hikes in this book, but you might have to hike farther than you expected or be delayed in returning if you lose your way. Review the map and trail descriptions in this book before setting out. A topographic map and a compass can be useful, assuming you know how to use them. And, of course, be sure to bring along this guidebook!

Tell someone where you're going and when you expect to be back. Explain the circumstances under which the person should call the authorities for help if you do not return as expected, and *don't forget* to check in with this person when you return, prior to the time when a search would be begun!

These common-sense suggestions are easy to follow, but few of us actually carry all of the emergency gear described above. Still, ask six friends who spend a lot of time outdoors and you'll find that they have either used or had need of every item on this list at one time or another. So take a few hours on some cold, rainy stay-at-home day to upgrade your first-aid kit and emergency-gear bag, and store both of them permanently in your day pack. You may never need these items, but if by chance you ever do, you'll be grateful beyond all measure that you took the time to be prepared.

■■■■■■■■■■■■■■■■■■■■■■■■■■■■■■■■■■■■■■■

Ethical Behavior on the Trail

Most hikers are aware of their impact on the natural environment, and many are knowledgeable about how to minimize those impacts. Nevertheless, *someone* is responsible for all the trash, the short-cut trails, the damage to flowers and trees. At the risk of being labeled a prig, I offer some suggestions for minimizing your impact on the natural world while you hike.

Stay on established trails. Many of our most heavily used parks have a network of lightly used footpaths that act as short-cuts between popular, well-traveled trails. These renegade trails destroy habitat merely for the convenience of getting the hiker from point A to point B faster. Off-trail travel and walking on rarely used, unofficial footpaths have documented negative biological effects. For example:

▼ Plants are destroyed by continued trampling. For example, the endemic population of fringed gentians at Soldiers Delight has been declining in recent years, largely because the wildflowers have been trampled and the soil compacted. As a result, the trail where these beautiful plants are found has been closed, and now no one can enjoy what many consider Maryland's premier fall wildflower.

▼ The behavior of animals may be affected by cross-country travel and newly created trails. For example, if footpaths into previously unbroken tracts of forest are created, ground- and shrub-nesting songbirds are more likely to be discovered and preyed upon by raccoons, foxes, and feral cats.

▼ Erosion is more likely on trails established by bikers for their convenience than on those sited and designed on suitable soils and topography. While bushwhacking and dispersive hiking are acceptable in true wilderness areas that receive light use, trails in the Baltimore metropolitan area don't fit that category.

Avoid short-cutting trails. Although this common practice may be a subset of the previous problem, it is so widespread and egregious that a separate reminder is in order. Short-cutting is at its most harmful where trails approach one another at different elevations and hikers decide to walk directly downhill to shorten the distance. Clearly, a path running directly downhill becomes a chute where rainwater quickly erodes the soil down to bedrock. Always use switchbacks and the established trails to gain or lose elevation. Use of renegade trails and short-cuts by others can be discouraged by pulling dead woody debris across the trail in a natural-looking manner.

In wet weather, use less vulnerable trails. When trails are likely to be muddy, consider using those trails that are less susceptible to erosion. For example, many of the fire roads on Baltimore City watershed property are underlain by rock and gravel, since they were designed for emergency vehicle access. Paved or gravel paths in state parks make a fine alternative after a rain. Mountain bikers should not ride on trails within forty-eight hours of rainfall; unfortunately, this common rule is widely ignored.

Wade through puddles. Once a mud puddle is established on a trail, don't make the problem worse by creating a new trail to the side in an effort to remain dry-shod. The mud hole will only get wider. I've seen some trail aneurisms thirty feet wide on what was once a narrow footpath. Enterprising mountain bikers, to their credit, have taken to "corduroying" mud wallows by lining them with small logs laid perpendicular to the direction of travel. Unfortunately, horses are afraid of such constructs and can be injured when a hoof slips off. For this reason, trail managers discourage corduroying. The only truly ethical way to deal with a mud puddle is to slog through it!

Don't litter. If you pack it in, pack it out. Chances are that if you have bought this book, you're not the sort of person who litters. If you want to go the extra mile and help make up for all the slobs out there who drop litter on our trails, consider taking along gloves and a trash bag on your walks and fill the bag as you walk. (Use common sense about what you pick up; metropolitan-area parks have been known to contain dangerous debris.) If you find dragging a trash bag several miles through the forest to be extreme, consider doing your trail maintenance in the final quarter-mile of the walk. Most trash is found within a short distance of the trailhead, because most litterers are too lazy to carry even their trash farther than this. Remember, trashy areas tend to get trashier, while clean areas tend to stay clean; so if we keep our trails debris-free, they're more likely to stay that way.

What about biodegradable garbage? While it is true that organic materials, like apple cores, will likely be eaten by animals or broken down by insect or microbial activity, I believe you should pack out orange and banana peels, fruit cores, and pieces of food you do not finish. Trails around Baltimore are heavily used, and what you dispose of today is unsightly garbage to the hiker who comes down the trail tomorrow. Please pack it out.

Answering nature's call. From time to time, we all have to answer nature's call. Make sure you are at least 100 feet from any stream or wetland. Urinate on dry ground away from creeks or drainages. Fecal matter should be disposed of on dry ground as well, in a small trench and covered with several inches of soil. The depth of such a trench depends on the soil composition. The plentiful microbial flora of topsoil helps degrade the waste faster, but a shallow covering layer makes it more likely that an inquisitive animal will dig up the site. In general, dig down about six inches, more if the topsoil is deep, less if it is shallow. Toilet paper may be buried with the fecal matter, although hard-core environmentally conscious hikers insist it should be packed out in a sealed plastic bag. If that's your belief, be my guest. Never burn toilet paper, as the fire may smoulder in the detritus layer of the soil and spread after you leave. After use, cover the waste with all the soil you excavated. A rock placed over the site will discourage digging by animals.

Keep your dog on a leash or leave him or her at home. Rounding a bend in the trail and seeing an unsupervised dog can be disconcerting until the owner comes into view. Of course, *your* dog would never attack anyone, but the oncoming hiker doesn't know you or your dog. Dogs off-leash *will* chase deer and other animals and, when thus distracted, will not respond to your commands; I've seen it happen many times. All dog owners think their dog is different and won't exhibit these behaviors; they are wrong. Please pick up your dog's fecal matter using a sealable plastic bag or bury it as you would human waste.

Give way to horses. Some horses may be skittish and hard to control, and you can do a favor for the rider by stepping off the trail and waiting patiently for the horse to pass. On slopes, choose the downhill side, as it is less threatening to the horse. I recommend that hikers give way to mountain bikers as well. Although mountain bikers are supposed to slow down and warn hikers of their passage, it is simpler for the hiker to merely step aside. Although the great majority of mountain bikers I have encountered while hiking are friendly and courteous, a few are overly self-absorbed; with them, insistence on your right to the trail may be at your peril.

Rules for mountain bikers. If you are exploring these trails by mountain bike, there are a few ethical issues that apply specifically to you. Ride only on trails that are open to mountain biking. In the state parks, most trails are open to bikes. The exceptions are trails in state-designated Wildlands and trails that are so steep and rocky that you'll end up walking anyway. Trails in Baltimore County parks are generally closed to mountain biking. On city watershed lands, only certain fire roads are open for mountain biking. Maps of those trails are included in this book. Don't ride within forty-eight hours of rain. Walk your bike through areas that are rapidly eroding, so as to cause no further damage. Warn hikers of your passage, and slow down as you pass. I recommend dismounting entirely as horses pass. Always wear a helmet.

Don't pick flowers. Leave them for the next person to enjoy. Most wildflowers wither quickly, often within a few minutes, so your pleasure will be short-lived. Some wildflowers are rare, while others set only a few seeds each year. Picking the flowers of such plants may have a serious impact on the population, or may kill the plant. Do not dig up flowers, ferns, grasses, or shrubs for transplantation; it is not only unethical but illegal to do so on public lands. Many woodland wildflowers do not transplant well, requiring specific soil types or unique soil fungi. Pollination of woodland wildflowers may depend on specific forest insects not found in suburban gardens.

Leave room for others to pass you. On busy trails shared by hikers and bicyclists, please walk or ride in file or at most two abreast, so as to permit passing. Cyclists should always call out a warning of their intention prior to passing ("passing on your left" is a commonly accepted notification). Some trails, like the Northern Central Railroad Trail, require use of a bell as a warning.

In summary, ethical behavior on trails is really very simple: merely follow the biblical directive to do unto others as you would have them do unto you. Courtesy and thoughtfulness will go a long way toward minimizing unpleasant interpersonal conflicts on the trail and toward keeping our environment clean and healthy.

MARYLAND

STATE PARKS

PATAPSCO VALLEY STATE PARK

Patapsco Valley State Park is one of Maryland's largest and most heavily used parks. It occupies the floodplain and adjacent hillsides of the Patapsco River, a significant tributary of Chesapeake Bay. The river starts near Mount Airy, Maryland, at Parrs Spring, and flows in a southeasterly direction to tidewater near Elkridge. For much of this distance, the state owns the land bordering the river, although there are many gaps in this public ownership. Patapsco Valley State Park encompasses approximately 15,000 acres.

The park began in 1907 when John Glenn donated 43 acres of land to the state in what is now the Hilton area of the park. It was called the Patapsco State Forest Reserve. The initial goal of this and other state forests was to slow erosion by revegetating land that had long been used for agriculture and timber harvest. However, use as a "public pleasure ground" quickly became established, and Maryland citizens flocked to Patapsco for picnicking, camping, and hiking. Since the park was served by train from Baltimore City, citizens without automobiles could easily spend a day in the country. Thus was born Maryland's first state park.

The Patapsco Valley is a much quieter place now than in that era. It is known locally as the "river of history." In 1762 the Dorsey family established an iron forge at Avalon which produced cannon barrels and nails for the army during the American Revolution. General Rochambeau's army crossed the Patapsco just downstream of Avalon in September 1781, on their march to Yorktown. The first railroad in America passed through the valley, terminating at Ellicott City, and was the site of the famous 1830 race between the steam engine Tom Thumb and a horse-drawn carriage (the horse won!). The Thomas Viaduct, the world's first multiarch stone railroad bridge, spans the Patapsco near Relay. Virtually everyone but the architect thought the bridge would collapse under the weight of the first train; it is still in use today. The world's first commercial telegraph service opened in 1844 along the Baltimore and Ohio Railroad's tracks through the Patapsco Valley. In the second half of the nineteenth century, Patapsco Superlative Patent flour was one of America's leading brands, produced at the large mill at Orange Grove. In 1907, Bloede Dam was constructed, the first hydropower dam to have turbines inside the dam. From 1933 to 1942, a Civilian Conservation Corps camp provided employment for young men during the Depression and built trails and structures that still exist today. A small museum highlighting local history opened at Avalon in 2000.

There are four major developed areas in Patapsco Valley State Park; each contains picnic sites, restrooms, and recreation fields. From southeast to northwest, they are Elkridge to Ilchester (containing the Avalon, Orange Grove, Hilton, and Glen Artney sections), Hollofield, Pickall, and McKeldin. All except Pickall contain fine hiking trails. In addition, there are many good trails traversing the undeveloped sections of Patapsco. Several are described in the following pages.

The Elkridge to Ilchester region, near the original donation of land, has long been the most heavily used portion of Patapsco. Running along both the Baltimore County and the Howard County sides of the river between Elkridge and Ilchester, the area is crisscrossed by dozens of trails. In order to describe these trails in an understandable way, this part of the guide has been divided into sections corresponding to the park's management units Glen Artney, Hilton, Avalon, and Orange Grove. On the ground, however, you'll find that the trails ignore these arbitrary divisions and connect with one another quite seamlessly. The paved Grist Mill Trail / River Road Circuit, which links these four units, is described first. Access to the trails of Glen Artney, Avalon, and Orange Grove is from the park entrance off Route 1 in Halethorpe. An entrance fee is charged. There are parking lots at each of these three areas so that your trail time can be maximized. The Hilton area has separate vehicular access.

Park headquarters are found in the Hollofield section of the park, just off Route 40 in Howard County. For more information about Patapsco, call the park at 410-461-5005.

Directions to Avalon, Orange Grove, and Glen Artney areas:
From the Baltimore Beltway (I-695), take exit 10, Washington Boulevard, south for 2.6 miles. Pass under I-195 and, just before

crossing the Patapsco River, turn right on South Street. The entrance to Patapsco Valley State Park is just beyond on the left. The park entrance road passes a fee station, goes under the historic Thomas Viaduct, and runs about a mile to a T-intersection. To reach Glen Artney, turn right and then left, following the park road to the end at Lost Lake. To reach Avalon, turn left at the T-intersection, cross the bridge over the Patapsco, and turn right into the large parking lot. To reach Orange Grove, pass by the Avalon parking area on River Road and continue upstream for 1.1 miles to the Orange Grove parking lot.

Directions to the Hilton area: From the Baltimore Beltway, take Frederick Road (Route 144) west, through Catonsville for 1.2 miles. Turn left on Rolling Road. After about 100 yards, Rolling Road bears left; stay straight, on Hilton Avenue. Proceed 1.6 miles to the entrance to the Hilton area.

▼ **Grist Mill Trail / River Road Circuit**

Distance: 4.1 miles, with a 0.7-mile (one way) spur
Difficulty: Easy

The Patapsco River flows at a stately pace between Ilchester and tidewater at Elkridge, alternately dancing brightly over short rock gardens and pooling up in long flat stretches. Surrounded by forest climbing steeply more than 100 feet up to ridgetops, this trail is Maryland's Piedmont at its finest. Fortunately for hikers, bicyclists, and families with small children, it is also the most accessible portion of Patapsco Valley State Park. A paved, wheelchair-

wood frog

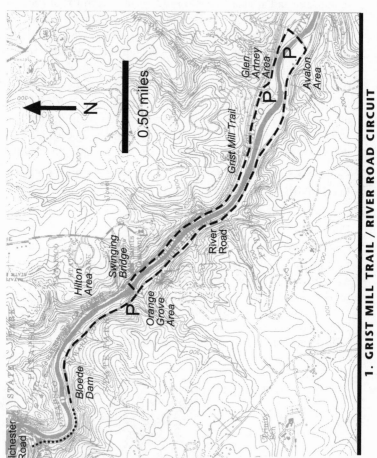

Ilchester Road

Bloede Dam

Hilton Area

Swinging Bridge

Orange Grove Area

River Road

Grist Mill Trail

Glen Artney Area

Avalon Area

N

0.50 miles

1. GRIST MILL TRAIL / RIVER ROAD CIRCUIT

accessible trail runs for over a mile along the Baltimore County side of the river, while a lightly used park road parallels the river on the Howard County side. Together, they constitute a 4.1-mile loop, joined at the upstream end by the Swinging Bridge, popular with generations of Marylanders. In addition, all the upland trails of Glen Artney, Hilton, Orange Grove, and Avalon can be accessed from this circuit.

The Grist Mill Trail begins at the parking lot next to Lost Lake in the Glen Artney section of the park. There is parking and a composting outhouse here; more-modern facilities may be found at the Avalon picnic area. Lost Lake is always worth a glance; Canada geese, mallards, and gulls are usually seen here. Fishing is limited to senior citizens and children. The Grist Mill Trail occupies high ground between the river and the adjacent railroad track, passing under the big trees of this riparian forest. There is good birding here in all seasons, and breeding wood frogs, spring peepers, and American toads can be heard in spring.

After 1.1 miles, the paved portion of the trail ends at the Swinging Bridge. A few old rock walls are visible between the trail and the railroad track here; they are all that is left of the Orange Grove flour mill, which thrived between 1856 and 1905. At one point, this mill was the largest flour mill east of Minnesota, standing six stories high. A dam across the Patapsco here supplied water power to the mill's rollers.

The park has plans to extend the paving of the Grist Mill Trail for about a mile farther upstream, as far as Ilchester Road. Part of this proposed trail will occupy the original 1828 rail bed of the Baltimore and Ohio Railroad, the first segment of track laid in the United States. For the present, however, cross the Patapsco on the Swinging Bridge. This swaying footbridge is the fourth incarnation on this site, previous bridges having been washed away in the floods of 1868, 1933, and 1972.

The Howard County side of this portion of the park is known as Orange Grove, for the osage orange trees planted here by mill workers residing in company housing on this site. Only a few of these trees are left today. Before completing the circuit, hikers may want to turn right and walk upstream on River Road, now closed to vehicular traffic. There are lots of Christmas ferns on this shady, north-facing slope that in winter never sees the sun. A prominent landmark is Bloede Dam, one of the first reinforced concrete dams used for power generation in the United States. Beyond the dam, River Road was completely washed away in Hurricane Agnes in 1972. A rough foottrail extends to Ilchester Road.

From Bloede Dam, return to Orange Grove, where there are bathroom facilities. Even if you aren't prepared for trail hiking, a 250-yard walk up the Cascade Trail is a worthwhile diversion. This trail leads uphill from the Swinging Bridge to a small waterfall in an attractive wooded valley.

To complete the circuit from Orange Grove, proceed downstream on River Road. Although open to vehicles, it is lightly traveled, and even small children on bicycles are safe if supervised. The Avalon picnic area, 1.4 miles from Orange Grove, offers ballfields, a playground, bathrooms, parking, and lots of room for kids to run around. Cross the Patapsco into Baltimore County on the road bridge, and turn left onto the park road that leads to the Glen Artney / Lost Lake area. This circuit, including the trip to Bloede Dam, covers 5.5 miles.

GLEN ARTNEY AREA

This section of the park has a lightly used picnic area, fishing pond (Lost Lake), parking, and a portion of the paved Grist Mill Trail. Backcountry trails include the Soapstone Trail (previously called the Vineland Trail), the Vineyard Spring Trail, and the Santee Branch Trail. Each is described as an entity, but most hikers will wish to complete a circuit that uses more than one of these trails. In addition, there are footpaths in this vicinity that are not described here; once you become familiar with the major trails, you may enjoy exploring these minor ones.

The Glen Artney area has been forested for about a century, so there are many large trees, good displays of wildflowers and ferns, and plenty of birdsong in season. Deeply incised stream valleys insure cool shade even on a hot summer day.

Access to the Glen Artney trail system is described from the parking lot at Lost Lake. Most hikers pay the park entry fee, park at Lost Lake, and hike from there. A great many mountain bikers, however, park at the Southwest Park-n-Ride on South Rolling Road (Route 166); the entrance to the Soapstone Trail is immediately across South Rolling Road. Hikers who use this access

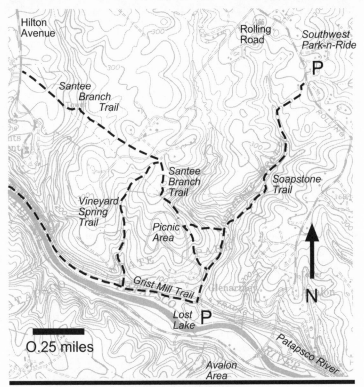

2. GLEN ARTNEY AREA

should be alert for hard-riding mountain bikers, especially on the one steep hill.

▼ Soapstone Trail

Distance: 1.2 miles one way, with a 0.6-mile loop spur
Difficulty: Easy to moderate

Begin your hike from the Lost Lake parking area. Walk through the railroad underpass into the Glen Artney picnic area. At the fork, continue straight, taking the road along Soapstone Branch. After 0.3 miles, the road ends at a picnic area with two shelters and a comfort station. The unpaved portion of the Soapstone Branch Trail begins at the far end of the parking lot and is blazed in purple. Cross the creek on a series of steppingstone rocks and you will enter a ravine. The trail runs alongside Soapstone Branch, crossing it many times on an always muddy course. This narrow, shady valley harbors excellent displays of spring wild-flowers, including spring beauty, bloodroot, windflower, jack-in-the-pulpit, violet, and wild geranium. There is also a wide variety of birds to be heard and seen during spring migration, in late April and early May, including the distinctive Louisiana wa-terthrush. As the trail nears Rolling Road, it rises steeply up the ridge in a curving trough. The gray clay lining this eroded chute makes it slippery when wet, and you need to be especially alert for mountain bikes here. The trail emerges from the forest at Rolling Road after 1.2 miles.

The upper portion of this trail, running through the valley of Soapstone Branch, may well be the most heavily used back-country trail in Maryland. Most mountain bikers that ride in Pa-tapsco access the park by this trail, and it shows. There is heavy erosion on steep slopes and at stream crossings. Hikers should stay alert for the occasional out-of-control novice cyclist, but most riders are friendly and courteous. Interestingly, this trail was little known, very lightly used, and mostly overgrown until the advent of mountain biking in the late 1980s.

A spur trail forms a loop near the picnic area and is useful in accessing other trails in the Glen Artney area. The entrance to this spur trail is behind the comfort station. It leads steeply up-hill on an old gravel road, eventually reaching the paved road. From there, it descends on a narrow footpath to a point near the railroad underpass.

▼ **Santee Branch Trail (Glen Artney section)**

Distance: 1.2 miles one way
Difficulty: Easy to moderate

The Santee Branch Trail, blazed in white, connects the Glen Art-ney picnic area and the Soapstone Branch Trail spur with the Hilton area of the park. It is an upland trail that follows a power line for much of its distance.

This trail begins at the highest point on the paved road through the Glen Artney picnic area, within 100 yards of the pur-ple-blazed Soapstone Branch Trail spur. Passing a small shed and aircraft antenna, the trail rises to the top of a hill decorated with the ruins of an old stone cistern. Proceed down the back side of this hill, through a forest of young red maples, to a major trail intersection; the red-blazed Vineyard Spring Trail terminates here, as does an old gravel road and at least one footpath.

Continue on the Santee Branch Trail by crossing the adjacent Foxhall Farm Road. The trail passes through an old pasture, now grown up in grasses, brush, shrubs, and small trees. Whitetail deer are commonly found here, and birding is frequently rewarding in this early successional habitat. The trail eventually crosses Santee Branch, rises steeply, and continues under the power lines to Hilton Avenue.

▼ Vineyard Spring Trail

Distance: 0.7 miles one way
Difficulty: Moderate

The Vineyard Spring Trail is a scenic and pleasant way to reach the uplands of Glen Artney from the river. It is most often used in conjuction with other trails in the area to form a circuit. From the Lost Lake parking area, walk upstream on the paved Grist Mill Trail, which parallels the river and the railroad tracks. At mile 0.3, turn right and walk through a railroad underpass. Although built to accommodate a stream, there is enough room for a hiker to pass dryshod except after major storms. The trail now rises steadily but never steeply on an eroded path. The forest is a mature one, with big old trees and lots of spring wildflowers. The adjacent stream tumbles over rocks in an enchanting fashion, making this an altogether pleasant place to hike. Eventually, the trail passes through a power line cut and ends at the major trail intersection near Foxhall Farm Road.

HILTON AREA

The Hilton area of Patapsco Valley State Park contains a picnic site, a recently reopened family campground, and the very popular Tire Park, a playground composed of thousands of old automobile tires, both intact and shredded. Hikers, however, will eschew these developed sites for several fine trails. There are five major trails: the Sawmill Branch Trail (red blazed), the Buzzards Rock Trail (yellow blazed), the Forest Glen Trail (blue blazed), the

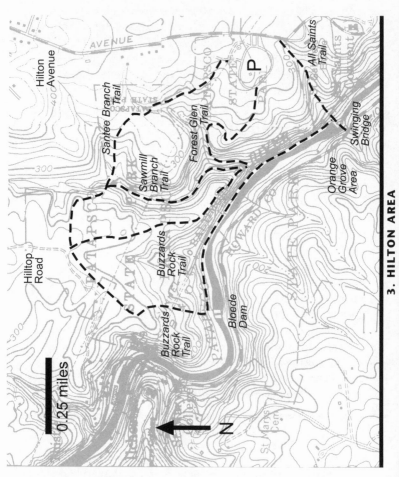

0.25 miles

Hilton Avenue

Hilltop Road

Santee Branch Trail

Sawmill Branch Trail

Forest Glen Trail

Buzzards Rock Trail

Buzzards Rock Trail

Bloede Dam

Orange Grove Area

Swinging Bridge

All Saints Trail

AVENUE

P

N

3. HILTON AREA

Santee Branch Trail (white blazed), and an unnamed, unblazed trail that leads directly downhill from the picnic area to the river at the Swinging Bridge. Most of these trails have very steep sections where mountain biking is prohibited.

▼ **Forest Glen Trail**

Distance: 0.5 miles one way
Difficulty: Moderate

This blue-blazed trail is narrow and rocky, precluding mountain bikes, and is very pretty besides. Begin from the parking area on the south side of the Hilton loop, three-quarters of the way around the one-way road. The trail, rerouted here in 1999, leads along the side of the ridge past the group campsite, eventually reaching Pig Run. The trail becomes steeper and very rocky as it parallels the little creek. In April, look for superb displays of hepatica, spring beauty, windflower, bloodroot, wood anemone, and trout lily here. Pig Run eventually dumps into Sawmill Branch; continue downstream and downhill. The Forest Glen Trail terminates at a tunnel under the railroad track at mile 0.5. From this point, there are four connections to other trails: (1) walk through the tunnel and then turn left to walk along the river, toward the Swinging Bridge and the Grist Mill Trail; (2) walk through the tunnel and then turn right to walk along the

wood anemone

river upstream on the Buzzards Rock Trail; (3) before the tunnel, ascend the steep cliff to the right on the Buzzards Rock Trail; (4) before the tunnel, take the Sawmill Branch Trail by crossing the creek and walking upstream along its western bank. Each of these possibilities is described below.

▼ Sawmill Branch Trail

Distance: 0.9 miles one way
Difficulty: Moderate

This red-blazed footpath is narrow, rocky, and even disappears completely in one place. Mountain bikes are prohibited for much of its short length. From where Sawmill Branch flows under the railroad tracks, walk upstream on the west bank (the Forest Glen Trail occupies the east bank). The trail soon narrows and then seemingly disappears near a small cascade, known to local kids as Pee Wee Falls. The trail is actually in the streambed here, since there is no room for it along the steep streambanks. In a hundred feet or so, the trail becomes evident again, and runs parallel to and above Sawmill Branch. At mile 0.4, the trail bears left, uphill; note the white-blazed Santee Branch Trail entering from the right. The Sawmill Branch Trail ends at the Buzzards Rock Trail, within sight of South Hilltop Road.

▼ Buzzards Rock Trail

Distance: 1.7-mile loop
Difficulty: Moderate to extremely strenuous

The entire yellow-blazed Buzzards Rock Trail traverses a forested landscape, and ranges in difficulty between very easy and extremely strenuous. Mountain bikes are prohibited on the steepest portion, down the side of Buzzards Rock itself. The trail is described as a counterclockwise loop, starting near the railroad tracks.

From the point where Sawmill Branch flows under the railroad tracks and into the Patapsco, climb up to the level of the railbed. Both the Forest Glen Trail and the Sawmill Branch Trail are visible in the valley below. Look west along the railroad tracks; a very steep hillside, virtually a cliff, runs parallel. The Buzzards Rock Trail climbs the side of the cliff and parallel to it.

This is a greatly eroded, mountain goat sort of path that will require use of your hands as it ascends 120 feet in about 50 yards. Birding is often rewarding as you climb the hill, and not just because it gives you an excuse to rest; the steepness of this narrow ridge allows views into the adjacent treetops. At the top of the hill is an overlook with very pretty views up the Patapsco Valley. This is Buzzards Rock, so named for the vultures that once soared on the warm updrafts created by the adjacent cliffs. In the 1990s, most of these vultures moved upriver to the Oella and Ellicott City area.

The Buzzards Rock Trail turns away from the cliffs and runs level on an old road, passing under a set of power lines and eventually reaching South Hilltop Road after 0.7 miles. Note that the red-blazed Sawmill Branch Trail joins from the right in this vicinity. Turn left on South Hilltop Road and follow it to a small parking area. The footpath enters the forest again and begins to lose elevation. It becomes increasingly steep, until it eventually reaches the long-abandoned railbed of the B&O Railroad. This was the location of the first railroad in America, and a few of the original granite crossties are still visible.

Turn left, downstream. The remains of Bloede Dam, one of the first dams in America used to generate electricity, are visible from this point. Until about 1980, adventurous kids were able to climb into the bowels of the dam, wondering when their bodies would be found if the dam chose that exact moment to collapse. Continuing downstream, the Buzzards Rock Trail soon drops onto the narrow floodplain, running between the railroad track and the Patapsco River. The loop is complete when the mouth of Sawmill Branch is reached, after a circuit of 1.7 miles.

■■

▼ Santee Branch Trail (Hilton section)

Distance: 0.6 miles one way
Difficulty: Moderate

This lightly used, white-blazed trail acts primarily as a way to connect the parking lots at the Hilton area with the upland portions of the Sawmill Branch Trail. Since a paved park road runs parallel to the Santee Branch Trail for more than half of its distance, many hikers just use the road.

The Santee Branch Trail originates at the parking lot under

the power lines just off the Hilton loop road. From this lot, walk past the gate that closes access to a paved road. Within 100 feet, turn left onto a wide trail that drops gently downhill. At the bottom, cross Pig Run, a tiny stream in a wetland filled with skunk cabbage. The trail then rises, crosses the park road, and continues through an oak and tulip poplar forest. The Santee Branch Trail eventually descends to Sawmill Branch, where it joins the trail of the same name.

The Santee Branch Trail also runs east from the Hilton area and connects with the Glen Artney trail system. This portion of the footpath begins where the power lines cross Hilton Avenue. Walk east under the power lines; the trail is either directly underneath them or is off to one side but parallel. See the trail description and map in the Glen Artney section of this book for articulation.

■ ■

▼ All Saints Trail

Distance: 0.3 miles one way
Difficulty: Moderate

This unofficial but frequently used trail is the fastest and most direct route from the Hilton area to the Swinging Bridge, the Grist Mill Trail, and the Orange Grove area. It became established in the 1980s, when trees were cleared for a sewer line. To reach this trail, walk downhill on Hilton Avenue from the park gate. Just before reaching the stone pillars at the entrance to All Saints Convent, turn right on the obvious trail. At the bottom of the hill, cross the railroad tracks with care and walk directly downhill to the Swinging Bridge. Turn left on the paved Grist Mill Trail to reach the Glen Artney area of the park, about a one-mile walk, or cross the Swinging Bridge to reach the Orange Grove area and access to the many trails on the Howard County side of the Patapsco River.

AVALON AREA

Perhaps Patapsco's most heavily used section, Avalon occupies the Howard County side of the river, across from Glen Artney. There are two large picnic pavilions here that are frequently filled with merrymakers, but most of these folks rarely venture beyond

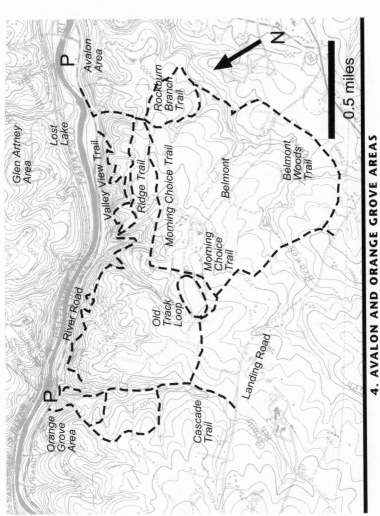

Glen Artney Area

Lost Lake

P

Avalon Area

Valley View Trail

Rockburn Branch Trail

Ridge Trail

Morning Choice Trail

River Road

Belmont

Belmont Woods Trail

P

Orange Grove Area

Old Track Loop

Morning Choice Trail

Cascade Trail

Landing Road

N

0.5 miles

4. AVALON AND ORANGE GROVE AREAS

the surrounding athletic fields. There are also restrooms and a playground at Avalon.

Avalon has more miles of trail than any other portion of Patapsco Valley State Park. Like the Orange Grove and Glen Artney areas, it is heavily used by mountain bikers, so only on weekdays will there be a sense of isolation. Nevertheless, this is a beautiful forest, with large mature trees, lots of wildflowers, frequent sightings of all sorts of animals, and cascading streams. This is the Maryland Piedmont at its best!

There are five named trails in Avalon, and one unnamed but heavily used footpath. The Ridge Trail and the Valley View Trail (orange and white blazed, respectively) were part of the designated trail system on the park's 1984 map. Since then, the Rockburn Branch Trail, the Old Track Loop, and the Morning Choice Trail have all been added to the official map, published in 2001. They are blazed in purple, red, and yellow, respectively. An unofficial trail, which I call the Belmont Woods Trail, is a long-established and well-used unblazed footpath. Since a portion of this trail traverses private property, its use cannot be sanctioned by the Park Service.

Both the Ridge and Morning Choice Trails connect with the Cascade Trail network of the Orange Grove area to the west.

■ ■

▼ Ridge Trail

Distance: 2.2 miles one way
Difficulty: Moderate

The Ridge Trail alternates between stretches of fairly level, wide trail (actually an old road) and very steep sections crosscutting narrow stream valleys. It runs parallel to the Patapsco, but only briefly comes in sight of the river. The trail's hilly nature, coupled with heavy use by horses, hikers, and mountain bikers, has resulted in severe erosion. Automobile-size divots in the trail contain mud in even the driest season, and that has led to widening of the trail, as hikers and cyclists try to avoid getting muddy. Still, for a moderately challenging walk through a beautiful, mature forest, don't miss the Ridge Trail.

Begin your hike from the parking lot at Avalon, where there is always an empty parking space, even when both pavilions are in use. From the gate at the west end of the parking area, walk uphill on River Road for 0.25 miles to the trailhead, marked by a sign and blazed in orange. Continue through a tiny dell heavily shaded by hemlocks to an old, unused road leading steeply uphill alongside a tiny stream. Water bars have been installed to slow erosion, but they have been only partially effective; heavy use and a frequently wet trail have left gullies and exposed rocks strewn randomly about. At the top of the hill, the Ridge Trail turns sharply right. (The Rockburn Branch Trail, described below, can be followed from here by continuing straight.)

Although there are some flat sections over the next mile, the trail also drops steeply into several ravines. These sheltered coves often include large tulip poplar trees mixed among the oaks and beeches, whereas the ridgetops feature black, white, and chestnut oaks almost exclusively. There are fine displays of wildflowers all along the trail in early spring. The trail also passes the ruins of a small picnic shelter and two outhouses, whose presence implies that automobiles used a portion of this trail in the 1940s and early 1950s! The structures and the trail were built by the Civilian Conservation Corps in the 1930s.

Eventually, the previously wide Ridge Trail becomes a narrow footpath, and for the next half-mile there are winter views of both River Road and the Patapsco River. Finally, the trail ascends away from the river, tops out at a small rock outcropping, and merges with the blue-blazed Cascade Trail at a sylvan dell and waterfall. Turn right, downhill, on the Cascade Trail to reach River Road, the Orange Grove parking area, and the Swinging Bridge. You may return to the Avalon parking lot on River Road or by crossing the Swinging Bridge and taking the paved Grist Mill Trail downstream or by any of several backcountry trails; consult the maps.

▼ **Valley View Trail**

Distance: 0.9 miles one way
Difficulty: Moderate

This white-blazed footpath is limited to hikers, because of its narrowness. As its name implies, there are some good views of the river far below, at least in winter. The Valley View Trail runs roughly parallel to the Ridge Trail.

Enter the Valley View Trail from a set of white-blazed

Night Gliders

AN ARMADA OF CLOUDS SWEEPS ACROSS THE FULL MOON, ALTERNATELY lightening and darkening the bare limbs of the November forest. Gone is the springtime cacophony of singing amphibians, and the deafening stridulations of forest insects are now silent, stilled by the recent frost. All is quiet; no breeze stirs the windrows of leaves underfoot. Suddenly, a dark shape glides ghostlike across the footpath, angling downward, and lands with a slap against the silver-gray trunk of a beech. The animal quickly scampers around to the back side of the tree and is gone.

This seldom-seen mammal of our woodlands is the southern flying squirrel, *Glaucomys volans*. Mostly nocturnal, flying squirrels are more common than people realize. The large tracts of forests that constitute our state parks and watershed lands in Baltimore County host flying squirrel populations. Even residential neighborhoods, if they have lots of mature, nut-bearing trees, may harbor this beautiful, fascinating animal.

The southern flying squirrel is smaller than the familiar gray squirrel but larger than a chipmunk. Despite its impressive size when gliding, a flying squirrel weighs only a few ounces. It has silky, grayish fur, except for the underbelly, which is white. Large luminous eyes adapted for vision at night lend it an appeal few other mammals have. The most unusual adaptation of the flying squirrel is the patagium, a loose fold of skin that runs from the foreleg to the hindleg. These act as little parachutes, providing both lift and directional control during gliding. Flying squirrels do not actually fly; they launch themselves from high in a tree and glide downward, steering around obstacles. To land, the squirrel drops its tail and raises its forelimbs, slackening the patagia and flaring out just before arrival. To glide again, it must climb up the tree to a suitable height. Flying squirrels are agile aloft but slow and clumsy on the ground. Owls are common and effective predators of this rodent.

Flying squirrels eat a variety of foods, but nuts are the primary component of their diet. Acorns are usually eaten promptly, but hickory nuts may be cached for winter dining. Fruits, moss, fungi, and insects each compose a minor portion of the diet. Flying squirrels have even been observed eating the eggs and young of forest songbirds.

These animals nest in tree cavities, frequently in holes excavated by woodpeckers. Other cavities serve as feeding stations; flying squirrels can dine in leisurely fashion in these woody chambers, safe from the depredation of owls. Because such cavities are more common in older trees, cavity-nesting squirrels prefer mature stands of hardwoods. In order to supply enough food for these squirrels, forests must be large; a single male requires about three acres of prime forest. Logging therefore affects flying squirrel populations, but the species is not rare or endangered. Housecats and raccoons also take a toll on their number.

Flying squirrels typically breed in late winter. Gestation lasts forty-one days. The young mature quickly and leave the nest by six weeks. They need no instruction in "flying" and quickly become accomplished aerialists. In the wild, these creatures live for five to six years.

Most Marylanders never see a flying squirrel. However, if you live in a neighborhood with many large nut-bearing trees and you feed birds year-round, you may wish to dimly illuminate your bird feeder and observe it well after dark. You may be rewarded with a glimpse of one of our prettiest but least-known mammals. Good luck!

wooden steps on River Road 0.3 miles west of the Avalon gate. After a long uphill, the trail winds along the edge of the upland ridge. The most striking aspect of this walk is the large number of dead oak trees, many of which still remain standing. Most were killed by a heavy infestation of gypsy moths in the late 1980s. Weakened by their ridgetop exposure to wind, and growing in dry, thin soils, these oaks succumbed to insect damage more easily than did those trees in sheltered areas.

After a bit more than a half-mile, the Valley View Trail rejoins the Ridge Trail for about fifty feet before branching off again to the right. After more pleasant walking on a narrow footpath, one reaches the end of the Valley View Trail at the orange-blazed Ridge Trail.

▼ **Rockburn Branch Trail**

Distance: 1.1-mile loop
Difficulty: Easy to moderate

This short circuit trail traverses an upland forest, despite its fluvial name. Only at one point, for perhaps 100 yards, does it reach
the floodplain of beautiful Rockburn Branch. One portion of the
Rockburn Branch Trail is heavily used; it provides a link between
the Ridge Trail and the unofficial Belmont Woods Trail. The remainder of the Rockburn Branch Trail is lightly traveled.

To reach the Rockburn Branch Trail from Avalon, take the
Ridge Trail to the top of the hill. Where the orange-blazed Ridge
Trail bears sharply right, continue straight for about seventy-five
feet to a four-way trail intersection. At this point, the yellow-
blazed Morning Choice Trail is on the right, while the outward
and return portions of the Rockburn Branch Trail are to the left
and straight ahead, respectively. Turn left.

The trail meanders through a forest of large trees that seem
always to host a lot of bird life. Woodpeckers are especially common, as there are many dead standing trees in this woods. Where
these snags have fallen, light reaches the forest floor and viny
tangles flourish, providing food and shelter for cardinals, chickadees, and nuthatches. The trail gradually descends, reaching the
floodplain of Rockburn Branch. Turn right, following the little
creek upstream. Within 100 yards, the Rockburn Branch Trail in-
conspicuously bears right and uphill. Should you miss this turn,
the trail on the floodplain (the Belmont Woods Trail) soon
crosses the creek. This is your clue to retrace your steps to find
the Rockburn Branch Trail junction. Continuing uphill, the
Rockburn Branch Trail again meanders through a sun-dappled
forest, reaching the four-way intersection noted earlier and completing a 1.1-mile loop.

▼ **Morning Choice Trail**

Distance: 1.8 miles one way, with an additional 0.8-mile spur
Difficulty: Moderate

This beautiful trail traverses a diverse upland landscape of forest
and open fields. Whitetail deer abound, and bluebirds are frequently sighted. The Morning Choice Trail generally runs paral-

lel to the Ridge Trail, but it is much more level. It is a favorite among mountain bikers of all abilities.

To reach the Morning Choice Trail from Avalon, take the Ridge Trail to the top of the hill. Where the orange-blazed Ridge Trail bears sharply right, continue straight for about seventy-five feet to a four-way trail intersection. At this point, the yellow-blazed Morning Choice Trail is on the right, while the outward and return portions of the Rockburn Branch Trail are to the left and straight ahead, respectively. Turn right onto the Morning Choice Trail.

This narrow footpath rises gently and then runs level through a maturing forest. At one point, a great many young saplings of the magnolia family have begun to grow, their huge, two-to-three-foot-long leaves lending a tropical feel to the woods. The trail soon emerges into the open fields of the colonial estate known as Belmont, and there are long views across many acres of grassland. The trail runs along the edge of the field, and if you are quiet, you will almost certainly see deer grazing on wildflowers and grasses. Once the trail returns to the forest, bear left at the collapsing remains of an old house (the right fork leads to the Ridge Trail).

The Morning Choice Trail again emerges into a field for a few hundred yards and then enters the forest for good. At mile 0.9, the trail makes a sharp left; the right fork again connects to the Ridge Trail. Another 200 yards of walking brings you to a major trail intersection with the red-blazed Old Track Loop (described below). A few yards to the left of the trail is the iron fence surrounding the cemetery at Belmont. Many of the headstones are so old, dating back to the 1700s, that they can no longer be read.

Continue south on the Morning Choice Trail along the edge of the Belmont property. Much trash has accumulated here over the decades; most of it is slowly being covered by vines and other creeping forms of plant life. The next half-mile of trail is excellent for birding, for it offers a variety of habitats in close proximity. When the trail reaches a T-intersection, bear right. (The left fork is a 0.8 mile spur that eventually reaches Landing Road.)

The Morning Choice Trail now proceeds directly in a westerly direction, crossing the private Norris Lane at mile 1.7. It then drops downhill, joining the Cascade Trail.

▼ Old Track Loop

Distance: 0.5-mile circuit
Difficulty: Easy to moderate

This short, oval circuit was once used as a race track for the horses of the Belmont estate, according to old maps. To the modern hiker, however, it no longer bears any resemblance to a race track. Instead, it seems like any other foottrail in Patapsco, with a number of short elevation changes and a twisty course. It serves primarily as a short cut between two arms of the Morning Choice Trail and is blazed in red.

▼ Belmont Woods Trail

Distance: 1.5 miles one way
Difficulty: Moderate

One of Maryland's largest but least-known eighteenth-century manor houses, Belmont is the heart of an estate that once encompassed much of this part of Howard County. Now greatly reduced in size, the most recent sale of land, in the 1980s, was to the state and became part of Patapsco Valley State Park. Thus, the approximately 80 acres of open fields around the mansion are surounded by public land that is frequently used by hikers, equestrians, and mountain bikers. Belmont is presently owned by the American Chemical Society and is used for retreats and meetings.

An unofficial, unblazed trail encircles Belmont, connecting with the Rockburn Branch Trail at one end and the Morning Choice Trail at the other. Since the trail traverses an upland landscape, there are only minor changes in elevation. Natural seeps make the trail muddy in a few places, but overall, this is easy walking.

To reach the Belmont Woods Trail from Avalon, take the Ridge Trail to the top of the hill and then bear left on the Rockburn Branch Trail. On the floodplain of Rockburn Branch, bear left at the fork, staying low, rather than continuing uphill on the Rockburn Branch Trail. The Belmont Woods Trail soon crosses Rockburn Branch; this is the best clue that you're on the proper trail, since there are no blazes.

This beautiful woodland stream has become wider and more scoured by floodwaters as development has occurred in its headwaters over the past twenty years. Nevertheless, birds like scarlet tanagers, parula warblers, pewees, ovenbirds, wood thrushes, and vireos abound in spring and summer, while the sunny, sheltered winter forest hosts titmice, chickadees, woodpeckers, and nuthatches. Trees arch high overhead, sunlight dappling the water. All in all, this is a most beautiful place.

The trail runs upstream on the eastern bank of Rockburn Branch, on private property. It then turns left, following a side stream uphill to the driveway for the mansion, Belmont Woods Road. The remains of an old trash dump mar this section of trail, but the many spicebush trees alleviate the visual pollution with their lemon-yellow flowers in spring and bright red berries in fall.

The trail continues west on the far side of the Belmont driveway and is again on park property. At one point, the trail crosses a pasture; in spring and fall this is an excellent place to see red-tailed hawks soaring overhead.

Eventually, a four-way trail intersection is reached. To the left, a walk of 100 yards brings you to Landing Road. To continue hiking in Patapsco Valley State Park, turn right at the four-way trail intersection. This is now the other arm of the yellow-blazed Morning Choice Trail, described previously. Another 0.8 miles of mostly level hiking brings you to the general area where the Old Track Loop and the Morning Choice Trail meet. Turn right to take the Morning Choice Trail back to Avalon; bear left to continue to the Cascade Trail system. Consult the map if this description seems confusing; there is a welter of trails in this small piece of park.

ORANGE GROVE AREA

Oranges? Growing in a grove in central Maryland? Well, not really. This section of Patapsco Valley State Park was named for a stand of osage oranges, a small tree with twisted branches. Osage orange trees produce greenish-yellow fruit, known colloquially as "monkey brains" for their odd appearance. The osage orange trees are now mostly gone, as are the mill houses that once stood on the site, replaced by a parking lot. Indeed, the parklike appearance of this area belies its industrial past. The Baltimore County side of the river was the site of a large flour mill until destroyed by fire in 1905.

A system of hiking trails winds up the stream valleys and

across the ridges of the Orange Grove area. Most are blazed in light blue to form the Cascade Trail complex. The orange-blazed Ridge Trail and the yellow-blazed Morning Choice Trail, both described in the Avalon section, enter the Orange Grove area from the east.

▼ Cascade Trail

Distance: 1.1 miles one way, with several spurs
Difficulty: Moderate

Begin your exploration of the Orange Grove area trails from the parking lot at the end of River Road. There is a comfort station and water fountain here, open when the temperature is above freezing. The trailhead is between the parking lot and the comfort station, across from the Swinging Bridge. The trail follows switchbacks up a short but steep hill shaded by hemlock trees and then proceeds straight and mostly flat for 200 yards. There are fine views of Cascade Branch below and excellent displays of spring wildflowers trailside. In April, look for bloodroot, spring beauty, wild ginger, jack-in-the-pulpit, windflower, star chickweed and cranesbill. The trail soon crosses the little stream on a series of steppingstone rocks. There is a beautiful twelve-foot-high waterfall and sylvan pool upstream, and Cascade Branch drops steeply over large boulders downstream. This area may well be the most scenic in Patapsco Valley State Park, and it is heavily visited.

The trail continues upstream in the valley of Cascade Branch, crossing and recrossing the stream. The shady vale is very scenic in all seasons; in winter, ice formations create a fairyland, and the sheltered valley is a haven for winter resident birds. The trail reaches Landing Road after 1.1 miles.

Although the main portion of the Cascade Trail parallels the stream of the same name, there are two other blue-blazed foottrails that branch off to the west. Both ascend minor drainages to a ridge, which trends north toward the Patapsco River. These trails unite and eventually drop steeply off the ridge to River Road just a few hundred yards northwest of the Orange Grove parking area. These side trails, well worth a visit, feature a deep forest with large mature trees, wildflowers, and forest interior–dwelling birds.

Flowering Dogwoods and Anthracnose

FOR THE THIRD TIME IN THE PAST CENTURY, A MICROSCOPIC FUNGUS IS changing the appearance and ecology of our forests. Anthracnose (*Distula destructiva*) was first discovered in 1977 in New York. It spread rapidly, reaching the southern Appalachians only ten years later. It is specific to flowering dogwood, and it kills the tree within a few years of initial infection.

A dogwood infected with anthracnose exhibits drying of the leaves, usually starting at the tips and margins. Lower branches are often infected first. Buds, typically swollen and healthy with life, become withered and release a greyish dust when broken. Infected trees produce fewer fruits. Seedlings and saplings are affected most heavily; mature dogwoods may be able to marshall stored reserves to put into fruits and new leaves for a year or two, but they too eventually succumb.

Anthracnose is Asian in origin and probably arrived in the United States on imported nursery stock. Unfortunately, whatever physical factors (weather, temperature) and biological factors (bacteria, viruses) that keep anthracnose from being a major problem in its native region are not present in North America. Therefore, this fungal pathogen is spreading rapidly on the wind, unconstrained by anything except the availability of host dogwood trees. Like chestnut blight in the 1930s and Dutch elm disease in the 1950s, anthracnose seems poised to dramatically alter the appearance and ecology of the eastern deciduous forest.

Dogwoods, despite their small size, play an important role in forest ecology. They form an understory layer, along with spicebush, cherry, and red maple, of trees ranging in height between ten and thirty feet. This understory intercepts light that filters through gaps in the leaves of large trees like oaks and tulip poplars, further shading the forest floor. Dogwoods grow densely and rapidly in gaps where large trees have fallen, competing for light and resources until dominant species of large, slow-growing trees restore the canopy. The bright-red fruits are an autumn food source for birds and squirrels. Dogwood leaf litter is rich in calcium; the tree thus recycles calcium from deep soil, where it is scavenged by roots, to the topsoil layer, where it is more available to the forest food chain.

Anthracnose is found in Maryland; flowering dogwood

declined by 97 percent in Catoctin Mountain Park in Frederick County between 1984 and 1994. The pace of infection and death seems a bit slower in the Baltimore metropolitan area. May still brings a glorious show of dogwood flowers to the forest, but careful inspection shows many trees to be infected. Even in residential neighborhoods, where dogwoods are commonly planted as ornamentals, trees are slowly dying off.

At present, scientists are very pessimistic regarding the future of dogwoods. There is no treatment and no cure. No naturally resistant trees have been found, and little is known about the molecular biology of disease resistance to fungi. In another generation, dogwoods may be relegated to stories told by oldtimers, a mythical tree of great beauty that once graced the spring landscape.

▼ Millrace Trail

Distance: 3.6-mile circuit
Difficulty: Moderate

Directions: From the Baltimore Beltway, I-695, take exit 14, Edmondson Avenue, west to the end. Turn right on Chalfonte Drive. Go one block and turn left on Rockwell Avenue. Go one block and turn right on Westchester Avenue. Park along the street in this residential neighborhood.

Before the days of electrical grids and high-tension power lines, manufacturing plants relied on water power to make the electricity they needed. And to keep a ready work force in these isolated river valleys, company towns were built surrounding the factory. Workers could rent basic housing inexpensively, and the company store could fill most of their needs. Throughout the nineteenth century and well into the twentieth, the big cotton mill at Oella filled exactly such a role.

Until Hurricane Agnes closed the mill for good in 1972, generations of Oellans lived in frame and stone houses on the steep slopes overlooking the mill. Public water and sewerage were obtained only in the 1980s. Soon thereafter, the quaint houses began to be rehabbed, the mill was made into artists' studios and

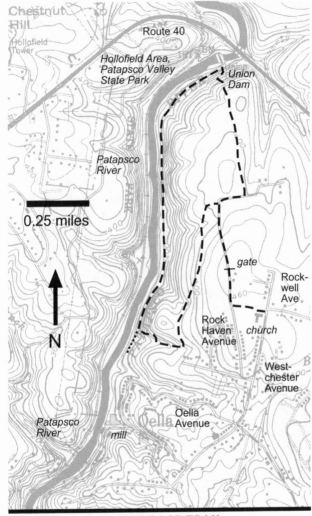

5. MILLRACE TRAIL

galleries, and an upscale lifestyle arrived on the shores of the Patapsco.

The millrace that supplied water for making power at the mill is still mostly intact and is now contained within Patapsco Valley State Park. The narrow path along its bank makes a pleas-

ant walking trail with good views of the river. A lightly used upland trail connects to both ends of the millrace, making an excellent circuit hike on which you are unlikely to see another person.

Begin your hike from the parking lot of Trinity United
Methodist Church at the corner of Rockwell and Westchester
Avenues in Catonsville. Walk through an old baseball field adjacent to the north side of the church and turn right on Rock
Haven Avenue. Although a local landowner has posted this lane,
the land on the west side belongs to Patapsco State Park. Within
200 yards, the paved road reaches a gate. Walk through the gate
onto a long-abandoned gravel road.

This old road runs level through a maturing forest of oaks
and tulip poplars. Whitetail deer are common here, yarding up
during the day before venturing out to eat the shrubbery of
Catonsville homeowners at night. After about a quarter-mile,
look for an obvious side trail bearing left. If you reach houses on
the old road, you've gone too far. This trail passes the remains
of a rusted old jalopy, becomes increasingly narrow, and soon begins to lose elevation. Finally, the trail leads directly downhill in
a very steep, erosion-prone gully; expect to use your hands to get
down.

At the bottom of the hill is the Patapsco River, backed up by
Union Dam. The dam was breached in 1972, and the river flows
around the far side of the dam. For this reason, the headrace is
dewatered, and nothing flows into the millrace on the near side
of the river. Turn left, walking downstream on the narrow path.

The millrace runs for more than a mile. In summer it is
mostly dry, but in winter and spring substantial portions hold
the seasonal rains. Both spring peepers and spotted salamanders
use the millrace to lay eggs, and it is a noisy place on warm
March nights. There are some good views of the river, but it is
mostly shielded by a screen of trees.

Look for a small wooden footbridge over the millrace near
its lower end. If you come to a place where large houses are
visible near the trail, retrace your steps for about 150 yards to the
footbridge. Prior to the late 1990s it was possible to continue past
these houses as far as the mill at Oella, but the millrace is now
posted private property in this area.

Crossing on the wooden footbridge, the trail leads steeply

uphill along a tiny stream. This portion of trail is blazed in turquoise. After 50 yards, the trail crosses the stream and then continues uphill on the opposite bank. Where a row of townhouses can be seen on the right, the trail turns left, crossing the stream and continuing steeply uphill. Once atop the ridge, the trail runs mostly flat for almost a half-mile before dumping out onto the old gravel road near the gate mentioned earlier. Turn right, go past the gate, and return to your car via the baseball field.

▼ Ole Ranger Trail (Hollofield Area)

Distance: 1.8-mile circuit
Difficulty: Easy to moderate

Directions: From the Baltimore Beltway (I-695), take exit 15, Baltimore National Pike (Route 40) west for 3.0 miles to the park entrance.

whitetail deer

The Hollofield area of Patapsco Valley State Park is the site of picnic areas and shelters, a quiet, pleasant, and large public campground, the park headquarters, and a regional communications center, all packed tightly within a few dozen acres, adjacent to a major highway. As one of the oldest units in Maryland's oldest park, Hollofield is a bit frazzled and worn, but it still gives good service. Many people visit this section of the park, but few take advantage of the short and pleasant hiking trail that encircles the northern portion of Hollofield. It is named the Ole Ranger Trail after a park employee who dressed up as and acted the role of a 1750s ranger of the Maryland frontier.

The trailhead for the Ole Ranger Trail is on the park road that connects the fee station with park headquarters. Park in any of the lots near the fee station and walk downhill; you will traverse an underpass below busy Route 40. The trail is about 80 yards ahead on the right, well marked by a sign. The Ole Ranger Trail is blue blazed.

The trail enters a forest dominated by oaks. But what is most striking to the hiker is the complete lack of green vegetation from the forest floor up to a height of five feet or so. Every tree and shrub has been completely denuded of foliage by whitetail deer. Development of open land for housing has been occurring steadily for years along the Route 40 corridor, and each acre of habitat lost forces the resident deer into smaller and smaller tracts. In response to the resultant overbrowsing, the park has set up a special hunting zone adjacent to this trail, but so far the strategy has failed to control the deer population. Meanwhile, the ecological balance of the forest has been greatly affected. In the 1970s, the Ole Ranger Trail had a lush herbaceous flora, featuring many woodland wildflowers. All of that is now gone. Even wood thrushes and ovenbirds, common summer residents of virtually every other forest tract described in this book, are missing from the Ole Ranger Trail, because there is no longer any vegetation to provide cover for these low shrub– and ground-nesters. Whitetail deer are beautiful large mammals with appealing big eyes, but they have become the ecological equivalent of a plague of locusts in suburban forests. (See "The Problem of Whitetail Deer," p. 225.)

When the trail reaches a fork at mile 0.2, bear right. The remainder of this footpath is a circuit, and you will return to this

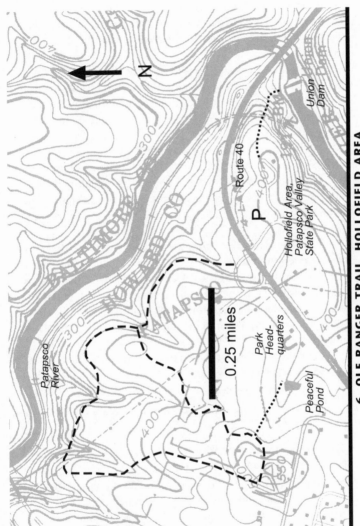

N

Patapsco River

BALTIMORE CO
HOWARD CO

PATAPSCO

400

300

Route 40

P

Hollofield Area, Patapsco Valley State Park

Union Dam

Park Head-quarters

Peaceful Pond

0.25 miles

6. OLE RANGER TRAIL, HOLLOFIELD AREA

point from the other direction. The trail passes underneath two sets of high-tension lines; wildflowers dot these sunny grasslands. A paved road that provides access to an electric substation forms the next quarter-mile of trail and is the most attractive portion of the Ole Ranger Trail. Tulip poplars soar far overhead, giving a cathedral-like appearance; their leaves turn a bright yellow in autumn.

Near the top of the hill, at mile 1.0, the trail turns left, leaving the road, and passes near a transmission tower. This was once the site of a wooden fire tower that was used to scan the surrounding "forest reserve" when the land was more rural than it is now.

From here, the trail angles downhill, and soon comes to a fork. An orange-blazed trail leads to Peaceful Pond within about 300 yards. This small cattail-edged pond in the middle of the forest is worth a visit; it is sometimes haunted by a great blue heron. Return up the orange trail to the trail intersection and rejoin the Ole Ranger Trail.

The trail winds through a transitional landscape that was mostly open twenty years ago. However, ecological succession has filled in the grasslands with shrubs and small trees, and in another twenty years the land will be entirely forested. When the trail reaches the fork mentioned previously, the circuit is complete. Turn right to return to the trailhead after a distance of 1.8 miles.

Peaceful Pond may be visited independently, via a short, 150-yard stroll. To do so, park in the lot at park headquarters; the trailhead is clearly marked.

▼ Daniels Trail

Distance: 2.1-mile circuit with a further 1.7-mile (one way) spur
Difficulty: Easy to moderate

Directions: From the Baltimore Beltway (I-695), take I-70 west. Take exit 85, Route 29, north for a few hundred yards to the end. Turn right onto Rogers Avenue (Route 99). Go 0.7 miles and turn left onto Old Frederick Road. After 0.6 miles, turn left onto Daniels Road. Go to the end, 1.0 miles. Park in the small lot by the water or in a larger lot just around the corner.

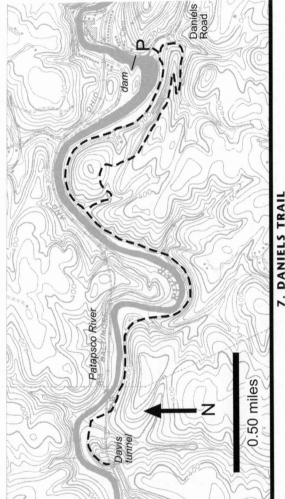

Ridges are special places. Obviously, there are good views into the surrounding valley, and if there is any breeze at all, you will catch it atop a ridge. But ridges are special in ecological terms as well. Rocks and boulders there tend to be exposed rather than buried under soil. Birds like vultures use the updrafts created by ridges to soar, while others, like sharp-shinned hawks and some song-birds, stick to the ridges during migration. The wind prunes tree limbs into odd shapes, and lichens grow richly on bark and rocks. Soils are drier, thinner, and more prone to erosion. The kinds of plants found atop a ridge are often different from those on the surrounding slopes. All in all, there's nothing like a good ridgetop trail for an interesting hike!

The Daniels area of Patapsco Valley State Park features a 1.1-mile ridgetop trail that ends at a level railbed next to the Patapsco River. The railbed then continues for another 1.7 miles upstream. Together, these two segments of the trail are as great a contrast as any you'll encounter on a hike, and make this walk a worthwhile experience.

Families with small children may prefer to do an out-and-back walk along the old railbed, avoiding the rigors of the ridgetop trail.

Daniels is the best site on the west side of Baltimore for flat-water canoeing. The dam backs up a reservoir of almost 2 miles, most of which is shallow and quite intimate. No permits are required and no fees are collected.

The trailhead is just off the small parking lot adjacent to the reservoir backed up by Daniels dam, so park in this little lot if a space is available. If this lot is full, continue 100 yards farther on Daniels Road to a large gravel parking lot near the dam. Before beginning your hike, examine the fish ladder built in the 1990s next to Daniels dam. Coupled with a similar fish ladder around Bloede dam several miles downstream, these structures have opened up much of the Patapsco River basin to anadromous fish. These fish, including shad and herring, return from the ocean to breed in the headwaters of freshwater rivers and have been declining in numbers for decades due to loss of breeding habitat.

Return to the small parking lot beside the river upstream of the dam. Cross the tiny stream and turn left on a gravel driveway. After about 50 yards, turn right on a narrow footpath marked with a white blaze. After another 50 yards up this trail, take a short detour to the Camel's Den. This well-known local landmark is a small cave that intrigues children. Although only a few yards deep, the cave is in a pretty setting next to a cascading stream where there are excellent spring wildflowers and fall color.

Return across the stream adjacent to the Camel's Den and continue uphill on the narrow footpath. At mile 0.3, take the first branch trail on the right, which switchbacks up to the top of the ridge. The next half-mile gives dramatic views of the Patapsco valley and river in winter, but the view is obscured between April and October. Chestnut oak is the dominant tree; look for a thick, deeply ridged bark and leaves with a wavy edge. There are lots of mountain laurels, and blueberry bushes cover the ground.

At mile 0.5, the narrow ridge begins to widen, and signs of a recent forest fire appear. Many of the trees, both upright and down, are charred, and there is little undergrowth. Surprisingly, a number of trees randomly scattered about the site seem to have avoided the fire completely.

The trail soon drops into a shallow valley, or swale, where the richer, moister soil has allowed tulip poplars to replace oaks as the dominant tree species. The trail then continues uphill, encircling a knobby hilltop, and drops down into another valley. At a stream, the trail forks; take the right fork downhill. The footpath reaches the railbed trail at mile 1.1. Turn right to return to your car after a total distance of 2.1 miles, or turn left to continue hiking along the river.

This railbed trail parallels the river and continues for another 1.7 miles to the far end of the Davis Tunnel. Since the path was once the railbed of the Baltimore and Ohio Railroad, it is level and wide, making easy walking or mountain biking. There are good views of the river for the entire length of the railbed. Birding is excellent in this riparian zone, especially during spring migration. Kingfishers, green herons, great blue herons, ducks, and geese are common on the river. In spring, blue-gray gnatcatchers, scarlet tanagers, pewees, and various warblers nest here, while Louisiana waterthrushes and rose-breasted grosbeaks usually pass through.

At the far end of the Davis Tunnel, where the trail once again meets the railroad, turn around and retrace your steps along the river to Daniels. The out-and-back trail on the railbed is 5.4 miles; use of the ridge trail adds another 0.1 miles.

▼ **Alberton-Woodstock Trail**

Distance: 7.0 miles one way
Difficulty: Easy at both ends, moderate in the middle

Directions: From the Baltimore Beltway (I-695), take exit 17, Security Boulevard, west for 0.6 miles. Turn right onto North Rolling Road. Go 0.5 miles and turn left onto Dogwood Road. Follow narrow, winding Dogwood Road for 2.1 miles to its intersection with Johnnycake Road. Cross the tiny bridge; the Alberton parking lot is on the left.

To reach the western terminus of the Alberton-Woodstock Trail, take the Baltimore Beltway to I-70 west. Take exit 85, Route 29, north. Route 29 ends within 200 yards; turn left at the traffic light onto Old Frederick Road (Route 99). Continue west for 3.9 miles and turn right onto Woodstock Road. Go 1.1 miles on Woodstock Road. At the bottom of the hill, just before the railroad tracks, there is a small parking lot opposite a tavern.

Looking for solitude in the Patapsco watershed? A long hike on the Alberton-Woodstock Trail may be just the ticket. Although each end of the trail is level, scenic, and moderately well-traveled, the upland portion that connects the two ends is hilly, far from any trailhead, and lightly visited. Hikers rarely make it as far as the midpoint of the trail, and mountain bikers have not yet discovered it. The trail is used and kept open by local equestrians.

The Alberton-Woodstock Trail is described from east to west, beginning at Alberton Road, the downstream end of this trail. Parking at Alberton is limited to eight vehicles, but there is typically a space available. Walk past the gate along what remains of the old roadbed. Parts of Alberton Road were washed out by Hurricane Agnes in 1972, closing it permanently to public vehicular use. In the first mile, there are pretty views of the river on one side and some large outcrops of rock on the other. This is a good winter walk; the southern exposure and sheltered valley make this as warm a place as you'll find on a sunny winter day.

At mile 1.1, a gravel road leads uphill to the right. Take a detour up this road for a hundred yards or so to visit what remains of the Catholic chapel of St. Stanislaus Kostka. The chapel burned in the 1920s, but the adjacent graveyard remained in use until about 1940. While long gone, St. Stanislaus Kostka is not forgot-

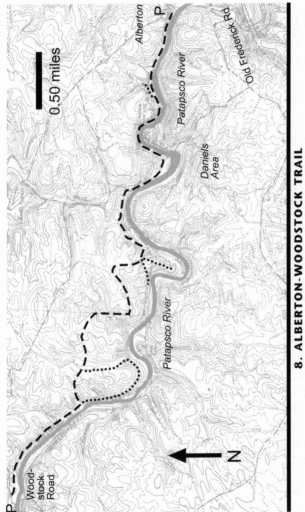

8. ALBERTON-WOODSTOCK TRAIL

ten: an informal shrine has been set up in a corner of the church, with prayer cards and worship books in waterproof bags.

Returning to Alberton Road, continue upstream. The old stone buildings of the C. R. Daniels cotton mill loom over the opposite shore of the river. Although Hurricane Agnes destroyed the mill as a functioning business in 1972, several other small companies have since reoccupied the site. The most obvious one is a mulch operation, whose pleasant fragrance fills the valley.

Over the next half-mile or so, a number of stone foundations are visible. This is all that remains of the once-thriving company town of Alberton. There were over a hundred dwellings here, but all were razed in 1968, unable to meet new federal housing standards. In a sense, abandonment of Alberton was fortuitous; had the town still been occupied in 1972, Hurricane Agnes would doubtless have taken the lives of many residents. Other than foundations, all that remains is the shell of a Pentecostal church built about 1940.

The trail continues on the floodplain past a series of long-abandoned automobiles, now rusting into oblivion, and reaches the mouth of Brice Run at mile 2.0. Cross the railroad tracks and take the foottrail that rises uphill, etched into the rock face. Judging by the exposed bore holes, this narrow bench of a trail was carved out by explosives during the construction of the railroad. There are some pretty views of the river from the top, framed among the branches of several Virginia pines.

The bench reaches level ground at mile 2.7 just as the railroad track enters a tunnel. Instead of following the river, the trail bears sharply right, rising up a hill to a four-way trail intersection. The left fork eventually peters out; proceeding straight will lead you to the river. Instead, turn right, and continue to a gravel road at the top of the hill. If you follow the road left you will reach a power line cut, where there are expansive views of the countryside from this high vista.

Power line cuts like this one are of great interest to naturalists. Utility companies maintain power line cuts as grasslands or shrublands through the use of herbicides or by cutting brush and small trees. In central Maryland, a hardy, handsome grass called broomsedge is frequently found under power lines. There is something inexplicably cheering about these tawny grasses, bright in the thin sun of a cold winter's day. Power line cuts are often frequented by bluebirds, who forage for insects among the grasses.

The gravel road runs downhill following the power line cut, crosses a stream, and rises up a steep slope. Halfway up on the left, a foottrail leads into the woods. Like the remainder of this trail, it bears horseshoe-shaped blazing marked by local equestrians using white paint.

The trail continues over hill and dale in a westerly direction, bordering a large horse farm. Eventually, a badly eroded gravel road crosses the trail. Turn left, downhill, on that road, since further travel straight ahead would lead to private property. Within 200 yards, the trail reaches the banks of the Patapsco again, at mile 5.0. Turn right, upstream, and follow the wide but sometimes muddy path for another 2 miles to the Woodstock Road bridge. This section of trail receives much more traffic and has very pretty views of the river. Once again, because of its southern exposure, snow melts from this trail sooner, so spring wildflowers bloom earlier here. Kingfishers, mallards, wood ducks, and great blue herons are commonly sighted along this portion of the river.

Should you choose to hike this trail in the opposite direction from that described, there is ample parking at Woodstock Road next to the railroad tracks and opposite a run-down tavern.

Families with children will find both ends of this trail eminently suitable for an out-and-back stroll. The Alberton end, in

brook trout

Baltimore Streams: Health and Status

EVERY TRAIL IN THIS BOOK RUNS ACROSS OR NEXT TO ONE OR MORE streams. The sound of running water enlivens and enriches the natural world, and all life depends on this precious liquid. In the late 1990s, the Maryland Department of Natural Resources conducted the Maryland Biological Stream Survey (MBSS), to assess the health of flowing waters in the state. The resulting data set was extensive and informative, and some of the more interesting conclusions are noted below.

For decades, scientists have monitored the chemical composition of streams and rivers, looking for changes in such parameters as dissolved oxygen, acidity, turbidity, and nutrient levels. The MBSS went a step beyond mere chemistry: diversity of aquatic life and habitat quality were also assessed. This ecological appraisal represents a new way to look at water quality, and it gives a more meaningful picture of the health of our waterways.

Two watersheds drain most of the area covered by this book. The Patapsco watershed is 680 square miles in size; 51 percent of its land is urban, 28 percent in agriculture, 17 percent forested, and 4 percent is wetlands. However, all of the more than fifty randomly selected sampling stations happened to be on small creeks upriver of Woodstock, where the landscape is significantly more rural. Most of the streams were rated "good" for overall stream quality; just seven were "fair," and none was found to be "poor." Only 4 percent of stream miles failed to meet the standard for oxygen concentration. On the negative side of the ledger, 68 percent of stream miles had creek bank conditions rated as "poor," and 85 percent of stream miles had elevated nitrogen levels. Since significant development is slated for Carroll County, most measures of future water quality are likely to decline.

The Gunpowder River watershed is smaller, at 478 square miles. It is about one-third forested, one-third agricultural, and one-quarter urban, with the rest in wetlands. Population in the watershed is expected to increase 15 percent by 2020. Once again, the MBSS yielded mixed results. All stream miles met the state standard for oxygen, but none met it for nitrogen. Riparian buffers were mostly in fair condition, but 80 percent of stream bank miles were rated "poor." Native brook trout were "abundant," occupying about 20 percent of basin streams. Brook trout are very sensitive to a variety of factors, including low oxygen, elevated temperature and turbidity, degraded riparian habitat, and competition from non-native fish. Therefore, the presence of brook trout augurs well for overall water quality in the Gunpowder River watershed.

The MBSS provides a snapshot of water quality, biotic diversity, and habitat stature that will be a valuable tool in assessing the impact of development and increasing population growth. As such, it can help us make decisions about the quality of life we aspire to in the Baltimore metropolitan area.

particular, is paved for more than a mile and has both historical and natural features of interest.

WOODSTOCK SEMINARY TRAILS

One hundred years ago, Woodstock College was a Jesuit seminary, a bustling center of intellectual thought and erudite education in a bucolic setting far from any city. The campus spread out over several hundred acres, much of it in farmland to supply the food requirements of the religious community. With time, however, the need for this seminary diminished. Much of the land was sold to the Maryland Department of Natural Resources and incorporated into Patapsco Valley State Park. The central campus remains, now converted into a Job Corps training center.

Evidence of some of the old roads from seminary days is still visible, both in the brick paving underfoot and in the width of the path and evenness of the grade. These old roads form the basis of a little-known and surprisingly extensive trail complex on the western edge of Baltimore County. Equestrians have kept the trails open, and, except on the section of trail along the river, you are far more likely to encounter a horse than a hiker.

Two hikes in the Woodstock portion of Patapsco Valley State Park are described. I have called them the Patapsco River Trail and the Nike Trail. No trails in the Woodstock area are blazed at present.

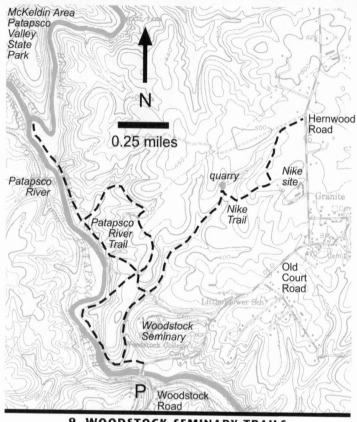

9. WOODSTOCK SEMINARY TRAILS

Directions: From the Baltimore Beltway (I-695), take I-70 west to exit 85, Route 29 north. Route 29 ends within 100 yards; turn left at the traffic light onto Old Frederick Road (Route 99). Continue west for 3.9 miles and turn right onto Woodstock Road. Go 1.1 miles on Woodstock Road. At the bottom of the hill, just before the railroad tracks, there is a small parking lot opposite a tavern.

▼ **Patapsco River Trail**

Distance: 4.1-mile circuit
Difficulty: Easy to moderate

This pleasant walk, a majority of it along the floodplain of the Patapsco River, features large trees and good birding. An upland section adds variety.

Access to the Woodstock trail system is via a gated paved road a few yards past the Woodstock Road bridge, in Baltimore County. The only parking is on the Howard County side of the river, by the railroad track and across the street from a bar. The access road turns to a dirt footpath as it reaches the floodplain. Cross the little creek and take the trail along the river, upstream. The first half-mile is flat and wide, with sandy alluvial soil underfoot. Large riverbottom trees shade the trail, and the occasional rock outcrop lends variety to the scenery.

At a bend in the river, the floodplain disappears as the Patapsco flows against a steep hillside; the trail bears uphill, away from the river. At mile 1.1, a trail intersection is reached; turn left. The footpath descends back to river level, passing through an unusual hemlock-strewn ravine. The trail continues adjacent to the Patapsco until it ends at the confluence of the North and South Branches at mile 2.1. The North Branch of the Patapsco has very little water in it, since Liberty Dam is only a few miles upstream. Nevertheless, you'll have to remove your shoes to keep them dry if you wish to continue upstream. Once across the North Branch, you're in the McKeldin area of Patapsco Valley State Park, described elsewhere in this book.

To continue with this hike, turn around and retrace your steps. Although a low-lying delta at the confluence of the two branches of the Patapsco, this spot has lots of big trees, which have been protected because the dam has prevented flooding. There is also a dense understory of shrubs and saplings. This is excellent habitat for birds, especially in winter, when the presence of water, shelter from the wind, late-day sun, and abundant food resources make it a refuge from the rigors of the cold season.

Shortly before a power line cut, a small stream enters the river and a trail runs beside it. Turn left and follow the creek uphill. After several hundred yards, the trail leaves the stream, bears east, and eventually reaches the power line right-of-way. Turn right under the power line, go about 100 yards, and look for an old road leading off to the left through an open field. As this road enters the forest, its underlayment becomes clear: old bricks with worn, rounded edges appear with frequency, protruding through the soil. The amount of work involved in paving a road with individual bricks is amazing to contemplate, and even more remarkable because this spot is almost a mile from the college center.

The trail soon reaches the intersection described at mile 1.1. Just beyond this point, bear left on a badly eroded, rock-strewn old road that leads downhill to a stream. With the buildings of the college ahead, a fine trail leads both left (upstream) and right (downstream). This intersection is at mile 3.7. The right fork passes an old pond and a trash dump, but the rest of the trail is very pretty, with an abundance of ferns and some good spring wildflowers growing in the shady ravine. At the bottom of the hill, turn left and walk 100 yards to Woodstock Road, completing a 4.1 mile loop.

■ ■

▼ Nike Trail

Distance: 2.2 miles one way
Difficulty: Easy to moderate

No, this is not a corporately sponsored trail, and you won't find the Nike "swoosh" logo instead of standard blazes. The trail is named for its destination, an abandoned Nike missile site off Hernwood Road. During the Cold War of the 1950s and 1960s, a great many missile sites were dispersed across the nation's countryside in obscure locations. Fortunately, those days are gone, and sites like this one are slowly moldering into the landscape, their concrete cracking, vegetation growing up walls and over rooftops. The scenery here is varied, including both maturing forests and abandoned fields.

This 2.2-mile (one way) trail can be be hiked as an out-and-back walk, or a car shuttle could be set. A car shuttle requires at least two vehicles, depending on the number of hikers. Both vehicles are driven to the terminus of the hike, where one is left. In the other, the hikers then drive to the trailhead and park. (Don't forget to take the keys to both with you!)

As you would to use the Patapsco River Trail, described above, park on the Howard County side of the Patapsco River by the railroad track and across the street from a tavern. Cross the river on the road bridge and turn left down a paved access road that turns to a dirt footpath as it reaches the floodplain. Cross the little creek and turn right, uphill, on a badly eroded unpaved road studded with loose, softball-sized rocks. At mile 0.6, there is a four-way trail intersection. To the right, a road leads uphill to the buildings of the seminary, while the path to the left is part of the Patapsco River Trail. Continue straight ahead on the old road that runs parallel to the stream.

This old road rises on an easy grade to an abandoned granite quarry at mile 1.3. The stone that was cut here was hauled down the road and used in the construction of the seminary buildings. This area of Baltimore County has several other quarries (hence the name of the nearby town, Granite), and was a major hub of commerce in the early 1800s. The quarry is no longer in use and is filled with water. This sylvan dell would be idyllic except for the grafitti on the rock walls of the quarry.

At the granite quarry, a narrow foottrail leads eastward, at a right angle to the old road you came in on. After about 200 yards, turn left at the first intersecting footpath you encounter. This hilly trail leads into an open field studded with brushy tangles and groves of small trees. At mile 1.8, the trail arrives at a barbed-wire-topped fence encircling the abandoned Nike missile site. The squat concrete buildings no longer have glass in their windows, and tendrils of Virginia creeper, poison ivy, and wild grape climb the walls in a cellulose embrace. Somehow, the whole place has a 1950-ish feel to it, a relic of our Strangelovean past.

A mowed path runs along the fenceline in either direction. Go right to get to Hernwood Road more quickly; otherwise bear left. When the fence ends, the mowed path continues for a few hundred yards more, emerging on a dirt road. Turn right to reach Hernwood Road and the completion of this walk at mile 2.2. There is space to park one or two cars at this trailhead.

▼ **Switchback Trail (McKeldin Area)**

Distance: 4.0-mile circuit; shorter loops possible
Difficulty: Moderate

Directions: From the Baltimore Beltway (I-695), take I-70 west. Take exit 83, Marriottsville Road, north. Go 4.2 miles to the park entrance on the right.

The McKeldin area of Patapsco Valley State Park occupies the triangle of land between the North and South Branches of the Pa-

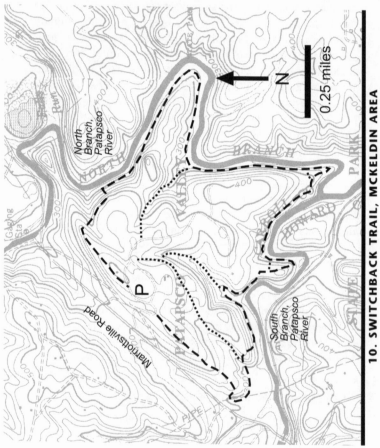

0.25 miles

10. SWITCHBACK TRAIL, McKELDIN AREA

tapsco River. The upland areas have been developed for recreation; there are picnic tables and pavilions, a playground, open fields for games, and modern comfort stations. The valley slopes and the riparian zone along the two rivers, however, remain in their natural forested state and make a beautiful destination for a walk.

There are other official, and some unofficial, trails in the McKeldin area, but the Switchback Trail is the longest, traversing two edges of the park. Any trail that leads uphill off the floodplain will return you to the upland, developed portion of the McKeldin area, should you want to shorten your walk. These other trails have not been described. Mountain bikes are allowed on many of the trails in McKeldin, and cyclists frequently outnumber hikers. All trail users should be courteous and obey park rules.

There are several parking lots at the McKeldin area; the most convenient is located just past the entrance station. While a fee may be charged here on busy weekends, the lot is often unstaffed during the week. A modern comfort station is located adjacent to this parking area, as is a playground for the kids.

Begin your hike by walking past the entrance station to the well-marked trailhead for the Switchback Trail. This sandy path is wide, level, and straight at first, passing through an oak forest with mountain laurels in the understory. The trail soon begins to descend and the path becomes littered with rocks. Most of these rocks are platelike, with two flat parallel surfaces. They are flagstones, a metamorphosed quartzite frequently used for patios and walkways in the Baltimore area. Several active quarries are located less than a half-mile from here, where Marriottsville Road crosses the South Branch of the Patapsco River. About halfway down the hill, a small abandoned flagstone quarry can be seen on the left.

The trail emerges onto the floodplain of the Patapsco at the bottom of the hill. Bear left; the right fork merely leads out to Marriottsville Road. The floodplain is a most interesting place ecologically. The soil is a sandy loam, the alluvium that settles out when major floods cover the area. Large trees are widely scattered, indicating that the last big flood was not strong enough to kill the really mature trees but swept away everything else. These trees are silver maples, box elders, and sycamores, three species characteristic of floodplains. Whitetail deer frequent this area, and a variety of birds can be found here. In particular, look for pileated woodpeckers year round—large birds with red crests and white patches on black wings—and for Baltimore orioles in spring and summer.

Two trails from the uplands join the Switchback Trail, but go right at each intersection to stay in the valley. The trail soon runs along the South Branch of the Patapsco; look for kingfishers, great blue herons, and geese in and over the water year round. Eventually, the trail rises to reach a paved road at mile 1.1. Turn right.

This road takes you past several picnic sites and ends at the largest single rapid on the river, the Falls of the Patapsco. This scenic spot is protected from further erosion by a fence and gabions. The river drops about eight feet over a series of ledges, the water dashing noisily and showing white.

The trail continues downhill, running near the water, and turns left where the river takes a 90° bend. At mile 1.4, the river makes another 90° turn, this one to the right. Bear right, following the river and the white blazes; the trail to the left leads uphill to the recreational areas of the park. The Switchback Trail soon runs over a sloping outcropping of gneiss, a very old metamorphic rock common in the Maryland Piedmont. The rock is scoured smooth by floods, and only a few mosses and grasses cling to life on it, in sheltered crevices. This rock slope can be very slippery in wet weather or in winter when ice covered, so use care.

The trail continues eastward with continuous views of the river, reaching the confluence with the North Branch of the Patapsco at mile 1.7. Follow the North Branch upstream through a forest dominated by large tulip poplars which is especially pretty in October. Once again, avoid any trails that lead uphill; all go to the recreational portions of the park.

After about a mile of level, pleasant walking, the floodplain ends, and the trail is squeezed between the river and the hillside. These slopes are covered with a rich collection of wildflowers in spring and ferns in summer. Very common are the necklace-shaped fronds of maidenhair fern. Although not rare, maidenhair fern rarely grows in the profusion it does here. Other ferns found here include cinnamon, hay-scented, Christmas, sensitive, and New York ferns.

At mile 3.3, no further progress upstream along the river is possible, and the trail goes straight up a very steep, erodable slope. At the top, the Switchback Trail bears right. After running north for a quarter-mile, the path arrives at a paved road lined with picnic tables and pavilions. Continue straight up this road, which returns you to your car at mile 4.0.

SOLDIERS DELIGHT NATURAL ENVIRONMENT AREA

Soldiers Delight is by far the most unusual landscape in the Baltimore metropolitan area. It is a serpentine barren: "serpentine" not because of its shape but for the unusual mineral, serpentinite, that is found in the underlying rock; "barren" for the open, sparsely vegetated nature of the countryside. Comprising about 2,000 acres in western Baltimore County, Soldiers Delight is owned by the state and managed by the Department of Natural Resources as a Natural Environment Area. As such, it contains no picnic shelters, playgrounds, ball fields, or other amenities typically found in state parks, and human activity is closely regulated. And with good reason: Soldiers Delight harbors at least thirty-nine species that are rare, threatened, or endangered. Among botanists, Soldiers Delight is well known as having some of the most interesting flora on the East Coast, but among Baltimoreans it remains surprisingly unknown.

There are 6.0 miles of hiking trails at Soldiers Delight. Mountain bikes and horses are prohibited on these trails, because their impact on the fragile vegetation would be too great. In addition, the very popular trail along Chimney Branch was closed to all use, including hiking, in 2000. Soldiers Delight's best-known wildflower, the fringed gentian, blossoms each October along Chimney Branch, but the number of plants present each year declined in the late 1990s. In addition, those plants that were present were often trampled. Please help conserve this fragile and beautiful species by staying away from the trail along Chimney Branch.

There are four hiking trails at Soldiers Delight. The red, orange, and yellow trails all share mileage on the east side of Deer Park Road and are in the Red Run watershed, a tributary of the Gwynns Falls. The Serpentine Trail, on the west side of Deer Park Road, is in the Chimney Branch watershed, a tributary of the Patapsco River. Access to all the trails is from either the Soldiers Delight Visitor Center parking lot (open 8 a.m. to dusk) or from the Overlook parking area on Deer Park Road.

For more information, contact Soldiers Delight Natural Environment Area, 410-922-3044.

Directions: From the Baltimore Beltway (I-695), take exit 18, Liberty Road (Route 26) west. Go 4.9 miles. Turn right on Deer Park Road. Go 2.1 miles and turn left into the driveway for the well-marked Visitor Center. The Overlook is another 0.2 miles north on Deer Park Road and is also clearly marked.

■ ■

▼ East Side Trails

Distance: 2.9-mile circuit; shorter loops possible
Difficulty: Easy to moderate

Trails on the east side of Deer Park Road are blazed with three colors: red, orange, and yellow. However, these are not three distinct trails, but actually overlap. The shortest circuit, 1.4 miles, is blazed in red. A longer circuit, 2.0 miles, picks up at the end of the red trail and is marked with orange blazes. Finally, an extension of the orange trail is blazed in yellow (2.9 miles). If all this seems confusing, consult the map.

Begin your walk from the Overlook parking lot on Deer Park Road. There is usually ample parking available here, and there is overflow parking on the opposite side of the road. There are excellent views of the rolling Piedmont countryside to the west from the Overlook, and this may be the best place in Baltimore to watch the sun set at day's end. From the Overlook, cross Deer Park Road with care and walk north along the road shoulder for about 100 yards. The trailhead is marked with red blazes and leads directly into the pine forest.

Virtually all the pines at Soldiers Delight are Virginia pines (also known as scrub pines) and are less than thirty feet tall. They are limited in growth by the thin, dry soils, which are poor in several essential nutrients, especially nitrogen. The soils here are usually only a few inches thick, and may even be nonexistent in some places. Other plants that grow in the forest at Soldiers Delight are also adapted to dry conditions. These include post oaks, blackjack oaks, greenbrier, blueberries, and several kinds of mosses and lichens.

At mile 0.35, the trail emerges from the forest into a savanna, where clumps of trees are randomly scattered about a

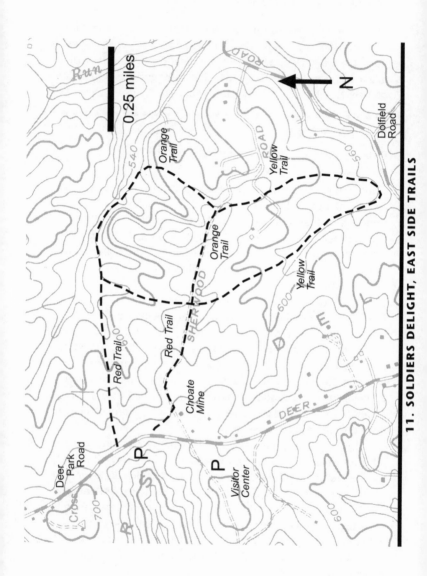

11. SOLDIERS DELIGHT, EAST SIDE TRAILS

grassland. Many of the trees here have recently been removed, in a long-term project to restore the serpentine grasslands. Photographs from the 1930s show that much of Soldiers Delight was once open areas dominated by grasses; scrub pines invaded the grasslands only in the past century. Since most of the rare plant species at Soldiers Delight are associated with open grasslands, it is important to remove the invasive pines. Soldiers Delight may be Maryland's most ambitious project in ecosystem restoration.

The first trail intersection is encountered at mile 0.7. The red trail bears right, returning to Deer Park Road after 1.4 miles. For a longer walk through more diverse scenery, continue straight ahead on the trail, now blazed in orange. The trail soon reaches a small branch of the headwaters of Red Run. Soils are richer here, along the creek, and there is a lush growth of ferns and wildflowers. Shrubs and small trees include mountain laurel, dogwood, sassafrass, and red maple. This is one of Soldiers Delight's most enchanting spots, especially in autumn or early on a dewy summer morning with the sun's rays slanting through the rising mist.

The trail soon leaves the floodplain of Red Run, rising through an oak forest. Houses become visible to the left, as the trail runs very near and parallel to the park boundary. At mile 1.3 the trail turns right, away from the nearby townhouses. This orange-blazed trail returns directly to Deer Park Road after a total distance of 2.0 miles. To continue hiking farther, however, look to the left for a yellow-blazed trail originating from the orange trail within sight of the townhouses.

This yellow trail proceeds through an abandoned orchard and then a field of thick grasses, goldenrod, and other wildflowers. It crosses Sherwood Road and then enters an oak forest. At mile 1.8, within earshot of Dolfield Road, the trail turns very sharply right and proceeds through a typical Soldiers Delight landscape of scattered grasslands, greenbrier thickets, and glades of scrub pine. At mile 2.5, a major trail intersection is reached.

At this intersection, the orange-blazed trail comes in from the right and the red-blazed trail comes in from directly ahead. Turn left to return to Deer Park Road; the trail is now blazed in red.

At mile 2.8, look for the Choate chromium mine on the left, surrounded by a fence. This is the best-preserved of many mines at Soldiers Delight (but is still very unsafe to enter). In the early

1800s, the serpentine rock of Soldiers Delight was mined, taken to Baltimore by wagon, and smelted to extract chromium. Isaac Tyson, the well-known Baltimore merchant, made a fortune off Soldiers Delight chromium, until richer deposits were discovered elsewhere in the mid-to-late 1800s. The Choate mine was briefly reopened during World War I, when foreign supplies of chromium were interrupted. The chromium mined at Soldiers Delight was used in paints and in the manufacture of steel.

The trail continues, arriving at Deer Park Road opposite the Overlook parking area after a total distance of 2.9 miles.

■ ■

▼ Serpentine Trail

Distance: 2.2-mile circuit
Difficulty: Moderate

The Serpentine Trail is the only footpath on the west side of Soldiers Delight. It traverses a fascinating and diverse landscape, with wide vistas of tawny grasses waving in the breeze. The scenery is reminiscent of the prairies of the midwestern United States; nothing else quite like it can be found in Maryland. The Serpentine Trail is blazed in white and is 2.2 miles long.

Begin your walk from the Visitor Center off Deer Park Road. The parking lot here is open daily 8 a.m. to dusk. If the Visitor Center is open, it is well worth a visit. In addition to water and bathrooms, there is an interesting collection of historical artifacts from the days when Soldiers Delight was mined. Other displays interpret the natural history of the serpentine barrens and explain the techniques used to manage the landscape.

Although the circuit can be hiked in either direction, it is described below in a clockwise loop. On the north side of the parking lot, turn left onto an old unpaved road. Walk about 100 yards to an old stone cabin set in a grassy area. This is Red Dog Lodge, built early in the twentieth century for use as a hunting lodge.

The area around Red Dog Lodge is dominated by large, mature oak trees. The understory has a lot of spicebush but has been heavily browsed by whitetail deer. Deer use park land, where hunting is prohibited, as a refuge during the day, fanning out onto surrounding farms and gardens to feed at night.

The trail leads downhill from the front lawn of Red Dog Lodge, emerging under a set of high-tension lines. There are ex-

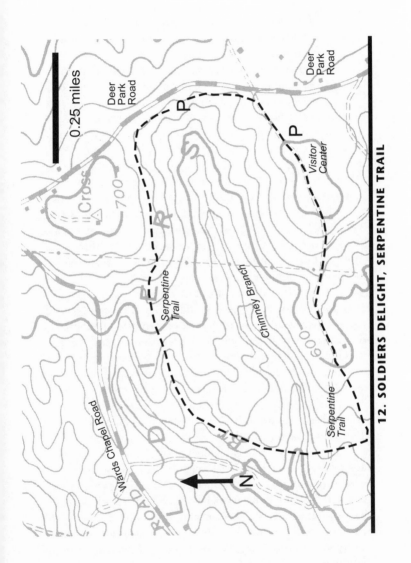

12. SOLDIERS DELIGHT, SERPENTINE TRAIL

0.25 miles

Deer Park Road

Cross

700

P

P

Visitor Center

Deer Park Road

Serpentine Trail

Chimney Branch

600

Serpentine Trail

Wards Chapel Road

ROAD

N

pansive views from here, both along the length of the power lines and over the trees to the west. Virtually all of the trees are Virginia pines, an invasive species that can grow in poor, rocky soils. Over the past sixty years, they have colonized much of the acreage at Soldiers Delight, land that previously was a sparsely vegetated landscape of grassland and barren rock.

After about a hundred yards, an experimental management plot appears on the right. In 2000, the pines here were girdled so as to kill them; they will be removed later. The forest floor was then burned, a process that recycles nutrients back into the soil, kills off some kinds of fire-sensitive vegetation, and opens up the soil for species that cannot otherwise compete or that may actually require fire to grow. Unfortunately, the fire was not hot enough to kill the greenbrier that choked the forest floor previously; it grew back vigorously within a few months after burning.

The trail continues downhill along the edge of state-owned land, passing a fenced grassland where horses sometimes graze. At mile 0.7, the trail turns sharply right. Of the three small streams the trail crosses, the second is Chimney Branch, the tributary that drains much of Soldiers Delight west of Deer Park Road. The shallow riffles of this tiny creek are habitat for many tiny aquatic insect larvae. The undersides of saucer-size rocks often reveal caddisfly larvae houses constructed of either large sand grains or woody debris. These houses protect the fragile insect larvae, which strain the passing water for algae and detritus. Other common insect larvae frequently seen include those of mayflies, craneflies, and dragonflies. Water striders skim across the surface of calm pools, looking for prey. Deeper pools often hold some very small fish. There's a surprising amount of life in these tiny, shallow streams!

The trail now rises gradually uphill and to the right, passing through a long stretch of serpentine barrens and grasslands. There are wide views of the open countryside, where considerable removal of Virginia pines has occurred. There are dozens of kinds of grasses at Soldiers Delight. The little bluestem is the most common, occupying more than half the vegetative cover. Every season brings a selection of wildflowers, many of them uncommon, blooming modestly among the grasses. In spring, look for lyre-leaved rock cress, serpentine chickweed, Small's ragwort and wild yellow flax. By mid-to-late summer, rose pink, grass-leaved blazing star, and fameflower all blossom. Early fall brings on several species of goldenrod. Photographs in the Visitor Center can help you become familiar with these unusual species.

At mile 1.5, the trail reaches and then crosses the power line cut. Much of the vegetation under the power line is atypical of Soldiers Delight, due to frequent disturbance. Over the years, the utility company has kept the vegetation low by mowing and by use of selective herbicides. Although the cut hosts numerous grasses, you will find none of the above-named wildflowers growing under the power line.

The power line cut hosts a selection of uncommon bird species. Bluebirds frequently perch on dead snags year round and nest in old woodpecker holes each spring. The distinctive calls of prairie warblers fill the the vernal air; Soldiers Delight may be the best location in the Baltimore area to see this vocal but otherwise shy bird. Towhees frequent the forest edge, scratching noisily in the leaf litter. Even the rare and beautiful painted bunting has been known to nest here on occasion.

prairie warbler

Ecosystem Restoration at Soldiers Delight

DURING MORE THAN A CENTURY OF POPULATION GROWTH AND INDUSTRIAL activity, we Marylanders have relentlessly exploited the land, air, and water that sustain us, and environmental quality has suffered. For example, the Maryland Biological Stream Survey rates only 12 percent of the stream miles in Maryland as "good," while almost half are rated "poor." Code-red air quality days make Baltimore's airshed among the worst in the nation with regard to ozone content. Development is gobbling up open space at an alarming rate despite antisprawl legislation that is considered a national model.

Maryland citizens are beginning to realize that we have a moral and ethical responsibility to restore and rehabilitate the natural environment that we have so heedlessly abused. For example, we are twenty years into an ambitious and expensive program to restore the Chesapeake Bay; progress is slow, and there is no end in sight. On a smaller scale, one of the most interesting experiments in ecosystem restoration is taking place at Soldiers Delight Natural Environment Area.

The goal of the ecological management program at Soldiers Delight is to restore the appearance and species composition of the landscape to an earlier historical condition. In the 1600s, the area that is now Soldiers Delight was a grassland. Native grasses and endemic herbaceous plants formed an open landscape with long vistas across the rolling hills. Islands of native oak trees studded the grasslands, giving a savannalike appearance to the area.

These grasslands were maintained by Native Americans, who set fires during the late autumn dry season to drive game animals toward hunters. These annual fires prevented the growth of invasive species like Virginia pine, red cedar, and greenbrier. Perennial grasses and wildflowers were unaffected; the above-ground portions had died back by late fall, while the underground rhizomes and roots were immune to the effects of such low-intensity fires. The seeds of annual plants were fire resistant, or lay in microhabitats of bare soil and rock where there was no tinder to support fire.

By the early 1700s, Native Americans had been driven out. Colonists could not farm the rocky soil, but they grazed livestock at Soldiers Delight. This grazing pressure was also effective in retarding the growth of woody vegetation that might otherwise have taken over the grasslands. When the State bought the land in the 1950s, cattle were removed, and the process of normal plant succession began. Photographs from this era show extensive areas of open grassland, with Virginia pines confined primarily to steep slopes along streams. Without fire or grazing to reset the clock of succession, the pines began to colonize the prairie. By 1990, a majority of Soldiers Delight was in pine; trees were out-competing the rare and unusual species characteristic of the grassland.

In 1995, with the input of scientists, conservationists, and concerned citizens, a management plan for Soldiers Delight was adopted. It called for the removal of pines from more than 1,000 acres, to be followed, where possible, by carefully monitored prescribed burns of the grasslands. Much of the pine removal is being done by volunteers; dozens of acres were cleared in 2000. Whether the many rare herbaceous species will be able to recolonize these newly cleared sites is as yet unknown. Certainly, however, the results of this ongoing experiment in ecological restoration will be fascinating to follow for years to come.

The trail enters an oak forest on the far side of the power line cut. When it approaches Deer Park Road, the trail turns right and runs parallel to and within a few yards of this surprisingly busy country road. The Overlook parking lot is reached at mile 1.9, an alternate trailhead. Follow the white blazes another 0.3 miles to the Visitor Center.

GUNPOWDER FALLS
STATE PARK

■■■

Gunpowder Falls State Park is one of Maryland's largest, comprising about 17,000 acres of river valley and adjacent uplands. It may also be the state's most dispersed park, for sections of it are spread all over northern and eastern Baltimore County, from tidewater to the Pennsylvania border. The focal points of the park are the river valleys of the Big and Little Gunpowder Rivers. ("Gunpowder River" and "Gunpowder Falls" are used interchangeably.) In addition, there are large tracts of uplands, some very high quality freshwater swamps and marshes, and even a Chesapeake Bay island within the park's jurisdiction. Some areas of the park see heavy visitation, while in others you are unlikely to encounter another person. Taken together, the lands that compose Gunpowder Falls State Park are of incredible ecological and recreational value, and we citizens are lucky to have them available to us.

Developed areas of Gunpowder Falls State Park, where visitor facilities are available, include Hammerman, Jerusalem Mill, and Monkton Station. Parcels with limited or no facilities include Big Gunpowder Wildlands, Pleasantville, Sweet Air, Hereford, the Northern Central Railroad Trail, and Hart Miller Island.

Park headquarters are in the Jerusalem Mill near Kingsville. For more information, call the park at 410-592-2897.

■■■

▼ Big Gunpowder Trail

Distance: 8.8 miles one way
Difficulty: Easy

Directions: To reach the upstream end of the trail at Harford Road, take the Baltimore Beltway (I-695) to Harford Road (Route 147). Go northeast for 2.9 miles. There is parking for about eight cars just before crossing the river.

To reach the trailhead near the middle of the Big Gunpowder Trail, take the Baltimore Beltway to Belair Road (Route 1). Go northeast for 5.6 miles. Just after crossing the river, turn right

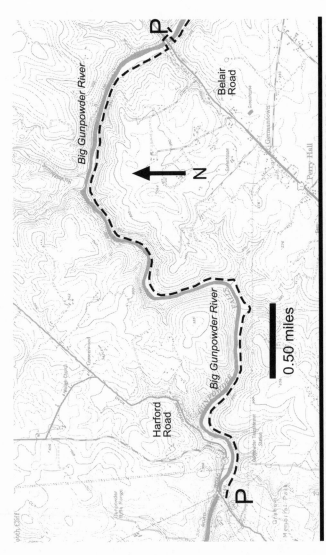

13. BIG GUNPOWDER TRAIL: HARFORD ROAD TO BELAIR ROAD

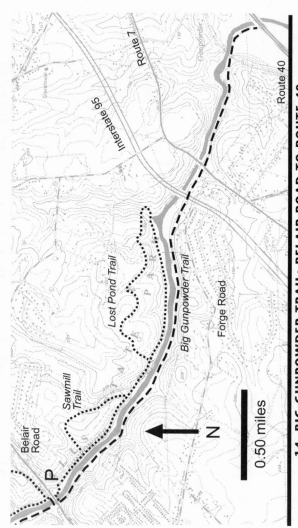

14. BIG GUNPOWDER TRAIL: BELAIR ROAD TO ROUTE 40

0.50 miles

N

Belair Road

Sawmill Trail

Lost Pond Trail

Big Gunpowder Trail

Forge Road

Interstate 95

Route 7

Route 40

into a large parking area. The trail is on the far side of the river, reached by walkways attached to the road bridge.

The Big Gunpowder River below Loch Raven dam displays two very different personalities. When the reservoir is full and water is flowing over the top of the dam, the river is alive, pouring forcefully and inexorably to tidewater over huge boulders and through narrow chutes. However, when Loch Raven is below capacity, the dam releases no water downstream, and the riverbed is an empty ravine of rocks. The contrast is interesting, and fortunately hikers have access to almost 9 miles of adjacent trail from which to contemplate it.

The Big Gunpowder Trail begins at Harford Road, Route 147, on the south side of the river. There is limited parking at this trailhead. Five miles downstream, Belair Road, Route 1, crosses the trail, and there is much more parking here. There is no parking at all where Philadelphia Road and Route 40 cross the trail.

The Big Gunpowder Trail is almost entirely level, but it is rocky underfoot. The trail runs within a few yards of the river for its entire length, and there are always pretty views of the river. Even when the river is dewatered, the scenery is interesting: one rarely is able to see the rocky bones of the land underlying a river. The trail is all within the confines of Gunpowder Falls State Park and is well forested.

This trail has white blazes, and mountain bikes are allowed.

This guide describes the trail in a downstream direction from Harford Road, the more western of the two trailheads. If you begin from Belair Road, near the midpoint of the Big Gunpowder Trail, you can proceed either upstream or downstream.

The Big Gunpowder Trail begins on the other side of the fence from the parking area along Harford Road. It is intially a rocky trail, and muddy spots have been filled with golfball-sized chunks of white limestone. About 100 yards from Harford Road, on the far bank of the river, is an interesting historical site. Several huge boulders mark the location of the Gunpowder Copper Works, in existence from 1804 to 1883. The dome of the United States Capitol was covered with copper from this mill a few years after the War of 1812. The only artifacts left are some huge eye bolts protruding from the riverside boulders.

The trail continues downriver, crossing several small

streams. The surrounding forest has lots of spring wildflowers, including bloodroot, spring beauty, windflower, ragwort, star chickweed, and even Virginia bluebells, uncommon elsewhere in the Baltimore area. By midsummer, however, the only wildflowers to be found are those on the riverbank, where there is some sunlight; they include dayflower, beggar ticks, white wood aster, tick trefoil, and jewelweed.

At about mile 3.0, the trail becomes somewhat rockier, as the surrounding hillsides press closer. The final mile to Belair Road resumes its mostly unobstructed path on the narrow floodplain. At mile 4.9, the trail emerges into the backyard of a restaurant-tavern; proceed along the driveway between the building and the river. The trail then crosses the Big Gunpowder River on a walkway below the grade of Belair Road. Once on the north bank of the river, walk under Belair Road through a large culvert, and re-cross to the south bank on a second walkway.

At mile 6.0, the trail again becomes somewhat obstructed with rocks, but it soon emerges onto a large outcrop adjacent to the river. This vantage point gives a good view of Pots Rock Rapid, a moderately difficult stretch of whitewater that requires paddlers to make a Z-turn among large rocks, strong currents, and irregular waves. The short pool below the rapid is a favorite fishing hole.

The trail passes under noisy I-95 at mile 7.3 and under Route 7, Philadelphia Road, at mile 7.5. This stretch of trail is unprepossessing, but it is home to several historical sites. Just upstream of I-95 is an area called Long Calm, used as a ford in the 1600s and plied by a ferry in the 1750s. By 1790, a covered bridge crossed the Big Gunpowder at Philadelphia Road. Reputedly, Lafayette and his troops camped near Long Calm during the Revolutionary War.

The remains of several old iron works and furnaces can be seen between here and tidewater. In the colonial era, much industry sprang up along the Big Gunpowder and other rivers situated along the fall line. Marking where rivers cascade off the Piedmont plateau onto the coastal plain, the fall line provided early industry with the water power necessary to run grinding wheels and turn gears.

Below Philadelphia Road, the trail becomes an old paved road. If the river has water in it, it's worth a side trip of a few dozen yards to view the Falls, the largest single rapid on the Big Gunpowder. More than 200 yards long, the river flushes markedly downhill through an ever-narrowing chute. Returning to the road, continue downstream. Where the pavement ends at mile 8.1, take the trail to the left. It leads down to the final rapid on the Big Gunpowder, Lorelei Ledge. Named after the generations of female sunbathers who have occupied these rocks, Lorelei Ledge is another Z-turn rapid. The churning whitewater dumps into tidewater at the bottom; this is a popular swimming and fishing hole.

Beyond the end of the pavement, the trail becomes very obscure, passing through a floodplain overgrown with shrubby trees and viny tangles in dry weather and flooded forest in wet. Few people venture into this swamp, since there is no access or parking at the far end. The intrepid hiker willing to slog through all this will reach Route 40 at mile 8.8.

▼ **Lost Pond Trail**

Distance: 4.2-mile circuit
Difficulty: Easy to moderate

Directions: From the Baltimore Beltway (I-695), take Belair Road (Route 1) north for 5.6 miles. Cross the Big Gunpowder River. The parking lot is on the right.

The Lost Pond Trail features pretty views of the Big Gunpowder River as it dashes, swirls, and foams against bedrock at Pots Rock Rapid. This hike also is a bit of a mystery quest, as one searches for the small man-made pond tucked unexpectedly among the big oaks of the rolling upland forest. Although each season has its charms along the Gunpowder River, spring is especially nice; the wildflowers that cover the floodplain and hillsides peak in April.

The Lost Pond Trail is clearly marked with light blue blazes and is typically in fair to good condition. Energetic hikers may wish to combine this walk with the adjacent Gunpowder Wildlands / Sweathouse Branch Trail.

The hike begins from the state park parking lot where Route 1, Belair Road, crosses the Big Gunpowder River. Although this lot is fairly large and can handle dozens of cars, it fills up fast on

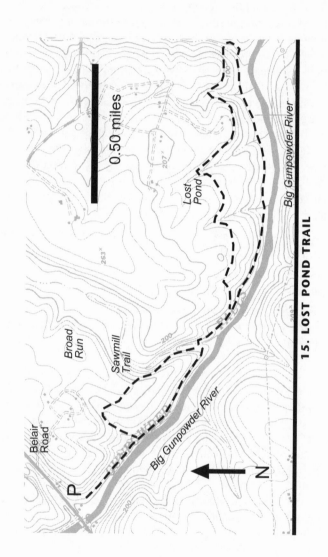

0.50 miles

Big Gunpowder River

Lost
Pond

263 ×

207 ×

209 ×

200

Broad
Run

Sawmill
Trail

Belair
Road

P

Big Gunpowder River

N

15. LOST POND TRAIL

spring and fall weekends. There is a small park-n-ride on the opposite side of Belair Road, uphill from the restaurant-bar.

The light blue–blazed trail originates at the east end of the parking lot and leads down onto the floodplain. This portion of the trail, paralleling the river, is often muddy. The rich alluvial soil is excellent for plant growth, and in April it is a reliable place to find Virginia bluebells flowering. This succulent perennial has beautiful blue vaselike petals that grow in clumps; it is widely considered one of Maryland's prettiest wildflowers. As always, leave these floral gems for the next person to enjoy; they wither almost instantly when picked. After 0.4 miles, a yellow-blazed branch trail appears on the left, leading uphill. This short loop, the Sawmill Trail, is best appreciated on the return trip, so continue downriver on the Lost Pond Trail.

At mile 0.9, the flow of the adjacent river necks down and drops over a steep rapid, called Pots Rock. At low water, the underlying potholed bedrock is revealed, with its sharp edges smoothed by erosion. Walk out on these rocks and enjoy their swirling grain; it's a popular sunbathing spot in warm weather.

Continue walking downstream on the blue-blazed trail for another 0.9 miles, at which point a trail sign directs you uphill, away from the river. The trail climbs gradually through a pleasantly wooded landscape, emerging on the shores of a now-drained pond at mile 2.5. This little wetland, less than an acre in size, seems incongruous in this forest setting, bordered by large trees. A man-made berm created the pond years ago, but the berm has been breached, so the pond is now merely a wetland. Still, this is a fine place to look for unusual flora. It attracts birds from the surrounding forest and in spring is alive with a cacophany of frog and toad vocalizations. The trail encircles the pond and then continues through the upland forest. Just before the trail drops back to river level, there is a beautiful, unobstructed overlook of Pots Rock Rapid. On the rare occasions when the river is running high, kayakers practice ferries, eddy turns, and pop-ups in the whitewater here.

Once back on the floodplain, turn upriver on the blue-blazed trail and continue for 0.3 miles. At the yellow blazes marking the Sawmill Trail, turn right and walk about 20 yards uphill. Look for a ditch to the left of the trail; this is an old hand-dug millrace associated with the Carroll Sawmill and dating back to

1833. At the downhill side of the millrace and on the right side of the trail is a short section of rock wall marking the sawmill's foundation. It is amazing that so much of this old sawmill is left after more than 150 years!

The Sawmill Trail ascends parallel to Broad Run and gives nice views up the stream valley. After meandering along the ridgetop, the trail drops back down to the river. Return another 0.4 miles to the parking lot, completing a 4.2-mile circuit.

▼ Big Gunpowder Wildlands / Sweathouse Branch Trail

Distance: 5.1-mile circuit; shorter hikes possible
Difficulty: Moderate

Directions: From the Baltimore Beltway (I-695), take Belair Road (Route 1), north for 5.6 miles. Cross the Big Gunpowder River; the parking lot is on the right.

The Big Gunpowder Wildlands / Sweathouse Branch Trail is an interesting circuit hike that begins by passing through a fairly dry upland forest, then drops into the steep valley of Sweathouse Branch, and finally returns along the banks of the Big Gunpowder River. The most distant point achieved by the trail, at the mouth of Long Green Creek, is especially scenic, featuring large boulders and tumbling waters in a shady, leafy setting. The entire trail lies within a designated wildland where no mountain bikes are allowed, so it is especially valued by hikers. This trail is well-blazed and clearly marked with trail signs at important intersections. Families with small children can avoid the more difficult upland sections and walk along the river to trail's end, and then return via the same route.

The hike begins from the Gunpowder Falls State Park parking lot where Route 1, Belair Road, crosses the Big Gunpowder River. This fairly large lot does fill up at popular hiking times. Additional parking is available at a park-n-ride on the opposite side of Belair Road, on the Baltimore County side of the river.

A wood chip trail leads from the parking lot upriver to a pedestrian underpass of Route 1. Within 50 yards of the underpass, the Wildlands Trail, marked with pink blazes, bears to the right. This wide, well-maintained trail leads uphill roughly par-

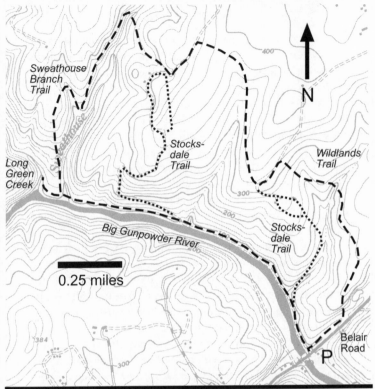

16. BIG GUNPOWDER WILDLANDS / SWEATHOUSE BRANCH TRAIL

allel to Belair Road; vehicle noise is obtrusive at this point, but it is soon left behind. After a climb of about 150 feet over a half-mile, the trail reaches the uplands, and there are no other significant uphills on the hike.

At mile 1.8, the Stocksdale Trail, blue-blazed, bears left and drops downhill to the river near Route 1. Take this short-cut only if you lack time, because the best part of this circuit is still ahead. Turn right instead, and go another 0.8 miles, where the other arm of the Stocksdale Trail bears downhill to the left. Again go right instead, where yellow blazes now denote the Sweathouse Branch Trail. The path soon drops steeply into the ravine carved by Sweathouse Branch, and follows the creek downstream for several hundred yards. This narrow valley is cool and shady in sum-

Wood Ducks

WOOD DUCKS ARE SOMETIMES SEEN ALONG THE GUNPOWDER RIVER, ES-pecially in the lower reaches near tidewater. Woodies are America's most colorful duck, and may also have the most interesting nesting habits.

You are most likely to see wood ducks in early spring, just as the first hint of green begins to freshen the trees. Female wood ducks travel up into swamps and river valleys in search of tree cavities suitable for nesting. In the early 1900s, hunting and forestry practices that removed many trees greatly reduced the numbers of wood ducks. Fortunately, wood ducks will nest in artificial nest boxes, which are often placed in swamps by wildlife agencies and private landowners, with the result that wood duck numbers have recovered nicely.

Once a satisfactory nest cavity is found, the hen lines it with wood chips and her own down. She soon begins to lay the first of about a dozen or so eggs. But since all the eggs should hatch on the same day, she will not begin to incubate until all her eggs have been laid. In the meantime, the hen frequently leaves the nest unattended as she looks for food.

While she is away, other females may climb into the nest and lay an egg of their own among hers! To biologists, this is known as "intraspecific brood parasitism." By the time the nesting female begins to incubate, she may be warming the eggs of several other hens. Hatching occurs after just over a month of incubation. Like the hatchlings of many ducks, these are precocial—downy and able to walk and swim at birth; within two days they have bailed out of the nest, tumbling to the water or ground

*female and male
wood ducks*

below. The female stays with the ducklings until they fledge a month or so later.

The advantages of brood parasitism are obvious for the renegade female, but why doesn't the nesting hen remove eggs that aren't her own? Since all wood duck eggs look similar, she probably can't tell which eggs are hers and which are not. And because she doesn't have to feed her young, as do most song-birds, there is little or no energy investment, and thus no penalty in raising the young of others. However, if there are too many eggs in the nest, the hen cannot keep all of them sufficiently warm, and mortality will be significant. High levels of brood par asitism occur where artificial nest boxes have been too closely spaced and where the boxes are in the open and thus easily lo-cated by parasitizing hens. Unfortunately, most artificial nest boxes are placed above water so that the boxes can be easily monitored by boat; they would be better off located several yards back into the swamp where the boxes are better concealed.

---

mer and would invite lingering but for the finer rewards ahead. The trail soon crosses the creek and climbs steeply uphill for 100 yards. Thereafter, the path parallels Sweathouse Branch from atop the low ridge, giving nice views of its mossy boulders below.

At mile 3.8, the trail drops off the ridge toward the Big Gun-powder River. Turn right, upstream, and you will reach the mouth of Long Green Creek within 200 yards. This is a perfect place for a picnic in any season; there's a huge rock ledge from which you can look upstream into the mysterious gorge of Long Green. A faint trail leads up Long Green Creek on the opposite (west) side, but you'll likely have to remove your shoes and wade the creek to get there. At low water, Long Green Creek is a great place to boulder-hop; look for tiny fish stranded in small pools, and crayfish along the shoreline and under rocks. At high water, Long Green Creek is renowned among expert local kayakers as a short, adrenalin-raising "steep creek": narrow, fast, boulder-choked, and dangerous. On only a few days each year is there enough water to paddle Long Green Creek, and then only within an hour or two of more than three inches of rainfall.

Return to Belair Road by the blue-blazed path running downstream parallel to the Big Gunpowder River. This trail is usually muddy but offers a variety of wildflowers, especially in spring, and good birding opportunities throughout the year. Upon arrival at Belair Road, the 5.1-mile circuit is complete.

■ ■

▼ Northern Central Railroad Trail

Distance: 40 miles one way
Difficulty: Easy

Directions: From the Baltimore Beltway (I-695), take I-83 north to exit 20, Shawan Road, to the east. Where Shawan Road ends, turn right (south) on York Road (Route 45). Within about 200 yards, turn left onto Ashland Road. The name of the road soon changes to Paper Mill Road. Go 1.1 miles to where the NCR Trail crosses Paper Mill Road; park in the adjacent parking lot. Almost every other road that crosses the NCR Trail has at least a few parking places; consult any good road map. "Official" parking lots are maintained at the Phoenix Pond, Monkton, White Hall, Parkton, Bentley Springs, and Freeland, all in Maryland. Recommended access points in Pennsylvania are New Freedom, Glen Rock, Hanover Junction, and York.

The Northern Central Railroad Trail may be Baltimore's best recreational amenity. Occupying the abandoned railbed of the defunct Northern Central Railroad, this crushed limestone path begins in Cockeysville and runs almost due north to York, Pennsylvania. In Maryland, a majority of the adjacent land is owned by the state and managed by Gunpowder Falls State Park. The trail passes through a landscape that is part natural forest, part pastoral fields and farms. For much of its length, a river or creek flows nearby. Wildlife is plentiful, especially in the early morning. Hundreds of thousands of people visit the NCR Trail annually, and although it can be crowded at times, it is still an enchanting and beautiful place to visit.

Although many people walk on the NCR Trail, it is more frequently used by bicyclists. Expect heavy bicycle traffic on weekends, and keep to the right side of the trail as you walk. It is difficult for more than two people to walk abreast. The first few cyclists who suddenly hurtle past you can be disconcerting, but most hikers adapt quickly to the surprise. Bicyclists are supposed to alert hikers with a bell, or a salutation like "passing on the

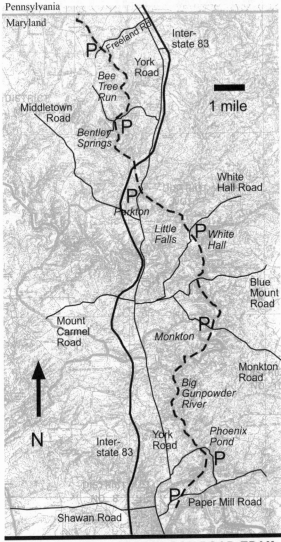

Pennsylvania
Maryland

Freeland Rd

Inter-
state 83

York
Road

Bee
Tree
Run

1 mile

Middletown
Road

P

Bentley
Springs

P

White
Hall Road

P

Parkton

Little
Falls

P White
Hall

Blue
Mount
Road

Mount
Carmel
Road

Monkton

P

Monkton
Road

Big
Gunpowder
River

N

Inter-
state 83

York
Road

Phoenix
Pond

P

P

Paper Mill Road

Shawan Road

17. NORTHERN CENTRAL RAILROAD TRAIL

left," but in reality this practice is followed only occasionally. Still, hikers and bicyclists must share the trail, and a little courtesy and tolerance go a long way toward making shared trails pleasant places.

The Northern Central Railroad Trail itself is managed by Gunpowder Falls State Park. For more information, call the park at 410-592-2897.

Most Baltimoreans begin their visit to the NCR Trail at Paper Mill Road, where there is ample parking, even on crowded weekend days. Therefore, this description of the trail is from south to north.

The first mile of this walk, to Phoenix Pond, is atypical of the rest of the NCR Trail, at least in ecological terms. The wide, flat path is sunny here, for the adjacent grassy shoulders are kept mowed. Summertime wildflowers abound, especially on the dry, sandy soils, and some are not common. Look for lyre-leafed sage, butter-and-eggs, scarlet pimpernel, viper's bugloss, spiderwort, and beardtongue, alongside more common species like yarrow, oxeye daisy, goldenrod, and thistle.

At Phoenix Road, walk to the far side of the parking lot to visit a shallow pond encircled by trees. This is an excellent place to look for birds year-round, but especially in spring. Baltimore orioles and orchard orioles nest in the sycamores, a variety of warblers and other migrants flit about, and a great blue or green heron can frequently be seen stalking the shallows. In early spring, listen for the calls of breeding amphibians like wood frogs, spring peepers, and American toads, while in early summer the croak of green frogs and the basso thrumming of bullfrogs take over.

As you continue north, the forest closes in, and the path is

beaver

shady except at midday. The adjacent Gunpowder River has extensive floodplain wetlands that support breeding salamanders in spring and a variety of interesting wetland plants in summer. Butterflies are common in summer, feeding on the nectar of these flowers, while damselflies and dragonflies sometimes stray near the trail during their patrols of the river. Birding continues to be good almost anywhere along the trail.

Monkton Station is another major public access point. The old railroad station has been converted into a small park office and gift shop, and you will find water, picnic tables, and restrooms here. Across the street, a small store sells refreshments, while another rents bicycles and tubing gear. Although the tiny parking lot is almost always full, there is plenty of parking on Monkton Road just west of the river.

A mile north of Monkton Station, the trail parts company with the Big Gunpowder River. Nevertheless, a major tributary, Little Falls, continues adjacent to the NCR Trail. From here north to Parkton, Little Falls tumbles through a rocky gorge, and a short detour down to the water's edge is well worth the time. From Bentley Springs northward, the NCR Trail follows an even smaller tributary, Bee Tree Run. This is beaver country, and over the years these industrious rodents have built dams in a number of locations, creating wetlands adjacent to the trail. These swamps support red maple, green ash, various willows, cinnamon ferns, sphagnum moss, jewelweed, and several kinds of turtles—altogether a fascinating landscape, one that changes every year.

Although the NCR Trail seems flat to hikers, bicyclists will notice that the grade increases significantly from Bentley Springs north. The height of land is just north of the state line, and by the first town in Pennsylvania, New Freedom, you will be in the Susquehanna River watershed. New Freedom is a pleasant little town, with small stores at which to purchase refreshments and a bike shop for any unexpected emergencies. There is ample roadside parking near the trail for hikers and cyclists who wish to begin from here, at the approximate halfway point of the NCR Trail.

Once into Pennsylvania, the landscape changes. While northern Baltimore County is very rural, with large farms and extensive woodlots, southern Pennsylvania has more houses near the NCR Trail, and more road crossings. It is still a very pleasant walk, and well worth the longer commute if you want to hike any part of the northern half of the trail. The final few miles into York are increasingly urbanized.

■ ■

▼ Gunpowder North / Gunpowder South Circuit

Distance: 14.6-mile circuit; shorter hikes possible
Difficulty: Easy to moderate

Directions: From the Baltimore Beltway (I-695), take I-83 north to exit 27, Mt. Carmel Road. Go right, east, for 0.5 miles to York Road (Route 45). Turn left, north. Go 0.8 miles to Bunker Hill Road. Turn left onto Bunker Hill Road and follow it for 1.1 miles to the parking lot by the Big Gunpowder River.

There is not a prettier stretch of river in Maryland than the Big Gunpowder River between Prettyboy and Loch Raven Reservoirs. Sure, the Big Gunpowder may lack the steep mountains and raging whitewater of the Youghiogheny, and it can't compare to the grand vistas and pastoral quiet of the Pocomoke; but for an intimate river with gin-clear, ice-cold water flowing through an unspoiled valley, nothing can touch the Big Gunpowder. Almost every rod of its shore is protected by state park. It is a world-class trout fishing stream, and a premier canoeing river. Wildlife abounds. The valley is even spared floods, usually, protected as it is by an upstream dam. And a wonderful trail circuit, the Gunpowder South and Gunpowder North Trails, makes it easy to visit and enjoy this aquatic gem.

As described, this is a very long trail. Fortunately, however, a number of road crossings make shorter circuits possible. Merely choose the distance you wish to walk, and go! This hike is described as a counterclockwise circuit from the most convenient access point, Bunker Hill Road. The trail on the north side of the river is called the Gunpowder North Trail, while that on the south side is called the Gunpowder South Trail. Both are blazed in white.

Mountain bikes are prohibited from the entire length of this trail, as the area has been designated a Wildland by the Department of Natural Resources.

Begin your hike from the large parking lot at the end of Bunker Hill Road. There is ample parking here, and bathrooms are available in warm weather at the cinder block comfort station

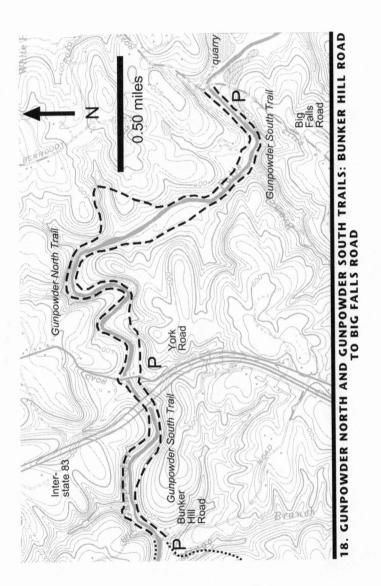

18. GUNPOWDER NORTH AND GUNPOWDER SOUTH TRAILS: BUNKER HILL ROAD TO BIG FALLS ROAD

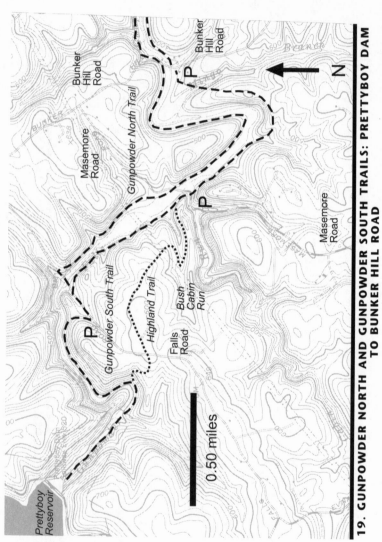

Prettyboy Reservoir

Bunker Hill Road

Bunker Hill Road

Masemore Road

Gunpowder North Trail

Gunpowder South Trail

Highland Trail

Bush Cabin Run

Falls Road

Masemore Road

0.50 miles

N

19. GUNPOWDER NORTH AND GUNPOWDER SOUTH TRAILS: PRETTYBOY DAM TO BUNKER HILL ROAD

nearby. Walk through the small open field on the east (down-river) side of the parking area, to the Gunpowder South Trail near the river. Like most of the major trailheads in Gunpowder Falls State Park, it is marked by an upright post with the name routered into the wood.

For the first few hundred yards, the trail runs adjacent to the river. The Big Gunpowder River is narrow enough to be entirely shaded, as large trees arch over the river, and in summer it has the appearance of a green tunnel. At all but the lowest water levels, the river flows with a brisk pace, but rapids are minimal. At the first bend in the river, the trail moves away from the river, now passing through a rich forest of ferns, wildflowers, and rocky outcrops.

The trail passes under noisy I-83, and crosses York Road (Route 45) at mile 0.9 to emerge at a grassy sward popular for picnics. There is parking at York Road for about a dozen cars, so this is an alternate access point. Continue downstream on the Gunpowder South Trail. The blue-blazed Panther Branch Trail (described elsewhere in this book) also originates here, so be sure to take the white-blazed trail.

The next 2 miles of trail are generally within sight of the river. Openings in the tree canopy let sunlight reach the forest floor. A luxuriant growth of vines and shrubs, many with thorns, makes for some difficult going in summer but lend variety to the landscape. The mouth of Panther Branch is reached at mile 3.1, and is worth a detour, especially in spring to see the excellent displays of seasonal wildflowers.

Continue downstream to Big Falls Road at mile 3.6, the easternmost point of the Gunpowder South Trail. Further progress downstream is barred by a large and active quarry that straddles the river. There is parking for about six cars at Big Falls Road. Cross the river on the road bridge, and turn immediately upstream on what is now called the Gunpowder North Trail.

Once again, the trail generally follows the river, although at one point it leaves the floodplain and climbs over a short but steep ridge. A highlight of this section of trail is Raven Rock Falls at mile 5.3. This is not a vertical waterfall; instead, water flows about eighty feet down a a steeply inclined rock face. Raven Rock Falls is a popular lunch site.

The Gunpowder North Trail continues upstream adjacent to the Big Gunpowder River, crossing York Road at mile 6.2, Bunker

Hill Road at mile 7.2, and Masemore Road at mile 8.5, before terminating at Falls Road at mile 9.3. As with this entire trail, there
are plenty of wildflowers spring through fall, especially in the riparian zone, where rich alluvial soil coupled with ample moisture
promote a riot of vegetation. Among the larger and more obvious
flowers, look for Joe Pye weed, yellow coneflower, cardinal flower,
and jewelweed in mid-to-late summer, growing near the water.

Falls Road marks the western terminus of the Gunpowder
North Trail. Cross the road bridge and turn right, upstream, on
the white-blazed Gunpowder South Trail. The next 1.6 miles, to
the base of Prettyboy Dam, form one of Maryland's best short
hikes. What makes this section different from the rest of the
Gunpowder North and South Trails is that the river changes from
a mild-mannered, pastoral stream to a brawling whitewater
creek. The Gunpowder pours through narrow slots and over large
boulders into short, deep, green pools before then resuming its
headlong pace downstream. This half-mile section of river is
more typical of a mountain creek than of a Piedmont stream just
a few dozen miles from tidewater.

The trail along the river is not steep, but it can be difficult
going. Watch your footing on the sometimes loose rock, and
avoid ankle-twisting crevices. But stop to look around and enjoy
the scenery! The hillsides are steep here, with a number of outcrops of exposed rocks covered in lichens and mosses. Hemlock
trees lend a deep shade. In late May, the hillsides appear to be
covered with an unseasonal snowfall, but it is the flowers of hundreds of mountain laurels. And on a hot summer day when tem-
peratures reach triple digits in Baltimore, the air temperature
never rises out of the seventies near the river.

As the trail continues upstream, the steep rapids disappear
at a U-shaped bend in the river. Above this point, the Gunpowder assumes its more typical placid course. The adjacent trail is
narrow and at one place ascends to a point where there are good
views of the river valley. Prettyboy Dam soon comes into view.
The trail terminates at the base of the dam at mile 10.9. A long
flight of steps leads to the top of the dam. There is no parking
allowed anywhere near here, so Prettyboy Dam Road cannot be
used as an access point. Turn and retrace your steps downstream
on the Gunpowder South Trail.

Falls Road is reached at mile 12.5 and Masemore Road at

mile 13.3. There is parking for about ten cars at Falls Road and twenty cars at Masemore Road, alternative access points. About a half-mile downstream from Masemore Road, the trail leaves the river, angling directly across the upland to the Bunker Hill Road trailhead at mile 14.6.

There are several side trails that enter the Gunpowder South Trail. Near the U-shaped bend in the river downstream from Prettyboy Dam, the pink-blazed Highland Trail runs steeply uphill from the river. This 1.0-mile trail eventually returns to the Gunpowder South Trail near Masemore Road. The Highland Trail is used primarily by hikers who park at Masemore Road and who wish to walk a circuit without repeating any section of trail. The Mingo Forks Trail and the Panther Branch Trail each share a portion of the Gunpowder South trail. These two fine trails are described separately.

■ ■

▼ Panther Branch Trail

Distance: 4.2-mile circuit
Difficulty: Moderate

Directions: From the Baltimore Beltway (I-695), take I-83 north to exit 27, Mt. Carmel Road. Go right, east, for 0.5 miles to York Road (Route 45). Turn left, north. Go 0.8 miles to Bunker Hill

columbine

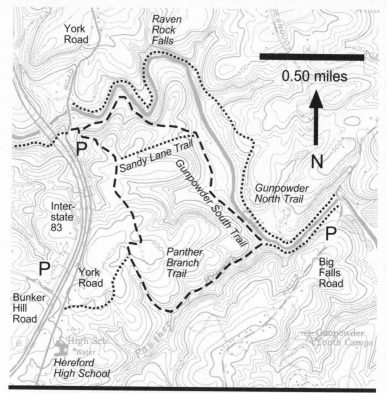

20. PANTHER BRANCH TRAIL

Road. Turn left onto Bunker Hill Road and follow it for 1.1 miles to the parking lot by the Big Gunpowder River.

Springtime wildflowers are the glory of the vernal season, and nowhere is there a more diverse collection of these colorful natives than along the Panther Branch Trail in Gunpowder Falls State Park. In addition to wildflowers, this footpath features a wide variety of habitats that make interesting hiking. Finally, this tiny, obscure watershed has a surprising amount of human history associated with it.

The walk begins (and ends) where York Road, Route 45, crosses the Big Gunpowder River in northern Baltimore County. There is a small parking lot, for perhaps a dozen cars, and some additional roadside parking here. Cross York Road with care and enter a grassy area that leads down to the river. In warm weather, this area is heavily congested with picnickers, tubers, fishermen, sunbathers, and assorted other park users; almost all of them will be left behind in the first 100 yards of trail. Entrance to the trail is about halfway up the hill, indicated by a vertical post incised with the trail name and dark blue blazes.

The trail rises uphill, and a strange phenomenon suggests itself almost immediately to an observant hiker. You will see a grove composed almost exclusively of black cherry trees, and all of them are leaning downhill! Whether these trees were influenced by wind or heavy snow is uncertain, but they certainly make an odd-looking forest.

After 0.5 miles of steady but not steep climbing, a confusing five-way trail intersection is reached. The pink-blazed Sandy Lane Trail runs downhill to the river. An old roadbed, wide and inviting, is unmarked and merely loops back upon itself. Be alert for the blue blazes marking the Panther Branch Trail as it continues uphill.

Within 100 yards, the trail emerges from the forest into a mixed landscape of shrubs, brush, small open grassy areas, and occasional large trees. This is good habitat for birds in all seasons, and cottontail rabbits are common. By far the most unusual feature of this area, however, is the tamarack trees that have been planted here. Tamaracks are native only to the westernmost portions of Maryland, so to find them in Baltimore County is a real surprise. Their foliage turns a brilliant yellow in late autumn, competing handily with maples for dramatic autumn color.

The trail soon joins an old road running along the edge of a large field under the shade of a stand of white pines. Within 100 yards, an upright trail marker indicates that the Panther Branch Trail veers left, downhill, across the field. An assortment of early summer wildflowers graces this field, and in the colder months the dried stalks of broomsedge lend a pleasant warmth to the scene. Abandoned farmland like this can be maintained free of shrubs and trees by an annual mowing.

The path now enters the forest, and the headwaters of Panther Branch appear to the right. The trail descends steadily for almost a mile, the sound of flowing water always close at hand. Where the stream meanders, alluvial terraces have been deposited, and these are rich locations for spring wildflowers like trout lily, false hellebore, skunk cabbage, and several species of violet. Under the forest canopy look for spring beauty, toothwort, may apple, windflower, jack-in-the-pulpit, wild ginger, and even the occasional orchid. Columbine and early saxifrage may be found on rocky outcrops. But in late April, one wildflower dominates this entire valley in an uncommon profusion: dwarf ginseng. A close relative of the medicinal herb ginseng (but without any economic value), dwarf ginseng is a modest plant only an inch or two high with an upright panicle of tiny white flowers that are reminiscent of an exploding firework. This whole group of native wildflowers are known as spring ephemerals: they grow and flower before the trees leaf out, taking advantage of a short season of direct sunlight. By late May, the green foliage of many of these species has died back completely, and only the underground portion of the plant persists, awaiting yet another spring.

In addition to its botanical treasures, Panther Branch has features of historical interest. Several ruins of small buildings built of native stone are scattered along the lower portions of the trail. Even more interesting are several deep ditches that obviously once channeled the flow of the creek. In the 1700s, gunpowder was made here, using water power to grind the powder to an appropriate grit. The small buildings were used for storage.

Panther Branch empties into the Big Gunpowder River at mile 2.2. Turn left, upstream, on the white-blazed Gunpowder South Trail. This narrow footpath parallels the river most of the way back to York Road. Nevertheless, there is enough variety to the landscape to keep the walk interesting. The trail alternately passes by wetlands dominated by a lush growth of skunk cabbage, dry rocky slopes rich with mountain laurel, open areas where brushy tangles threaten to overgrow the trail, and maturing forest with good views of the river. One highlight is the view across the river toward Raven Rock Falls at approximately mile 3.0, where a small stream cascades eighty or so feet down a jumbled rock face.

Birding is good all along the Gunpowder, and this portion is no exception. Look for sparrows and cardinals in the thick underbrush and forest songbirds in the tall trees. The most common summer resident is the red-eyed vireo, a visually nondescript bird with an easily recognized call. It is just two notes, but they are repeated up to fifty times a minute, a rate unmatched by any other local bird.

What's in a (Latin) Name?

MANY PEOPLE WHO READ ARTICLES IN THE POPULAR PRESS ABOUT PLANTS and animals are confused about scientists' curious insistence on calling organisms by a Latin name. For example, we humans are called *Homo sapiens*. Why this strange practice, in a dead language?

The answer is both practical and historic. In practical terms, common names are sometimes ambiguous. For example, birds called "robins" are found in both North America and Great Britain, but American and British robins are remarkably different birds. Similarly, a single species can be known by multiple common names. For example, *Houstonia caerulea* is variously called bluets, innocence, and Quaker ladies.

Every kind of organism known to science has been given its own unique Latin name. It consists of two names, the genus and the species. These words usually reflect some aspect of the organism's structure, use, or discovery. For example, *homo* is Latin for "man," while *sapiens* means "having sense."

Latin binomials are given to a newly discovered organism by the scientist who first publishes a valid description of it in a scientific journal. Many common species were named in the eighteenth century by Carolus Linnaeus, who first used this system to classify organisms on the basis of similar morphologies. Linneaus chose Latin not only because it was the language of educated people at that time, but so that there could be no confusion about how a name would translate from one language to another.

The etymology of these Latin names is frequently obscure but almost always fascinating. Here are a few examples of genus names given to wildflowers:

Achillea: the common garden plant and wildflower yarrow was named for the Greek hero Achilles. According to legend, Achilles carried this plant with him to war, using it to staunch the flow of blood from wounds.

Panax: the well-known herb ginseng. Its Latin name is derived from two Greek words, *pan,* meaning "all," and *akos,* meaning "cure." Hence, ginseng is literally a panacea, a cure-all, reflecting the great value some societies place on its root as a tonic and aphrodisiac.

Sanguinaria: the beautiful white spring wildflower whose common name is bloodroot. The Latin word "sanguis" means blood. The reference is to the red rootstock, which exudes an orangish liquid.

Aquilegia: another equally beautiful spring wildflower, columbine. The genus name is derived from the Latin for "eagle" and refers to the resemblance between the five spurs and an eagle's claw.

Helianthus: this plant has the closest possible correlation between its Latin genus and its English common name, sunflower. From the Greek words *helios,* meaning "sun," and *anthos,* meaning "flower."

Tussilago: our earliest spring wildflower, coltsfoot, looks like a dandelion and grows in the disturbed soil along roadsides. *Tussilago* means "cough dispeller"; an extract was used in colonial American cough medicines.

These are just a few of the Latin names of common wildflowers. Many of the references are much more obscure, but their investigation is always a fascinating and rewarding endeavor!

The trail reaches York Road after 4.2 miles of prime hiking.

Some hikers choose to access the Panther Branch Trail from Bunker Hill Road, parking on the road shoulders underneath I-83. Cross York Road (Route 45), walk up the paved road to the Hereford High School stadium, and walk around it to the back side. The open field alluded to previously is behind the stadium; walk through it until you cross the Panther Branch Trail.

▼ Mingo Forks / Bunker Hill Circuit

Distance: 3.8-mile circuit
Difficulty: Moderate

Directions: From the Baltimore Beltway (I-695), take I-83 north to exit 27, Mt. Carmel Road. Go right, east, for 0.5 miles to York Road (Route 45). Turn left, north. Go 0.8 miles to Bunker Hill Road. Turn left onto Bunker Hill Road and follow it for 1.1 miles to the parking lot by the Big Gunpowder River.

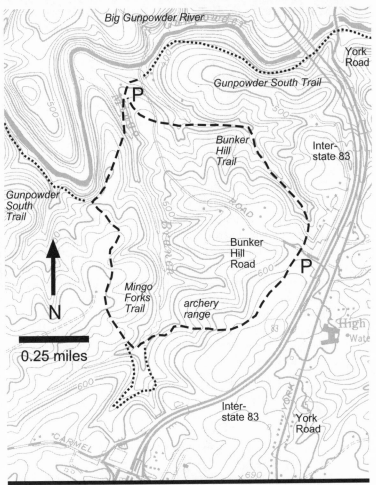

21. MINGO FORKS / BUNKER HILL CIRCUIT

This beautiful circuit hike passes through a variety of landscapes as it loops around the Bunker Hill section of Gunpowder Falls State Park. Traversing narrow stream valleys, upland forest, and abandoned agricultural fields now growing up in brush, the Mingo Forks and Bunker Hill Trails encompass most of the natural habitats typical of northern Baltimore County.

The parking lot at the foot of Bunker Hill Road is a good

place to begin this circuit. This is a popular area with tubers in the summer and fishermen year-round. During warm weather, the comfort station on the hill provides water and bathroom facilities. Youth group camping is allowed nearby with permission. Before you begin your hike, view the river from the bridge pier, now all that's left of a bridge that was damaged in Hurricane Agnes (1972) and later removed. Ample sunlight reaching the crystal clear waters of the Big Gunpowder River promotes growth of underwater grasses that sway in the current. The area is excellent for birding, with grassy fields, riparian forest, and brushy tangles harboring a diversity of avian life.

The trail begins behind the concrete block comfort station just uphill from the parking lot. The circuit can be hiked in either direction but is described clockwise. Therefore, follow the blue-blazed trail uphill rather than the white-blazed Gunpowder South Trail that branches off downhill. The Bunker Hill Trail soon crosses Bunker Hill Road and ascends gradually but steadily through a forest of mixed hardwoods and pines. Most notable is the crowsfoot virtually carpeting the forest floor. This primitive nonflowering plant also goes by the descriptive monikers "ground pine" and "running pine," for its recumbent, trailing, and evergreen nature. You'll no doubt recognize it as a component of holiday wreaths. In winter, the crowsfoot and Christmas fern make this one of the greenest trails around.

Christmas fern

The trail soon arrives at a tiny stream, and runs alongside it to a second crossing of Bunker Hill Road at mile 0.9, just a hundred yards from I-83. Directly across the road, continue up a fire road. The trail is now considered the Mingo Forks Trail, even though the blazes are still the same blue color. You soon pass through the midst of a woodland archery range. Use care if archers are present, but this range is lightly used. In a clearing, the fire road bears left, while the Bunker Hill Trail again becomes a footpath, turning right, downhill; look for the blue blazes.

The trail soon reaches a narrow valley where two forks of Mingo Branch unite at mile 1.7. A yellow-blazed horse trail leads up one branch, while the narrower blue-blazed foottrail initially heads downhill. Both will eventually arrive at the same point, so you can take either. The Mingo Forks Trail skirts a ridge and then runs up one of the forks. Within sight of a pasture, the trail bears right and ascends a hill through a stand of white pines to emerge on the uplands on a gas pipeline right-of-way. The trail continues through fields of grasses reverting to shrubs. This open stretch is a good place to look for fox, groundhogs, and birds of field and brush, like sparrows and indigo buntings.

Eventually, the trail reenters the forest and soon is united with the white-blazed Gunpowder South Trail. Despite the trail's name at this point, the river is not in sight, and in fact lies far below. Turn right; the trail runs gradually downhill, crosses a small stream, and reascends to its union with the Bunker Hill Trail within sight of the comfort station. The complete circuit is a fairly hilly 3.8 miles.

LITTLE GUNPOWDER TRAIL

The Little Gunpowder River flows nondescriptly along the eastern edge of Baltimore County. Compared to its larger brother, the Big Gunpowder River, the Little Gunpowder is far less frequently visited. And in some ways that's a shame, for the riverside scenery is every bit as beautiful, and it is superior in its sense of isolation and intimacy.

The Little Gunpowder Trail parallels the river for 5 miles. In this distance, the river changes from a Piedmont stream, sparkling and dancing through gravel bars, to a brawling creek slamming over steep drops and between large rocks. The sound of flowing water is always close at hand.

The trail is described as two sections, joined at the public access at Jerusalem Mill, headquarters of Gunpowder Falls State Park. With a car shuttle, energetic hikers could easily traverse the entire length of the trail in a day's hike. However, since most hikers rarely set shuttle, the linear nature of the trail doubles the mileage to an uncomfortably high total.

You might begin your walk with a tour of Jerusalem Mill, if it is open. In warmer weather there are often weekend events here, including blacksmithing demonstrations and acoustic music. There is a small history museum in the mill, open on weekend afternoons.

The Little Gunpowder Trail is clearly marked with white blazes.

Directions: From the Baltimore Beltway (I-695), take Belair Road (Route 1) north for 7.6 miles. Turn right on Jerusalem Road. Follow Jerusalem Road for 1.9 miles to the mill and nearby parking lot.

▼ **Jerusalem Mill downstream to I-95**

Distance: 5.7-mile circuit
Difficulty: Easy to moderate

Depart from the mill by crossing the river into Baltimore County on Jerusalem Road. The trailhead is just a few feet from the end of the bridge and is marked by an upright post with the trail name carved into it. This section of trail is meticulously maintained, as it is the most heavily used, connecting the mill with the wooden covered bridge at Jericho Road. Even so, the surrounding forest is very beautiful, with tall trees and lots of woodland wildflowers. May apples seem especially common and large all along the Little Gunpowder Trail. Shaped like little green umbrellas, may apples grow only in rich, undisturbed soil. Plants with one leaf will not flower; only those with two leaves bloom, the flower arising in the V-shaped cleft between the two leafstalks. The round green fruit, a bit smaller than a ping-pong ball, develops slowly over the late spring and summer and is typically ripe for a brief period in mid-August.

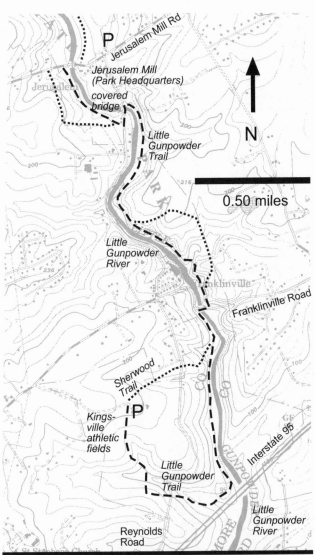

P

Jerusalem Mill Rd

Jerusalem Mill
(Park Headquarters)

covered
bridge

Little
Gunpowder
Trail

N

0.50 miles

Little
Gunpowder
River

Franklinville

Franklinville Road

Sherwood
Trail

P

Kings-
ville
athletic
fields

Interstate 95

Little
Gunpowder
Trail

Little
Gunpowder
River

Reynolds
Road

22. LITTLE GUNPOWDER TRAIL, JERUSALEM MILL
DOWNSTREAM TO I-95

At Jericho Road, mile 0.4, walk through the old wooden bridge, watching for vehicular traffic. Mud wasp nests adorn the roof, and phoebes nest in the rafters. On the far side of the bridge, the trail turns downstream. Very soon, the river's gradient picks up as it flows over outcrops of the local stone. These same rocks are obstacles to the trail, which climbs and then descends over them. For this reason, there is much rock scrambling on this section of the Little Gunpowder Trail, even though elevation gains are minimal.

The rapids increase in intensity, culminating at Factory Falls, a five-foot stairstep drop at mile 1.2. The trail is briefly difficult here, but there are good views of the river. At Franklinville Road, mile 1.4, cross the road bridge to the Baltimore County side and continue downstream.

The stream valley becomes less steep and congested with rocks below Franklinville Road. The forest is a maturing woodland with a complex understory and plenty of wildflowers. Among the more unusual plants flowering in midsummer are two of our native orchids, cranefly orchid and rattlesnake plantain. There is abundant birdlife, with kingfishers and great blue herons searching the little river for fish.

great blue heron

At mile 1.7, turn right on the Sherwood Trail, blazed in light blue and well marked. This trail leads steadily but not steeply up-hill to the Kingsville athletic fields, where there is parking that provides an alternative access point to the Little Gunpowder Trail. As the trail crosses the access road next to a baseball field, it again becomes the white-blazed Little Gunpowder Trail. This wide footpath descends into the river valley to within sight of I-95. The trail then runs upstream along the Little Gunpowder, completing a small circuit at the Sherwood Trail junction noted above. In sum, a round trip from Jerusalem Mill, around the Kingsville loop and back to the mill is 5.7 miles.

▼ **Jerusalem Mill upstream to Harford Road (Route 147)**

Distance: 2.9 miles one way
Difficulty: Easy

Once again, begin your walk at Jerusalem Mill. The trailhead is at the back end of the grassy area between the river and the blacksmith shop. The first mile of the Little Gunpowder Trail is typically only a few feet away from the river, and this intimacy lends an excitement few trails have. Not only do you look for-ward to seeing what's around the next bend in the trail, but you also anticipate each new view of the tumbling river. It has been said that turbulent water creates negative ions in the air that hu-mans find pleasurable and stimulating, and whatever the valid-ity of this claim, certainly rivers and streams are charismatic places. Each season along the Little Gunpowder has its own par-ticular charm: the long vistas of winter, the blush of lime green on spring trees, the lush flora and cool shade of summer, and the clear light and fall color of autumn.

At mile 0.3, the blue-blazed Jerusalem Mill Trail branches to the right. This 0.8-mile alternate route traverses the forested up-lands, eventually rejoining the main trail. The Little Gunpowder Trail, by contrast, only briefly leaves the river to cross Wildcat Branch and soon returns to the floodplain. After more fine scenery, Belair Road, Route 1, is reached at mile 2.0. Cross busy Belair Road with care.

The Little Gunpowder Trail continues upstream, but now on the opposite, Baltimore County, side of the river. It remains close

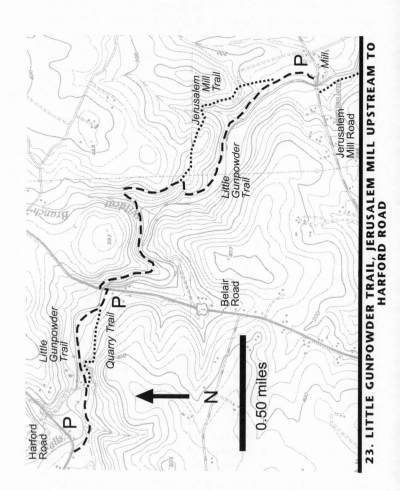

23. LITTLE GUNPOWDER TRAIL, JERUSALEM MILL UPSTREAM TO HARFORD ROAD

to the river at all times, arriving at Harford Road at mile 2.9. An interesting side trail in this area is the Quarry Trail. This blue-blazed trail branches left upstream of Belair Road, winds through an upland forest, and rejoins the Little Gunpowder Trail at mile 2.6. From the top of the quarry, a short stroll from the highest point on the Quarry Trail, there are wonderful views of the Little Gunpowder valley. The vista of steep hills and one isolated farm is reminiscent of a hollow in rural West Virginia.

Upstream progress beyond Harford Road is not possible, because the riverfront land is privately owned.

SWEET AIR AREA

Of all the acreage in Gunpowder Falls State Park, perhaps no area is less known or more lightly used than the Sweet Air section. Located near the headwaters of the Little Gunpowder River, near Jacksonville, this very diverse landscape offers fine hiking through fields and forest. There are several trails of varying lengths, to suit walkers of all abilities and energy levels.

Directions: From the Baltimore Beltway (I-695), take exit 27, Dulaney Valley Road, north. Just after crossing Loch Raven Reservoir, the road bears left and becomes Jarrettsville Pike. Turn right onto Hess Road, 11.7 miles from the beltway. Go 1.1 miles and turn right onto Park Road. Go 0.3 miles and turn left onto Moores Road. Go 0.9 miles and turn right onto the gravel Dalton-Brevard Road. This road ends at the parking area for the Sweet Air section of Gunpowder Falls State Park.

▼ **Little Gunpowder Trail**

Distance: 3.6-mile circuit
Difficulty: Moderate

Not part of the longer trail of the same name described above, this diverse, white-blazed loop is a good introduction to the pleasures of the Sweet Air section. The route passes through cornfields, hedgerows, uncultivated fields, and both upland and riparian forest. The section that runs directly beside the Little Gunpowder River is especially pretty.

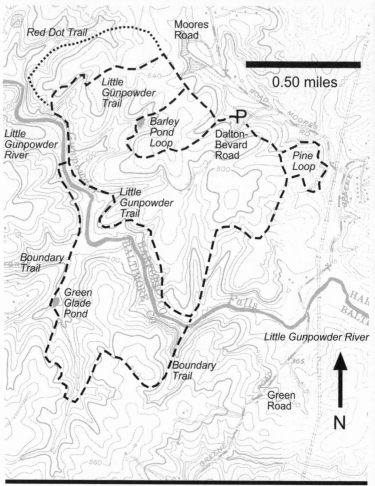

24. SWEET AIR AREA

Begin your hike from the parking area, which is merely a mowed grassland and where there are no facilities of any sort. The trail begins at the west end of the lot, near the corner of a fenced horse pasture. The trail sign calls this the Barley Pond Loop, but the white blazes indicate it is the Little Gunpowder Trail (it provides access to the Barley Pond Loop). The old farm road soon passes through a field of corn, which in August towers overhead like some tropical jungle. At mile 0.4, just past an adjacent suburban backyard, the Little Gunpowder Trail turns left. It passes through hedgerows of multiflora rose, the plentiful thorns of which can make passage in summer a painful affair. This thick growth provides shelter for animals that like overgrown, shrubby habitat. Look for rabbits, snakes, and birds like towhees, yellowthroats, white-eyed vireos, catbirds, and various sparrows.

The trail soon crosses a pipeline cut and enters the forest. This very open woods gives long vistas over extensive fern beds among red maples, as the path winds downhill. The trail meets the Little Gunpowder River at mile 1.0; turn left, downstream. (The red dot trail, designated for hikers only, bears right and returns you to the uplands near the pipeline.) The Little Gunpowder River is very narrow here near its origin, flowing smoothly past small rock outcrops over a bed of gravel. The shallow valley features large trees shading the river and lush vegetation streamside, making a very pretty scene. The trail runs a few feet from the river; look for floodplain flowers like day lily, jewelweed, and stinging nettle, and flowers of rich soil like bloodroot, jack-in-the-pulpit, wild ginger, and enchanter's nightshade. Birds include veeries, ovenbirds, wood thrushes, red-eyed vireos, parula warblers, and several kinds of woodpeckers. The only drawback to this trail is the frequent mud bogs churned up by horses, which make passage a messy affair.

red maple leaves

At mile 1.4, the trail leaves the floodplain, but still generally parallels the river, and views of the river are frequent, especially in winter. The Little Gunpowder Trail joins the light blue–blazed Boundary Trail at mile 2.4. These united trails lead uphill, away from the river, passing an abandoned field lush with milkweed, tasty raspberries, and fragrant thistles. After another cornfield, the trail reenters the forest; it arrives back at the parking lot at mile 3.6.

▼ **Barley Pond Loop**

Distance: 1.6-mile circuit
Difficulty: Easy to moderate

This short, yellow-blazed loop features a woodland pond popular with kids fishing for bluegills. The trail is short enough to be comfortable for small legs. Begin this walk using the same route as the Little Gunpowder Trail. After 0.1 miles, just past a row of trees, the trail bears left. Running at first along the edge of a cornfield, the path enters the forest at mile 0.6. There are lots of ferns along this portion of the trail; they include hay-scented, New York, cinnamon, and Christmas ferns. Turn right at mile 0.8. If you encounter a pipeline right-of-way, you've gone a bit too far; retrace your steps for about twenty feet and look for the yellow-blazed trail leading uphill through the forest.

Barley Pond is reached at mile 1.1. This is an old impoundment in a pretty woodland setting and is an enjoyable spot for a picnic. Bluegills are the most common catch here, and turtles sun themselves on logs; both of these animals seem to hold a fascination for youngsters that is out of all proportion to their size. Continue uphill past the pond; as the trail emerges from the forest, it joins the white-blazed Little Gunpowder Trail. Turn right and return to the parking area at mile 1.6.

▼ **Boundary Trail**

Distance: 4.9-mile circuit
Difficulty: Moderate

At 4.9 miles, the light blue–blazed Boundary Trail is the longest footpath in the Sweet Air portion of Gunpowder Falls State Park. It is mostly upland in character, descending into the floodplain only to cross the Little Gunpowder River. Because it is not possible to ford the river without getting shoes and socks wet, the Boundary Trail is not recommended for hiking in winter or in cooler weather.

The first portion of the Boundary Trail is contiguous with the Little Gunpowder Trail (see p. 97). Where the Little Gunpowder Trail turns left at mile 0.4 into some hedgerows, continue straight. Within another 0.1 miles, the light-blue-blazed Boundary Trail turns left, downhill. Be sure to follow the blazes, as there are several unblazed side trails in this area. The trail eventually reaches the Little Gunpowder River, where a gas pipeline crosses. Remove your shoes and wade the river, about thirty feet wide and knee deep even in summer. On the far side, the trail turns downstream and runs along the floodplain for about 0.5 miles. At Sawmill Branch, the trail turns away from the river, rising uphill to Green Glade Pond. This pretty little woodland pond is home to amphibians in spring and attracts many different birds in the nesting season. Beyond the pond, the trail continues uphill to its most distant point, a trail intersection marked by a large boulder. Turn left, carefully follow the blazes downhill, and eventually arrive at the Little Gunpowder River. Wade the river again. Within 100 yards, the white-blazed Little Gunpowder Trail intersects the blue-blazed Boundary Trail. The unified trail leads uphill, reaching the parking lot at mile 4.9.

▼ **Pine Loop**

Distance: 1.5 miles
Difficulty: Moderate

This short, yellow-blazed loop merely extends the Boundary Trail at the northeastern corner of the park. It passes through and then alongside a planted white pine forest.

▼ **Pleasantville Circuit**

Distance: 5.5-mile circuit
Difficulty: Easy to moderate

Directions: From the Baltimore Beltway (I-695), take exit 31, Harford Road (Route 147) in a northeasterly direction. Go 8.0 miles and turn left on Fork Road. Go 1.7 miles and turn right on Bottom Road. Proceed 2.0 miles and park at any of several roadside pullouts within view of the river. More parking is available by crossing the bridge over the Little Gunpowder River, turning immediately right onto Guyton Road, and parking at any of several more pullouts.

A walk along the Little Gunpowder River certainly fits the moniker Pleasantville. Tall trees shade this narrow, gently flowing creek incising a shallow valley. The river is visible for much of the walk, and there are plenty of wildflowers and birds. A portion of the trail is on the railbed of the late, lamented Ma and Pa (Maryland and Pennsylvania) Railroad.

Trails run along both the Baltimore County and Harford County sides of the river, and the route is described below as a loop using both. The trail on the north side of the river is designated the Ma and Pa Trail and is blazed in yellow. The Little Gunpowder Trail, with white blazes, runs along the south side of the river. Finally, the white-blazed Pleasantville Loop is an upland trail west of Pleasantville Road. Hikers who want a route with fewer elevation changes, a wider footpath, and more continuous views of the river should choose the Ma and Pa Trail.

Begin your walk where Bottom Road crosses the Little Gunpowder River. There is roadside parking for a dozen cars at several pullouts on either side of the river. Cross the road bridge into Harford County on the north side of the river and walk uphill along the road shoulder for 0.2 miles. At this point, a wide, conspicuous trail leads left uphill from the road, joining the abandoned railroad grade within 200 yards. For the next mile, the trail is wide and flat.

Construction of a railroad through rolling country like the Maryland Piedmont required frequent cuts and fills in order to keep the railroad bed level. Hills were carved through using drilling and blasting, and valleys were filled in. In addition, since valleys frequently contain streams, viaducts were constructed to allow the water to flow underneath the roadbed without eroding it. There are some fine examples of fills along this section of the Ma and Pa Trail, where you can look up the stream valley from a high perch atop the roadbed.

At mile 1.3, the old railroad once crossed the Little Gunpowder on a trestle; because only the approaches remain, the trail now descends to river level. It then runs upstream parallel to the river

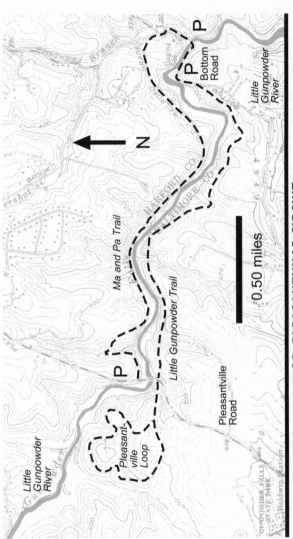

N

Little Gunpowder River

Ma and Pa Trail

Little Gunpowder Trail

Pleasant-
ville Loop

Pleasantville
Road

Little
Gunpowder River

Bottom
Road

P
P
P
P

0.50 miles

25. PLEASANTVILLE CIRCUIT

on the floodplain. In summer, vegetation impinges on these narrower portions of the trail. There are beautiful wildflowers like day lily, wild ginger, and jewelweed, and nasties like stinging nettle, poison ivy, and the thorny multiflora rose. The beauty of this trail far outweighs these vegetable detractions, however. As the trail nears Pleasantville Road, it rises from the floodplain, goes over a short but steep hill, and terminates at mile 2.2. There is parking for several cars along the surprisingly busy Pleasantville Road.

Cross the Little Gunpowder into Baltimore County. You may return directly to Bottom Road by taking the Little Gunpowder Trail downstream (described below) or continue west on the Pleasantville Loop.

The Pleasantville Loop is 1.3 miles long. It is very lightly used, and the trail may be difficult to follow in places. Keep alert for the white blazes, however, and you'll avoid getting off-trail.

The Pleasantville Loop trail starts a few feet past the bridge, on the Baltimore County side, and rises steeply to the top of the ridge. It twists and winds through a maturing forest in a complex fashion, hitting every point on the compass several times. Faint game trails intersect at several places, and a double-laned renegade trail carved by an all-terrain vehicle further confuses the issue. If you reach agricultural fields, you've missed the park trail. Keep the white blazes in sight; if you lose sight of them, backtrack until you find one. The trail eventually loops back on itself and then descends to Pleasantville Road.

Cross the road and continue downstream on the white-blazed Little Gunpowder Trail. This footpath quickly rises to the railroad grade, now on the Baltimore County side of the river. However, this portion of the railbed is a bit farther from the river, and vegetation obscures the view in summer. At the trestle approach, the trail narrows, dips into a ravine, and crosses a small tributary creek. For the next mile, the Little Gunpowder Trail generally parallels the river, crossing several small streams, before emerging at Bottom Road. From Pleasantville Road to Bottom Road on the Little Gunpowder Trail is 2.0 miles. The riverside circuit composed of the Ma and Pa Trail and the Little Gunpowder Trail totals 4.2 miles. Addition of the Pleasantville Loop brings the mileage to 5.5.

A Short History of the Ma and Pa

THE NINETEENTH CENTURY IN AMERICA WAS THE ERA OF RAILROADS. THE iron horse helped open up the west and made the Industrial Revolution possible by enabling goods to be moved long distances. As automobiles, trucks, and buses gained ascendancy in the twentieth century, many of the smaller, locally oriented railroad lines quit operation. Older citizens fondly remember these local lines and their romantic appeal in the age of steam. And perhaps the best-loved in the mid-Atlantic region was the Maryland and Pennsylvania Railroad, known universally as the Ma and Pa.

This colorful local railroad ran from Baltimore to York, but on a circuitous route that included the slate quarries at Delta, Pennsylvania, very near the Susquehanna River. Baltimore and York are only 49 miles apart, but the Ma and Pa's peripatetic route covered 77 miles! Winding through the countryside, the Ma and Pa had 476 curves and passed over 111 trestles and bridges. The one-way trip took 4 hours and 10 minutes, with an average speed of less than 20 miles per hour.

The Maryland and Pennsylvania Railroad, incorporated in 1901, resulted from the merger of two smaller lines: the Peach Bottom Railroad and the Maryland Central Railroad. The Peach Bottom Railroad was the more ambitious of the two, formed in the 1870s to link York and Delta with Philadelphia and Pittsburgh. But most investors were local, and the railroad never came close to completing its grandiose plan. The Maryland Central was never much more than a local line, hauling mostly agricultural products to Baltimore from points in Harford County.

The Ma and Pa made a modest profit for a few years. In its heyday in the early teens, it had 573 employees, and the Bel Air station hosted sixteen trains a day. Corporate offices were in Baltimore, and most service facilities were found along the Jones Falls in the area that is now the Baltimore Streetcar Museum. The changing character of transportation, with the advent of trucks and buses, spelled trouble, however, and the Ma and Pa was in financial difficulty by 1915. Thereafter, a series of consolidations and cost-cutting measures yielded just enough revenue for the company to remain solvent through the Depression and World War II. The quaint old steam engines lasted until 1956, when diesels reduced operating costs, but by then, the railroad's death knell had already sounded, even if the patient was still alive. The contract to carry mail was lost in 1954, precipitating cancellation of passenger service (which was down to about twelve passengers a day anyway). The train no longer carried milk from the farms to the city, and coal shipments had declined greatly as well. In 1958, the route from Baltimore to Whiteford in northern Harford County was abandoned. Sections of track in Pennsylvania were gradually abandoned in the 1980s. Today, the Ma and Pa is merely a switching operation in the York railyards. However, an 8-mile section of track around Muddy Creek Forks has been preserved, and the Ma and Pa Railroad Preservation Society hopes to offer excursion trips for rail fans on this scenic portion of the line.

To longtime residents of rural northeastern Baltimore County, few memories are as nostalgic as the haunting whistle of an old steam train in the gathering dusk of evening. The Ma and Pa is gone from the landscape, but not forgotten.

NORTH POINT STATE PARK

Our parks and other recreation areas are used more frequently every year, and at times, the more popular parks can seem overrun with people. But North Point State Park is an anomaly: far more people visited this site in the first half of the twentieth century than ever will in the twenty-first. This 1,320-acre tract of land was the site of the very popular Bay Shore Park, a swimming beach, dance hall, restaurant, promenade pier, bowling alley, and gardens, operating between 1906 and 1947. The history of this site goes back even further; British forces advanced up this peninsula during the War of 1812, only to be repulsed at the nearby Battle of North Point. The agricultural fields within the park have been farmed continuously for more than 350 years.

When Bay Shore Park closed in 1947, the land was bought by Bethlehem Steel, as a possible site for future expansion. The Department of Natural Resources acquired the land in 1987, to be used as a state park. Almost half the acreage of North Point State Park is a designated Wildland, where resource protection is the only priority. Black Marsh Wildland is considered one of the finest examples of a freshwater marsh in the Chesapeake watershed and is home to an endangered species of marsh bird, the black rail.

Considerable improvements to the park occurred in 2000. A 3.8-mile bike trail, separate from adjacent roads, was established on a route that spans the entire width of the North Point peninsula. The entrance road was paved and hiking trails have been clearly blazed. Dozens of signs giving information about plant and animal species that might be seen have been posted on the trails.

The route for hiking described here is a 4.8-mile circuit that includes all of the Wildlands Trail (where bicycles are prohibited) and part of the Defenders Trail (the hiker/biker trail).

North Point State Park is presently managed by Gunpowder Falls State Park. For more information, call 410-592-2897.

▼ North Point State Park Trails

Distance: 4.8-mile circuit with a 2.2-mile (one way) paved spur
Difficulty: Easy

Directions: From the Baltimore Beltway (I-695), take exit 41 to North Point Boulevard, Route 151, south. Just before the road passes under the beltway, turn left onto North Point Road (Route 20). Continue 1.9 miles to the park entrance, on the left.

Begin your hike from the parking lot next to the fee station, located 0.5 miles from the entrance on North Point Road. The Wildland Trail is blazed in white and begins from one corner of the parking lot. The initial few hundred yards pass through an old field now grown up in small trees and dense underbrush. White mulberry trees are very common, their tasty fruits weighing down the branches hanging over the trail. The berries, which ripen in June, are especially attractive to birds, and there is much avian activity in the trees then.

At a huge old scarlet oak, the narrow footpath emerges from the forest into Black Marsh. You won't get your feet wet, however, because the trail is on the bed of the old trolley that brought visitors to Bay Shore Park. Constructed of slag and other waste materials from the nearby Sparrows Point steel plant, the roadbed is well drained and solid. A screen of small trees blocks the view of the marsh in warm weather, but in winter there are long vistas over cattails, common reeds, and mud flats. Midsummer brings the most spectacular views, when tens of thousands of crimson-eyed rose mallows blossom across the marsh. This large, showy flower, a member of the hibiscus family, is cottony white except for a rich crimson splash of color inside the corolla.

The trail reenters forest and soon reaches a side trail well worth a detour. This 0.3 mile (one way) footpath, blazed in light blue, leads to an observation deck with wonderful views across the marsh toward a pond of open water. Among the bird life you might see are great blue herons, green herons, snowy egrets, American egrets, osprey, red-winged blackbirds, various gulls, and even a bald eagle. Although Black Marsh supports a few black rails, you are unlikely to see any. This secretive, tiny bird is active only at night and had never been photographed until the 1980s!

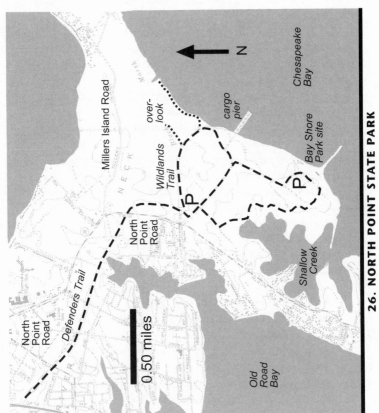

N

Millers Island Road

N E C K

Marsh

over-
look

Wildlands
Trail

cargo
pier

Chesapeake
Bay

North
Point
Road

P

P

Bay Shore
Park site

Defenders Trail

North
Point
Road

Shallow
Creek

0.50 miles

Old
Road
Bay

26. NORTH POINT STATE PARK

Return to the Wildlands Trail and turn left to continue your walk. The forest here is a mix of low, wet places that support moisture-loving plants, such as royal fern, jewelweed, and red maple, and higher, drier habitats dominated by oaks and hollies. Eventually you will see the hulking concrete shell of the powerhouse, once used to generate the electricity that ran the trolley. Just past the powerhouse, turn left on the red-blazed Powerhouse Trail.

This detour is also quite worthwhile. Within 100 yards, the trail ends at a long stretch of isolated Chesapeake Bay beach. At lower tides, walk north along the narrow beach, where much bleached driftwood accumulates. After about 250 yards, the beach ends in a tangle of common reed, and no further progress is possible. Return to the Powerhouse Trail.

Rejoining the Wildlands Trail, continue walking south. The path soon curves away from the water and reaches the paved park road after an estimated distance of 1.9 miles. You may return to the parking lot by bearing right on the park road, but to complete the circuit, turn left. A walk of 0.6 miles brings you to the activity hub of North Point State Park.

Located on the Chesapeake, this was the site of the old Bay Shore Park. There is very little left. The trolley barn has been refurbished and is used for picnics. Nearby, a large fountain has been charmingly and lovingly restored. Only the concrete footings of other structures remain, and they are largely obscured by encroaching vegetation. The beach is open for wading, although it is unguarded. There is a small visitor center that contains some interesting photographs from the glory days of Bay Shore Park.

At the south end of this activity hub, walk out onto the jetty that was once the site of the promenade pier. Jutting out more than 100 yards into the bay, it is popular for fishing and birding, and there are great views of Chesapeake Bay.

The hiker/biker trail, known as the Defenders Trail, begins at the south end of the trolley barn. For the next 1.2 miles, this stone-surfaced trail winds through a young forest and past many small agricultural fields. During migration seasons, birding is good, in the forest for songbirds and in the fields for some shorebirds and open-land birds like bobolinks. When the trail reaches the paved park road, follow it for 0.3 miles to the parking lot.

The remainder of the Defenders Trail is paved. It quickly leaves the park proper and runs west across the North Point peninsula. Opened in 2000, this trail parallels Bay Shore Drive but is separate and thus safe for young cyclists. It is screened by trees for its entire length, but there are three road and two driveway crossings. The hiker/biker trail is 2.2 miles in length from its western terminus at North Point Boulevard to the parking lot at the fee station.

BALTIMORE

COUNTY PARKS

▼ Trolley Trail / Benjamin Banneker Trail

Distance: 3.4 miles as described
Difficulty: Easy

Directions: From the Baltimore Beltway (I-695), take exit 14, Edmondson Avenue, west for 2.6 miles to the end. The Trolley Trail may also be accessed from the western end. To reach this trailhead, take Route 144, Frederick Road, toward Ellicott City. Just before crossing the Patapsco River, turn right on Oella Avenue and park in the lot on the right just beyond the tavern. The trail is on a berm above the parking lot.

Some of our most popular trails occupy the abandoned right-of-ways of trolleys and railroads. Such railbeds have many advantages as recreational trails: their gradient usually changes very gradually, the trail surface is already solid and well-compacted, the narrow right-of-way is unsuited for business or housing, and the cost of land purchase is relatively inexpensive. As a result, foresighted local governments have bought and developed dozens of such "rails-to-trails."

The Trolley Trail, in southwestern Baltimore County, is one such rail trail. It occupies a portion of railbed used by one of the old trolleys (called streetcars by Baltimoreans), the line that once ran from Baltimore City to Ellicott City. At first a narrow strip of woodland squeezed by surrounding houses, the trail eventually enters a narrow valley that makes it seem more remote than it is. Emerging from a steep rock cut onto the floodplain of the Patapsco River, the Trolley Trail provides walking access to the shops and restaurants of Ellicott City just across the river.

Adjacent to the Trolley Trail is a small county historical park on the site of the Benjamin Banneker farm. Known as America's first black man of science, Benjamin Banneker was a self-taught surveyor, mathematician, almanac writer, and farmer. A museum on the site offers a pleasant diversion and is well worth a visit. For more information, call 410-887-1081.

The Trolley Trail is paved and is popular with local residents, dog walkers, and the occasional bicyclist. The spur trail in Benjamin Banneker Park is unpaved and rarely used.

Begin your walk from the trailhead at the western end of Edmondson Avenue. There is always ample roadside parking here

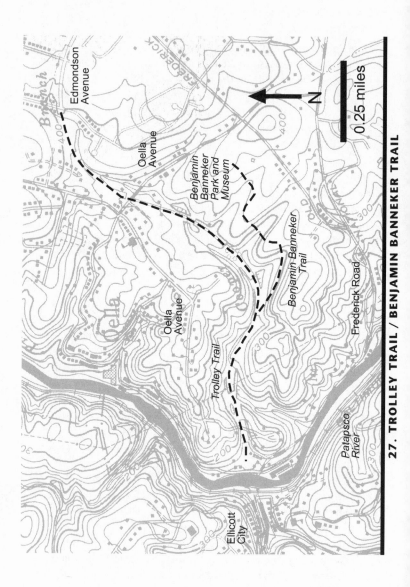

27. TROLLEY TRAIL / BENJAMIN BANNEKER TRAIL

N

0.25 miles

Edmondson Avenue

Oella Avenue

Benjamin Banneker Park and Museum

Benjamin Banneker Trail

Frederick Road

Oella Avenue

Trolley Trail

Ellicott City

Patapsco River

in this residential neighborhood. The first half-mile of trail is pleasant but unexceptional; houses are always within view through a thin screen of trees. Below Westchester Avenue, however, the trail enters a narrow valley that seals off all suburban noise and views. A family of barred owls occupies the defile, and their "who-cooks-for-you" calls are often heard at dawn and dusk.

At mile 0.8, you will see the entrance to the Benjamin Banneker Trail, denoted by a sign. This short spur is best explored on the return trip. Continuing downhill on the Trolley Trail, Coopers Branch begins to parallel the path. Ravaged by stormwater runoff from suburban Catonsville, Coopers Branch displays the characteristics of many local streams: erosion to bedrock, highly variable flows, and a dearth of aquatic insect life. Despite the degraded nature of this little stream, there are tall, handsome trees along its banks, and the overall sense is that of a secret place, sheltered from the surrounding development.

The trail enters a steep rock cut at mile 1.3. The narrow defile, hewn from solid rock to allow the trolley to reach Ellicott City, is a highlight of the Trolley Trail. Upon emerging from the cut, the trail ends at an overlook from which much of Ellicott City is visible. On winter afternoons, dozens of vultures congregate over the town, soaring on unseen thermals. After one has worked off some energy hiking, a drink, dessert, or meal at one of Ellicott City's many charming restaurants is certainly in order.

Return up the Trolley Trail for 0.7 miles and turn onto the Benjamin Banneker Trail. This unpaved footpath runs through a forest of large trees with an abundant understory of spicebush. Whitetail deer are common; they rest here during the day, before venturing out to eat the shrubbery of Catonsville gardens during the hours of darkness.

After a quarter-mile, bear right on a wood chip path that leads to the back of the Benjamin Banneker Museum. Should you care to visit, the museum is open Tuesday through Saturday, 10 a.m. to 6 p.m. There are displays of a few artifacts uncovered during an archeological excavation in the mid-1980s, as well as a series of rotating exhibits.

To reach the Trolley Trail from the Banneker Museum, walk down the driveway of the park to Westchester Avenue, turn left, and walk along the narrow road shoulder for 0.4 miles. Turn right on the Trolley Trail, which reaches Edmondson Avenue at mile 3.4.

Benjamin Banneker, America's First Black Man of Science

IF ONLY THE LANDSCAPE COULD SPEAK! MOST OF THE HIKES IN THIS BOOK are in forested areas that look undisturbed; we forget that every acre in Baltimore County has been used for farming or pasturage at some point in the past. And so we can only wonder: What sort of people lived on this land, what did they do with their days, and how did they live?

We know something of the answers for the land along the Trolley Trail. We know that in 1690, an English indentured servant, Molly Welsh, began to grow tobacco here, hacking out space between the trees of the forest primeval. By 1692, she had purchased an African slave, Banneka, then gave him his freedom and married him. They had four chidren. It was a tough life: no neighbors, racial prejudice, complete self-reliance. But the family had what few other families of color had at the time—freedom and land.

In 1731, Molly's daughter Mary had a son, Benjamin, who was destined to become a renowned amateur astronomer, mathematician, and author—America's first black man of science. The extended family lived on a 100-acre farm in southwestern Baltimore County, wringing an ever-improving living from the land.

The young Banneker was fortunate enough to attend a nearby Quaker school, learning to read and write in an era when that was highly unusual for a black child. He was precocious with mathematics and machinery but had little use for those abilities on the isolated farm. At age 22, Benjamin borrowed a pocket watch, made meticulous drawings and measurements, and carved from wood all the gears, wheels, and cogs needed to make a functional clock. For this feat he gained a measure of local fame, and the clock ran for more than fifty years.

Banneker's life changed in the 1770s when the Ellicott brothers established a mill on the Patapsco River only about a mile away. Ellicott's Lower Mills soon became a thriving center of commerce, and the Banneker farm was no longer so isolated. Even better, Benjamin was befriended by the Ellicott family, especially George, who treated him as an equal. George Ellicott was an experienced surveyor, even though he was only 18, at the time he met the 47-year-old Benjamin. Seeing Banneker's interest in and aptitude for things mechanical and mathematical, George lent Benjamin a good telescope and some textbooks. Fascinated, Banneker taught himself astronomy, calculating the motions of stars and predicting eclipses.

Benjamin Banneker left home for the only time in his life in 1791, to help another Ellicott, Andrew, survey the boundaries of the new District of Columbia. Although too old to participate in the field work, Banneker kept records and notes and made the astronomical calculations necessary for the survey. Using the finest instruments of the time and being taught by the new nation's "geographer general," Banneker greatly increased his knowledge and abilities.

Upon his return home, Banneker assembled his astronomical observations and calculations into an almanac, which was sold in the mid-Atlantic states yearly from 1792 to 1797. It was very popular and made Banneker a famous name in the young country. In an era of extreme prejudice, the almanac was touted as evidence that black men could learn complex subjects and be intellectual equals to white Americans.

By 1798, Banneker was in poor health. He did not publish his almanac again, but he continued to enjoy local acclaim and reputation. He died in 1806 and was buried on the farm. Banneker's one-room log house, containing his famous clock, inexplicably caught fire during his burial service and burned to the ground.

Benjamin Banneker left an inspiring legacy, having overcome poverty, isolation, poor education, and racial prejudice by hard work and intelligence. His life and work remain lessons for us even today.

OREGON RIDGE PARK

Most Baltimore-area residents know Oregon Ridge as a wonderful site for outdoor concerts, fairs, and fireworks and for the popular swimming lake, an old quarry now filled with water. But a minority have hiked any portion of the 6 miles of trails that wind through the property. And that's a shame, since the Oregon Ridge trail network is scenic, well-maintained, and traverses varied terrains. Whether you're looking for a quiet thirty-minute stroll in the woods or a heart-pumping, fast-paced hike over hill and dale, Oregon Ridge can satisfy you.

There are two major loop trails at Oregon Ridge. The shorter of the two, called the Loggers Red Trail, climbs to the top of the ridge, runs along the hilltop in an easterly direction, and then bears downhill to complete the circuit. This 1.6-mile trail is a pleasant and rather short introduction to Oregon Ridge. The second and longer loop includes much of the Loggers Red Trail (the name indicates the blazing color) but also extends south into the valley of Baisman Run. Various sections of it combine to form the Ivy Hill Yellow Trail and the S. James Campbell Trail. The second loop is 3.6 miles long.

All trails begin from the Nature Center, which has displays, live animals, knowledgeable staff, a small library and gift shop, and restrooms. Just outside the center are well-stocked bird feeders, which offer a good opportunity to see birds up close.

Mountain bikes are not allowed on the trails at Oregon Ridge, and dogs must be leashed.

For more information, contact Oregon Ridge Park (Nature Center) at 410-887-1815.

Directions: From the Baltimore Beltway (I-695), take I-83 north to Shawan Road, exit 20. Go west on Shawan Road for 1.0 miles. Turn left at the traffic light onto Beaver Dam Road. Go 50 feet and turn right into Oregon Ridge Park at the sign for the Nature Center. Follow this road 0.4 miles to the parking lot.

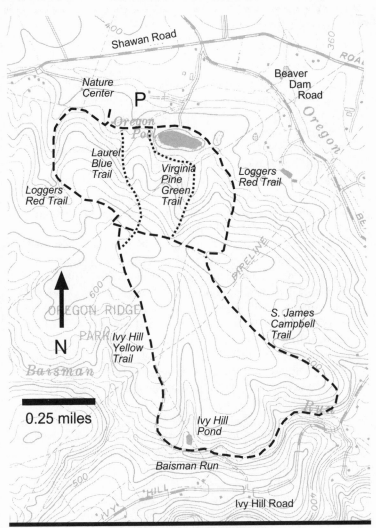

28. OREGON RIDGE PARK

■ ■

▼ Loggers Red Trail

Distance: 1.6-mile circuit
Difficulty: Moderate

Upon arrival at Oregon Ridge, park in the lot between the swimming lake and the nature center. There is usually adequate parking here, except during scheduled public events, when alternative parking arrangements in the fields will have been made. After visiting the nature center, cross the adjacent footbridge over a deep ravine. This is a good place to see birds, and not just those attracted to the nearby feeders; forest songbirds are common here, and the ravine bridge puts you closer to the treetops. On damp spring evenings, the ravine's vernal pools resound with the calls of love-struck amphibians.

At the far side of the bridge, turn right on the Loggers Red Trail. The initial few hundred yards pass through a mature forest with large trees, featuring both tulip poplars and oaks. There is lots of spicebush in the forest understory. This small tree, usually no more than ten feet tall, exudes a pleasant lemony scent when scratched. The trail soon begins to ascend along a small stream edged with water-loving plants, like skunk cabbage. But only a short distance away from the creek, the soil is rather arid, and plant growth is limited to xerophiles, like mountain laurel and blueberry.

At the top of the ridge, the trail emerges into a gas pipeline right-of-way. Since trees are kept down by mowing and light is plentiful, this is a good place to look for wildflowers. In spring the uncommon birdsfoot violet grows here, while later in the year Queen Anne's lace and goldenrod are prominent. The trail bears right along the pipeline for a hundred yards or so before turning into the forest; be alert for the red blazes. Two trails branch off to the right, the Short Cut Trail and the Ivy Hill Yellow Trail; these are described below as part of a longer circuit.

Continue following the Loggers Red Trail. This pleasant, easy walk runs for about a half-mile along the top of Oregon Ridge on a wide trail. The dominant tree species is chestnut oak, which is distinguished by deeply ridged bark and a wavy edge to its leaf. Woodpeckers, especially downy and red-bellied, are common in this forest. The Loggers Red Trail passes the Laurel Blue Trail and the Virginia Pine Green Trail, both of which merely lead directly downhill to the nature center; continue along the ridge. As a second gas pipeline right-of-way appears, the Loggers Red Trail turns left, downhill, eventually passing the lake and the parking lot before reaching the nature center.

■ ■

▼ Ivy Hill Yellow Trail / S. James Campbell Trail

Distance: 3.6-mile circuit
Difficulty: Moderate

Despite the two names, this is actually one trail that joins with the Loggers Red Trail to form a 3.6-mile circuit. The trail traverses the southern portion of Oregon Ridge Park, much of it in the deeply incised valley of Baisman Run. The tract containing these trails was purchased in 1990, and it is a welcome addition for hikers.

Begin this hike from the nature center and walk the Loggers Red Trail as described above to the top of the ridge at the first gas pipeline right-of-way. Soon after reentering the forest, turn right on the Short Cut Trail, or, if you should miss it, the Ivy Hill Yellow Trail that appears next. The Ivy Hill Trail runs south down the back of Oregon Ridge into the narrow valley of Baisman Run. Mountain laurel lines this trail; in May its large white flowers resemble clumps of snow clinging to the dark green leaves.

At the bottom of the hill, walk downstream for a few feet, and then detour upslope to Ivy Hill Pond. This beautiful little body of water sits in a hemlock-shaded dell, and it is as pretty a place to relax or picnic as there is in the Baltimore area. Several large boulders that block the pond's outlet are perfect for sitting on while you bird, read, or just think. Be sure to carry out all trash, including any that you might find, so that this sylvan dell remains equally beautiful for those who follow you.

Baisman Run flows clear and clean to the east, sparkling over gravel bars and dancing through tiny rocky chutes. In spring, a great variety of wildflowers abound near the creek. Look for bloodroot, hepatica, spring beauty, trout lily, toothwort, wild ginger, jack-in-the-pulpit, and dwarf ginseng.

The trail crosses the creek several times, seeking a firm footing, and after about a half-mile emerges within sight of Ivy Hill Road. At this point, the trail bears sharply left and rises steeply uphill to the top of the ridge. Cross a second gas pipeline right-of-way. When the trail ends at the Loggers Red Trail, turn right and follow it downhill, as described above, to the nature center.

CROMWELL VALLEY PARK

Baltimore County's newest major park is Cromwell Valley Park. Purchased in 1993 and 1994, the park encompasses 367 acres in the watershed of Minebank Run, a tributary of the Big Gunpowder River. Extensive open fields kept in grassland dominate the park. In addition, there are hedgerows and coverts, groves of mature trees, upland forest, fields still kept in agriculture, and riparian buffers. The northeast border adjoins Loch Raven watershed property, extending the acreage of undeveloped land beyond that of the park itself. Situated within a mile of the beltway, preservation of this tract was a coup for county government.

This land has been farmed since the early 1700s. Old but well-kept farm buildings, including the beautiful Sherwood House, are scattered throughout the property.

Hikers will find a half-dozen fairly short trails available for exploration in this passive-use recreational park. Some are very easy, while others have substantial elevation changes. There is not a clearly defined circuit of trails, so four of the longer trails are described individually; choose whatever combination strikes your fancy.

Cromwell, in the few years since it opened, has become a very popular venue for birding. The variety of habitats makes for a productive morning, especially in the spring and fall. Autumn brings a surprising number of raptors to the skies over the park.

Horses and bikes are not permitted on trails in Cromwell Valley Park. The park is heavily used by dog walkers; dogs must be kept on leash and droppings collected and removed.

Begin exploration of Cromwell Valley at the parking lot of Willow Grove Farm, down a long lane from the park entrance on Cromwell Bridge Road. There are portable restrooms available just uphill from the parking lot, behind a garagelike building. A bulletin board has information about the park and its programs.

For more information about Cromwell Valley Park, call 410-887-2503.

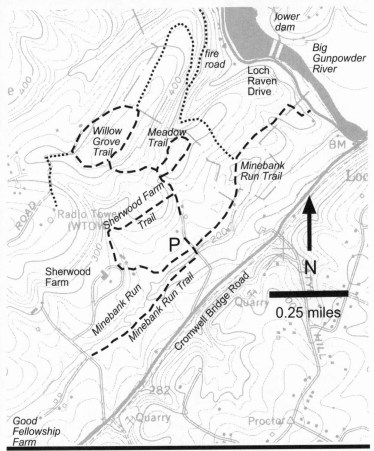

29. CROMWELL VALLEY PARK

Directions: From the Baltimore Beltway (I-695), take exit 29 north, Cromwell Bridge Road. Go 1.6 miles to the park entrance, marked Willow Grove Farm.

▼ **Minebank Run Trail**

Distance: 1.2 miles one way
Difficulty: Easy

This pastoral, blue-blazed trail runs the length of Minebank Run that flows within the park. Birders will find it quite productive.

From the parking lot, walk downhill to the stream and cross it. Turn right, walking upstream on a grassy trail that is kept mowed in the growing season. Although the creek is not visible from the trail, its presence and the adjacent riparian buffer of trees and shrubs make it prime habitat for birds. In addition to common species like robins, mockingbirds, chickadees, and starlings, look for indigo buntings, goldfinches, cedar waxwings, Baltimore and orchard orioles, yellowthroats, and red-winged blackbirds. A fencerow of mulberries and cherries insures substantial bird activity in June. Bluebirds nest in the many boxes set up for them along the trail. Bobolinks migrate through each spring and fall, feeding in the surrounding grasslands. Although the habitat is perfect, meadowlarks are surprisingly uncommon; their populations have declined in the past few decades, especially close to suburban areas.

At the driveway to Sherwood Farm, turn around and retrace your steps. Cross the bridge at Willow Grove Farm and continue downstream. Minebank Run is visible for the first few hundred yards. Kingfishers and great blue herons can sometimes be seen along the creek. As the trail bends away from the stream, several brick lime kilns are visible on the left. These ovens were used until the 1920s. Marble from quarries to the north was dumped into the top and heated over wood fires. The resulting lime powder was collected and used to make whitewash and soil additives to reduce acidity in agricultural fields and gardens.

The trail continues up a small hill through a field of grasses interspersed with summer and fall wildflowers. Look for oxeye daisies and a variety of goldenrods. The trail eventually reaches the remains of a paved road, which bears right and drops downhill to terminate at Loch Raven Road just downstream of the dam. Return by the same route. Note that at least two other footpaths join this portion of the Minebank Run Trail. They are not a part of the Cromwell Valley Park trail system but connect to fire roads on the adjacent Loch Raven watershed property.

▼ Willow Grove Trail

Distance: 1.1 miles one way
Difficulty: Moderate

This hilly, red-blazed trail runs perpendicular to Minebank Run, leading to the top of the ridge. Begin from the parking lot by walking uphill along the driveway toward the big farmhouse and adjacent outbuildings. The huge sycamore shading this area usually hosts Baltimore orioles in late spring and early summer. The open fields and occasional big trees are classic oriole habitat. Continue uphill past a barn and a private residence. Note the Sherwood Farm Trail branching off to the left, and, farther on, the Meadow Trail to the right (both described below). The Willow Grove Trail then proceeds through an older forest until it emerges into an open area atop the ridge. Bear right on a mowed path. Just before the mowed area ends, the red trail turns left into the trees, although this turn is difficult to find. If you miss it, you'll enter a mature forest on an unmarked trail that leads to a fire road in the Loch Raven watershed property. Assuming you've managed to stay on the Willow Grove Trail, continue for about 300 yards, and then make a hard left into another mowed area. This turn is unmarked; if you miss it, you'll soon come within sight of a radio transmission tower, cluing you to retrace your steps. Proceed uphill on the mowed path until you complete a

female and male
Baltimore orioles

loop atop the ridge. Turn right, downhill, to return to the parking lot.

▼ **Sherwood Farm Trail**

Distance: 0.7 miles one way
Difficulty: Easy to moderate

This orange-blazed trail connects the Willow Grove Trail with Sherwood Farm to the west. Running mostly flat about halfway up the hill, it offers dramatic views across the grasslands all the way down to Minebank Run and up the opposite hillside. Near the Sherwood Farm end, the trail enters a forest dominated by tulip poplars and enlivened by a tiny stream. The trail soon emerges at the outbuildings of Sherwood Farm. From this point, you may return to the parking area by walking downhill for a short distance, turning left at a barn, and continuing downhill to the dirt road parallel to Minebank Run.

▼ **Meadow Trail**

Distance: 0.4 miles one way
Difficulty: Easy to moderate

The yellow-blazed Meadow Trail is a short loop off the Willow Grove Trail, running along the edge of a hilly meadow. There are lots of oxeye daisies in this field in the late spring, milkweed in midsummer, and goldenrods in the fall. The two foottrails that veer off into the forest connect to a fire road on the Loch Raven watershed.

Rivers in the Sky: The Wonder of Bird Migration

A COOL, CLEAR SPRING NIGHT ON A RIDGETOP IN RURAL BALTIMORE County: the newly risen moon glows just above the treetops, and the stars glisten like spindrift snow. The wind has fallen with the evening, and the quiet here before the season of insects is almost disconcerting. But as your ears adapt to the night, you begin to hear noises far overhead: a rustling of sorts, with pips and squeaks and chip notes, soft and irregular. You look up at the moon, and a shadow crosses its face. Then another, and another, and more, several dozen over a minute. The northward migration of songbirds is on.

Most North American birds migrate. Some of our local residents, like crows and jays and robins, migrate only short distances; so even though these birds are around all year, the individuals here in winter have mostly arrived in fall from the north, and are not the same ones nesting here in summer. Others among our summer birds migrate longer distances, to the gulf coast of the United States, to northern Mexico, Central America, even the West Indies. And a great many more species merely pass through our area twice a year on their way north in spring and south in fall. The fascinating question is: how do they know where to go, where to stop, and how to get there? The answer is more complicated than most people realize.

Migration requires both orientation and navigation. Orientation is knowing in which direction to fly, and it is cued on physical features in the environment: the sun, the stars, and magnetic fields. Birds can orient to all three. Using the sun as a compass is intuitively straightforward for us humans to understand. But many birds migrate at night. Experiments using indigo buntings inside a planetarium showed that they use a generalized star map, not one particular star like the North Star. If the image of the stars projected on the planetarium ceiling was shifted 90° from the real sky, birds changed their orientation accordingly. Finally, some birds use magnetic fields; laboratory experiments in which the orientation of a magnetic field was altered have demonstrated this capability in birds. Many birds have tiny crystals of magnetite in their nasal cavities that act as sensors of magnetic fields.

Navigation entails staying on track during migration or getting back on track after encountering winds or a storm. Navigation also involves knowing when and where to stop. Many songbirds, for example, return to the same patch of forest year after year, and adults frequently return to their natal area. Solving the riddle of avian navigation is less amenable to experimentation, but scientists believe birds hold a sort of mental map based on the appearance of the landscape from above. Odors and sounds may also help identify the route and the destination.

Scientists are working to learn more about avian migration. Ultimately, that tiny birds weighing only a few ounces migrate hundreds of miles in a night and return to the same acre of land they left six months earlier is a wonderment seemingly beyond all human comprehension.

BALTIMORE
CITY PARKS

LEAKIN PARK

There are many advantages to city living, but access to hiking trails and other outdoor recreational amenities rarely tops the list. Of late, however, Baltimore City has recognized the recreational and ecological value of greenways and has been developing trails along both the Jones Falls and the Gwynns Falls. Leakin Park, on the west side of town, is host to the Gwynns Falls Trail, currently a 4-mile path with both paved and crushed limestone sections. Also traversing Leakin Park is a network of short foottrails suitable for hikers who are looking for an unimproved trail in a wooded setting. Both are described below.

Leakin Park is not heavily visited, in part because many citizens are afraid of criminal activity. Since the opening of the Gwynns Falls Trail in the late 1990s, a contingent of Baltimore City police has been working from an office in the park, patrolling the trail on a regular basis. As a result, some park employees now consider it one of the safer places in Baltimore City.

For more information regarding Leakin Park trails, contact the Carrie Murray Outdoor Education Center at 410-396-0808.

Directions: From the Baltimore Beltway (I-695), take exit 16, I-70, east to the end. The exit ramp dumps you onto Security Boulevard. Make the first right onto Forest Park Avenue, followed by an immediate right onto Franklintown Road. Proceed 1.6 miles to the Winans Meadow Trailhead.

The westbound #15 bus serves Leakin Park, stopping along Windsor Mill Road at the park's northwest corner.

▼ Gwynns Falls Trail

Distance: 4.0 miles one way
Difficulty: Easy

The bucolic nature of the Gwynns Falls Trail is surprising, given its location within the city limits. Much of the trail is quite iso-

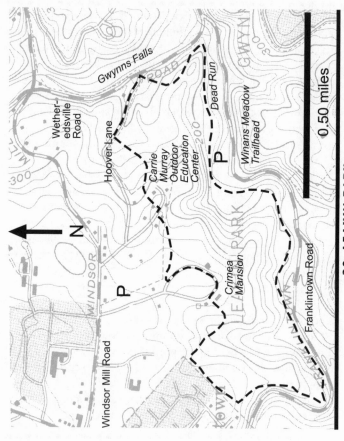

30. LEAKIN PARK

lated from the surrounding urban bustle, and the views from most parts of the trail are of a forested stream valley that could easily be mistaken for one in rural Baltimore County. Except for Franklintown Road, there are no signs of civilization at all.

Four miles of trail have been completed as of this writing, and there are definite plans to extend this trail another 8 miles downstream along the Gwynns Falls to where it joins tidewater near Oriole Park at Camden Yards.

Begin your walk at the Winans Meadow Trailhead, where you will find ample parking, restrooms, and an information kiosk. Official park brochures show a 0.25-mile paved "Children's Loop" in this area, suitable for bicycles, rollerblades, or a short, casual stroll, all within view of the parking area. However, a portion of the trail is subject to flooding, and the path may sometimes be wet, muddy, or rocky.

The portion of the Gwynns Falls Trail beyond the loop begins from the east end of the parking area. The paved trail parallels Dead Run, an aptly named major tributary of the Gwynns Falls. Virtually the entire watershed of Dead Run is developed, with very little surface area that is not paved or otherwise impervious to rainfall. Hence, even minor storms flash-flood the little stream with torrents of muddy, polluted water. Much of the riverbed has been scoured down to bedrock, and there is little aquatic life.

At mile 0.35, the trail crosses a pretty bridge spanning Dead Run and dumps onto Wetheredsville Road, permanently closed to vehicular traffic. Wetheredsville Road runs adjacent to the Gwynns Falls proper, a creek about thirty feet wide in winter and just a trickle during a summer drought. The river flows noisily over small rapids and would be a true delight except for the incredible amount of trash, especially plastic bags, that clings to riverside vegetation. Such seems the fate of urban streams, receiving the effluvia of hundreds of storm drains after every major storm event. Water quality in the Gwynns Fall is poor. But just when you're thinking about consigning this urban creek to the lower circles of environmental hell, the joyous rattle of a kingfisher or the watchful waiting of a great blue heron enlivens your day.

At mile 1.0, the trail reaches Windsor Mill Road. Bear right and cross the bridge, turning right again on the far side. The Windsor Mill Trailhead is located here, but parking is quite limited.

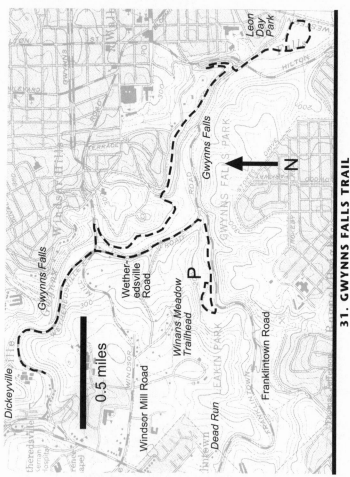

Dickeyville

Gwynns Falls

theredsville
Sherman
Hospital

Windsor Mill Road

0.5 miles

Wetheredsville Road

Winans Meadow Trailhead

Dead Run

EAKIN PARK

FRANKLINTOWN

Franklintown Road

Gwynns Falls

ROAD

P

Gwynns Falls

GWYNNS FALLS PARK

N

STOKES DRIVE

Leon Day Park

HILTON

300

200

200

31. GWYNNS FALLS TRAIL

This next section of trail has a unique historical character. In the 1800s it was a millrace, supplying water and its power to five mills in the Calverton (now Rosemont) community. By 1900, the millrace was no longer in use, and it was filled in to become the Mill Race Path, popular for strolling a century before it became the Gwynns Falls Trail. This portion of trail is not paved, however. There are frequent golf-ball-sized rocks in the trail bed and puddles in wet weather, so road bikes, children on training wheels, and strollers will find it difficult going. The drop-off is quite steep in places, so keep children well supervised.

The next 1.5 miles may be the best portion of the Gwynns Falls Trail. The path is far above the river and Franklintown Road, and in winter views of the river valley and its forest are wonderful. There are surprisingly many wildflowers here, including spring beauty, jack-in-the-pulpit, violet, day lily, and jewelweed. Big old trees, especially oaks, tulip poplars, and American beeches, tower over the path, keeping it shady even in the hottest weather.

Paving resumes at Hilton Parkway, and the trail drops steeply off the hillside to floodplain level. After crossing several busy streets, the trail encircles Leon Day Park, named for the Hall of Fame baseball player and Baltimore native. As of this writing, Leon Day Park is the trail terminus. This trailhead has parking and restrooms and is 3.0 miles from the Winans Meadow Trailhead. A circuit of Leon Day Park adds another mile to your walk.

Return on the same route, but don't miss a side trip that is not an official part of the Gwynns Falls Trail. At the intersection of Windsor Mill Road and Wetheredsville Road, continue on Wetheredsville Road as it parallels the Gwynns Falls in an upstream direction. A walk of 0.65 miles through a pretty forested landscape brings you to the historic mill community of Dickeyville. This is arguably Baltimore's most charming neighborhood, an isolated enclave of meticulously kept homes, many constructed from the native stone of the valley.

Once back at the Winans Meadow Trailhead, energetic hikers can explore the many short foottrails that connect the highlights of Leakin Park: the Carrie Murray Outdoor Education Center, the historic Crimea Mansion, and even a miniature railroad, which operates once a month in pleasant weather. A suggested 2.6-mile circuit of Leakin Park is described below.

Construction on Phase 2 of the Gwynns Falls Trail is expected to begin late in 2001. The trail will follow the river downstream from Leon Day Park to Carroll Park, a distance of about 2 miles. Phase 3 will follow soon after, finances permitting. This will be the longest and most complex leg of the Gwynns Falls Trail. After extending downstream from Carroll Park in the Gwynns Falls Valley, the trail will fork near tidewater. The northern branch will run near Oriole Park at Camden Yards, and then over to the Inner Harbor. The southern prong will follow the shoreline of the Patapsco River through Middle Branch Park and on to Cherry Hill Park.

▼ Leakin Park Circuit

Distance: 2.6-mile circuit
Difficulty: Moderate

A complex network of hiking trails winds through Leakin Park. Exploring them makes a very pleasant way to spend an afternoon. A surprising sense of remoteness permeates these lightly used trails; most hikers rarely even consider Leakin Park as a des-

racoon

tination. That's a shame, because the quality of the experience rivals nearby state parks.

The 2.6-mile circuit described below is the longest hike in Leakin Park. In large measure, it follows the perimeter of the park. A number of shorter trails intersect the described route; all lead back to the developed, northern portion of Leakin, on the uplands.

Begin your walk from the Winans Meadow Trailhead, off Franklintown Road. Ample parking, restrooms, and information are available here. At the west end of the parking area, cross Dead Run on a small footbridge. Turn right and follow the paved path downstream for about 200 yards. Where the paved trail turns right to recross Dead Run, continue straight on a foottrail.

The trail passes through a forest of large trees, most of the time staying within sight of Dead Run. A lush understory of shrubs and herbaceous plants implies that whitetail deer have not browsed the plant life here, as is so typical elsewhere in the region. There is good birdlife near the water, including a resident kingfisher, who apparently finds enough fish to sustain himself.

At mile 0.4, the trail arrives at a point overlooking the junction of Dead Run and Gwynns Falls. The trail bears left, uphill, but soon drops back down onto a much wider, wood-chipped path. This portion of the trail was improved in the winter of 2000 to accommodate filming of the movie Blair Witch Project II.

As the trail reaches Wetheredsville Road (now permanently closed to vehicles), turn left on Hutton Avenue, a gated, paved road. Continue for about 200 yards and turn left on a footpath. The first portion of this trail is on a boardwalk that keeps hikers dryshod; the soil is often very wet here. There is a rich understory of spicebush, multiflora rose, and poison ivy, as well as an inordinate number of spider webs across the trail. The trail passes through a younger forest of slender trees before emerging into a clearing at the Carrie Murray Outdoor Education Center at mile 1.0.

If the center is open, be sure to stop by to view the displays. There are often wild birds being rehabilitated here as well. To continue the walk, turn right up the paved service road. Go past some truly immense white oaks, and turn left onto a white-blazed foottrail opposite a small parking lot. At mile 1.2, the footpath merges with an old dirt road, bordered by huge boxwoods on one side and a line of osage orange trees on the other. At the paved road, Bald Eagle Drive, turn left.

The Crimea Mansion soon comes into view. This old stone building with wood accents was built in the 1850s by Thomas Winans, who made his fortune in railroading. During the Civil War, Winans was a vocal southern sympathizer, and rumors of escape tunnels and secret stashes of firearms on his property abounded.

Just past the Crimea Mansion, turn left at a climbing wall into a parking lot and pick up an old dirt road at its back end. Within 50 yards, make a right, and follow this foottrail through a forest studded with huge old trees. The occasional rock wall appears, reminiscent of a time when these were agricultural fields.

At a T-intersection at mile 1.5, turn left. The trail now runs along the border of the park, and there is much trash from a nearby group of apartments. Eventually, the trail leads downhill to Franklintown Road. Turn left, following the trail along a pipeline right-of-way that is overgrown with vegetation in the warmer months of the year. At the top of a small hill, Winans Meadow appears below, with the Trailhead parking area at its far end.

JONES FALLS TRAIL

The Jones Falls is Baltimore's river. Certainly the Gwynns Falls drains a larger watershed, and the Patapsco gives its name to the tidal waters of the harbor. But the Jones Falls carves its valley due south through the heart of Baltimore, topographically dividing East Baltimore from West Baltimore. Much of the city's early industry grew up on the banks of the Jones Falls, using its hydraulic energy to power mills and generators. Today, the Jones Falls is a quirky stream with many faces: its water quality is dismal, but it is still a surprisingly pleasant natural place, where herons and kingfishers play; its streambed is obscure, mostly forgotten and in part consigned to a drainage pipe, but the valley's wonderful potential as a recreational resource is just beginning to be recognized.

The City of Baltimore plans a paved recreational trail along a portion of the Jones Falls Valley. It will run from Pennsylvania Station in the south to Wyman Park Drive in the north, running parallel to Falls Road and generally within sight of the Jones Falls. Although this is only a little more than a mile of trail in the valley itself, it will connect to the open space of Druid Hill Park. The trail will emerge from the valley, cross the Jones Falls on Wyman Park Drive, and join the park road that encircles Druid Hill Park lake. One lane of this loop will be converted for pedestrian and bicycle use, much as is Lake Montebello Drive. Thus, there will be almost three miles of dedicated, off-road trail for use by recreationalists. Construction is expected to begin in 2001.

Citizen activists have even bigger plans for the Jones Falls valley. They envision the Jones Falls Trail extending northward to Cylburn Arboretum, and even to Robert E. Lee Memorial Park and Lake Roland. This would create a true urban greenway of significant length, connecting several of Baltimore's remaining islands of natural habitat with a "green" corridor. To the south, the Jones Falls Trail might be extended all the way to the Inner Harbor, along the route of the Fallsway. Although this segment

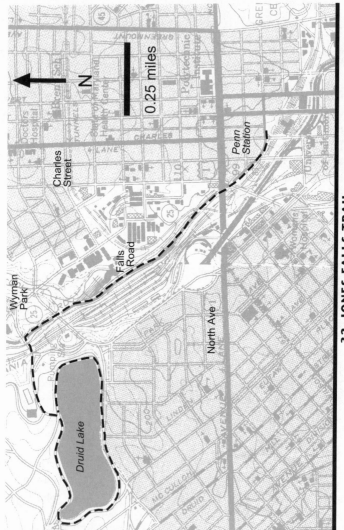

32. JONES FALLS TRAIL

would not provide habitat for wildlife, it would give citizens yet another prime recreational opportunity in an urban area otherwise lacking in such amenities.

Finally, a major branch of the Jones Falls Trail could be created without much difficulty. Stony Run flows into the Jones Falls at Wyman Park Drive. Much of the land bordering Stony Run is already in public ownership, the city having long ago bought this right-of-way from the defunct Maryland and Pennsylvania Railroad. A foottrail already exists in Wyman Park as far north as University Parkway and also between Cold Spring Lane and Northern Parkway.

Baltimore citizens have taken the lead in envisioning and designing this dramatic and valuable greenway in the Jones Falls Valley. To make this plan come true will take political influence and money. But opportunities like this come along only rarely, and I'm betting that the confluence of public activism and vision will make this dream a reality in the decade to come.

CYLBURN ARBORETUM

One of Baltimore City's best-known and most-loved parks is Cylburn Arboretum. Famous among gardeners, this botanical treasure offers extensive beds of flowering herbaceous plants and shrubs. A variety of trees, both native and exotic, are scattered about the grounds. Cylburn's botanical diversity attracts all sorts of birds during migration; in early May it is possible to see a dozen species of warblers here.

The center of activity at Cylburn is the mansion. Jesse Tyson, heir to the Tyson mining fortune, began building Cylburn in 1863 for his mother. Her death and the Civil War delayed the progress of construction on the Victorian mansion for about twenty years. When Jesse, then in his sixties, married nineteen-year-old Edythe Johns in 1888, the completed house and grounds became a focal point for Baltimore society. Lavish parties were frequently held on the grounds, and extensive formal and informal gardens were planted. When Edythe died in 1942, the city bought Cylburn Mansion and its surrounding 176 acres. The estate became a city park in 1958.

There is an extensive network of walking trails at Cylburn, but taken together they total less than a mile. For this reason, the trails are best suited to the slow pace of nature study, wildflower identification, and birding rather than hiking for exercise or recreation. To encourage this kind of use, many of the footpaths are mulched so as to be smooth, cushioned, and dry underfoot. Most of the trails form a semicircle around the mansion, either just inside or just outside the treeline of the surrounding forest. The sole exception is an old road that runs downhill from the back of the mansion to the light rail line. One hundred years ago, Cylburn hosted so many parties that it had its own rail station here on what was then the Northern Central Railroad!

Because the trails at Cylburn are so short, no trail description of a recommended route is included. Merely wander as you

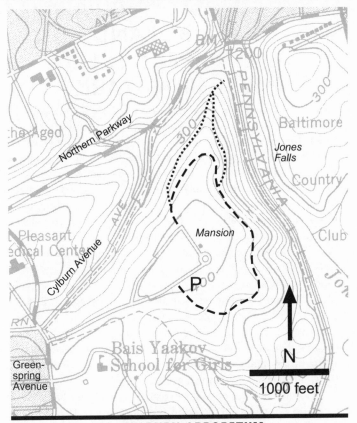

33. CYLBURN ARBORETUM

will; if you become disoriented, just walk uphill, where the mansion sits atop the crest.

Directions: From the Baltimore Beltway (I-695), take I-83, the Jones Falls Expressway, south. Take exit 10B, turning right, west, onto Northern Parkway. Go 0.2 miles and turn left onto Cylburn Avenue. Go 0.7 miles and turn left onto Greenspring Avenue. Make an immediate left into Cylburn Arboretum.

Cylburn is served by bus, near the terminus of the #1 line.

LAKE ROLAND
AND ROBERT E. LEE
MEMORIAL PARK

■■■

Tucked away in a quiet residential neighborhood inside the belt-way is Lake Roland, a wonderful nearby destination for an easy hike in any season. Lake Roland is among Baltimore's best locations for birding. The surprisingly large park encompasses such diverse habitats as mature upland forest, brushy coverts, riparian forest, serpentine grasslands, swamps, and open marsh. In autumn, the vibrant yellows of hickories and tulip poplars reflect golden off the water, lending a colorful accent to long views down the lake. The park is very popular and heavily used, but a walk to the far end of Lake Roland leaves most of the crowds behind and has an unexpectedly remote character.

Although everyone refers to this area as Lake Roland, the park's official name is Robert E. Lee Memorial Park, and it is this name you'll see on signs directing you to the park. During the Civil War, Baltimore was a city with a large number of southern sympathizers, and this heritage lives on in this park, named for the Confederacy's best-known general.

Lake Roland was once a water storage facility for Baltimore City's drinking water. Originally known as Swann Lake, it was created when a concrete dam was constructed across the Jones Falls in the early 1860s. The city's needs quickly outgrew Lake Roland's capacity, and a new dam was built on the Big Gunpowder River, creating Loch Raven, still Baltimore's major water source. Since then, the lands adjacent to the lake have been a well-loved park for passive recreation, used by generations of north Baltimore residents.

Lake Roland is heavily used by people walking their dogs. Fortunately, most owners pick up after their pet, so there are relatively few doggy "land mines." A minor controversy has erupted here in recent years between pet owners who let their dogs run free and other park users who feel dogs should always remain on leash. Whatever your feelings on this issue, you can expect to encounter lots of new canine friends on any hike.

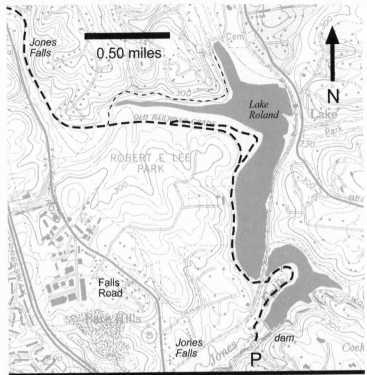

34. LAKE ROLAND / ROBERT E. LEE PARK

Mountain bikes are permitted on the trails at Lake Roland, and usage is heavy. Trails are narrow, and both hikers and cyclists should use caution and courtesy when passing.

Distance: 2.6 miles one way, with several spur trails
Difficulty: Easy

Directions: From the Baltimore Beltway (I-695), take exit 23, Falls Road. The exit goes north only. Turn left at the first stoplight onto the portion of Falls Road that runs south. Continue south for 3.4 miles. After crossing the Falls Road bridge, make an immediate left onto Lakeside Drive. Follow the signs to Robert E. Lee Park.

Lake Roland may also be reached by light rail, disembarking

at the Falls Road stop. Walk up Lakeside Drive for about a quarter-mile to the dam.

Begin your walk at Lake Roland from the footbridge over the Jones Falls. There are often ducks, herons, and other waterbirds in the shallow water below the dam, and they are easily observed from the walkway above. At the northern end of the footbridge is a peninsula where the developed portion of the park is located. Follow the paved road uphill and along the water, passing under huge old trees. When the paved path begins to circle back toward the footbridge, near a stone picnic shelter, take a badly eroded trail downhill to the right. Within 50 yards, carefully cross the light rail tracks.

The footpath now runs along the bed of an old railroad grade, continuing for 2 miles. Although level, it is narrow, because of encroaching vegetation, and is surprisingly muddy. The water is only a few feet away, and there are frequent views toward the far shore. In spring, the brush harbors cardinals, blue-gray gnatcatchers, towhees, catbirds, yellowthroats, white-eyed vireos, and sparrows.

The path forks at mile 1.0. Bear right onto a dike whose higher elevation allows views down into the wetland vegetation of Lake Roland. From this vantage point, ducks, grebes, herons, and red-winged blackbirds are often visible. The mature trees overhead harbor an assortment of warblers during spring migration and provide nesting sites for Baltimore orioles, red-eyed vireos, woodpeckers, and yellow warblers. It is this variety of habitats within a small area that makes the upper end of Lake Roland such a fine location for birding.

The trail continues to a footbridge over the Jones Falls at mile 1.8. Many hikers and birders turn around at this point, but it is possible to continue for another 0.8 miles on the old railbed to the trail's end at Falls Road. Another alternative is a narrow, muddy footpath beginning on the far side of the footbridge. This trail runs along the north shore of Lake Roland and then up Roland Run before ending at a neighborhood road after 0.7 miles one way.

On the return trip from the footbridge, you may wish to walk on the old railbed, where many of the wooden ties are still visible. This route is muddy in spring or in wet weather, however, since it is lower than the surrounding land. A number of trails

Raptor Migration over Baltimore

THE SEPTEMBER MORNING DAWNS COOL AND CLEAR, AN OVERNIGHT RAIN having cleared out the oppressive summer humidity. A steady breeze out of the northwest quickly dries out the remaining puddles, and the rising sun begins to heat the land. By 9 a.m., a few broad-winged hawks appear, flapping and gliding in search of rising columns of air. What at first is merely an occasional hawk soon builds into a steady stream of individuals, and by noon the sky explodes with boiling kettles of up to a hundred hawks, rising on unseen thermals to heights at the limits of human vision. The fall raptor migration, one of Baltimore's great natural phenomena, is under way. And almost no one notices.

Twice a year, raptors (which include hawks, owls, eagles, and osprey) migrate through Maryland. In spring, these birds of prey are heading north, toward forests and cliffs where they nest and raise young. In autumn, these same birds return south to wintering grounds where prey is more plentiful. Raptors tend to follow the same well-defined routes year after year. For example, one flyway is along the spine of the Appalachians, and thousands of birders congregate at Hawk Mountain Sanctuary in Pennsylvania each autumn to look for and count the birds. Another flyway follows the Atlantic coast; along it, Cape May, New Jersey, is widely considered the best place in the United States to see hawks. What very few people appreciate, however, is that still another flyway exists along the edge of the coastal plain and the Piedmont, roughly along the I-95 corridor. That means that a river of migrating hawks flows over Baltimore City; all you have to do (on the right day) is look up!

A small group of dedicated hawk watchers count the birds in these semiannual migrations. Their data are amazing. At one site in the Hamilton section of North Baltimore, almost 15,000 raptors were counted in fall of 1999. Of this total, more than 12,000 were broad-winged hawks. Broad-wings are rather chubby soaring hawks about the size of a crow, distinguished by alternating black and white bands on the tail. More than 7,000 of these broad wings were sighted on one day, September 18, 1999! Other interesting totals from that year were 32 bald eagles, almost 3,000 migrating blue jays, and 6,600 migrating monarch butterflies.

Broad-winged hawks are clearly the most numerous and easily sighted raptor over Baltimore. Their migration strategy makes them notable. As the sun warms the land, hot air rises; in some places, the warm air rises as a spiraling updraft. A soaring bird that catches such a thermal rises quickly, as if on an elevator, to as high as 10,000 or more feet. Other birds, seeing the updraft made visible by these soaring hawks, join in. Soon, hundreds of hawks may be circling and rising in the thermal, leading observers to aptly describe it as a "boiling kettle." Once the birds have attained a high altitude, they break out of the thermal and glide southward, slowly losing altitude, until they join another thermal. In this way, a migrating bird can drift hundreds of miles on the right day, expending little energy and preserving strength and body fat for those days when conditions are not quite so perfect.

We humans tend to be so self-absorbed that we ignore the daily occurrences in the natural world around us. Only when we pause from our daily routine to look and ponder and wonder do we begin to appreciate the rest of the species that share our planet. The migration of raptors, who embody power and freedom as they soar on rivers in the air, is one example of such wondrous events.

branch off to the right and lead into an upland portion of Robert E. Lee Park. Although not included in the trail mileage, this area is well worth a detour.

The character of the landscape quickly changes on these uplands. Stunted Virginia pines dominate on a dry, rocky soil; gaps in the tree canopy reveal grasslands reminiscent of Soldiers Delight. In fact, this area, known as Bare Hills, is underlain by the same serpentine rock as Soldiers Delight, and so bears similar vegetation. A number of old dirt roads crisscross the area; explore as you wish. To return to the trail along the edge of Lake Roland, merely walk downhill. Then bear right to return to the trailhead.

HERRING RUN PARK

■■

Set amid the neatly kept rowhouses of east Baltimore is a narrow strip of greenery that constitutes Herring Run Park. A paved path, favored by local residents for strolling, dog walking, and bike riding, follows the little stream for more than 3 miles through this park. Several short portions of it have a surprisingly remote feel for such an urban location. And urban it is: virtually the entire Herring Run watershed is densely populated, and the percentage of its land that is covered by impervious surfaces (like streets and houses) is greater than either the Gwynns Falls or the Jones Falls watersheds. For this reason, water quality in Herring Run ranges from poor to dismal. Nevertheless, open space enlivened by the sound of water music still makes magic, and Herring Run can be a wonderful city getaway.

For more information, call the Herring Run Recreation Center at 410-488-6634.

Distance: 2.1-mile paved circuit, with a 1.3-mile (one way) spur.
Difficulty: Easy

Directions: From the Baltimore Beltway (I-695), take Harford Road (Route 147) south for 4.5 miles. Turn right onto Lake Montebello Drive and park. Public transportation also serves this trailhead; bus #19 stops along Harford Road near Herring Run Park.

Herring Run Park can be reached from any number of adjoining neighborhoods, but perhaps the most convenient place to park is the road around Lake Montebello. This old city reservoir, constructed between 1875 and 1881, receives raw water from the Gunpowder and Susquehanna Rivers. Two adjacent filtration plants purify the water for drinking. There is ample parking along the 1.4-mile road that encircles Lake Montebello. The interior two lanes have been closed to vehicular traffic and are heavily used by walkers and runners in one and cyclists in the other. Park along the outside curb where there is space and walk

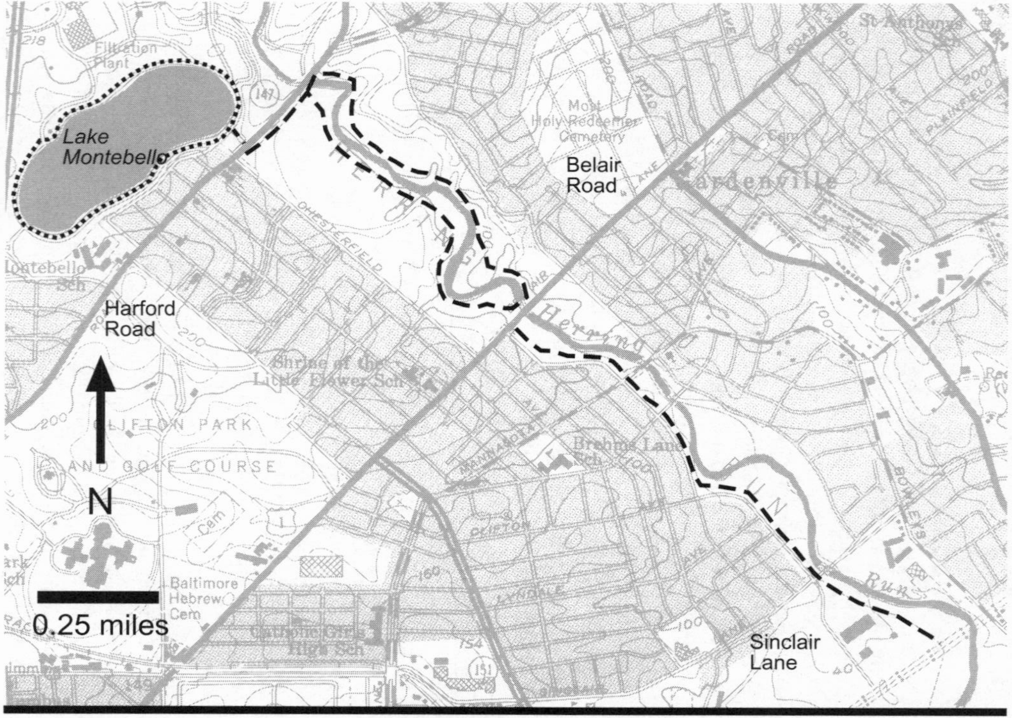

35. HERRING RUN PARK

Lake Montebello

Harford Road

Belair Road

Sinclair Lane

N

0.25 miles

to the easternmost end of the lake. Leave the walking oval at Lake Montebello Drive and cross busy Harford Road with care. From the east side of Harford Road, a large grassy expanse filled with various athletic fields is visible. Walk into Herring Run Park and turn left onto the paved path that runs parallel to Harford Road. In less than a quarter-mile, it intersects the main trail itself, running adjacent to the creek.

Turn right. For about 200 yards, the asphalt path divides the playing fields from a riparian buffer along the river. A number of native trees have been planted, including sycamores and various oaks. In the years to come, these trees will shade both Herring Run and its adjacent greenway edge, providing habitat for wildlife and protection against erosion. The trail soon enters a small forest, and here it is possible to feel like the city has been left behind. A tangle of vines festoons trailside shrubs and forms a green wall in summer. Birds like cardinals, sparrows, and chickadees flit back and forth in the dense vegetation. All too soon the trail emerges from the woods and rises to Belair Road.

Turn left and walk along the sidewalk, crossing the bridge over Herring Run. Within fifty feet, the paved trail bears left again, now running upstream on the east side of the river. Once again, this area is well forested. Only in the final half-mile does the trail approach Herring Run. Although there is much trash wrapped around streamside vegetation, the creek sparkles prettily on a sunny day. Herring Run is always active, having a moderate gradient that runs steadily over cobble bars, small rapids, and long-abandoned low dams. Under the Harford Road bridge, cross the river again and turn left (downstream), completing a 2.1-mile loop. Return to your car on Lake Montebello Drive.

Hikers looking for a longer walk in this area have the option of continuing downstream from Belair Road. The paved trail continues in a southeasterly direction for 1.3 miles. However, the stretch from Belair Road to Sinclair Lane is basically a sidewalk, just a few feet from Shannon Drive. The trail dies out in a tangle of underbrush and small trees a few hundred yards southeast of Sinclair Lane.

BALTIMORE
CITY WATERSHED LANDS

LIBERTY, LOCH RAVEN, AND PRETTYBOY

∎∎∎∎∎∎∎∎∎∎∎∎∎∎∎∎∎∎∎∎∎∎∎∎∎∎∎∎∎∎∎∎∎∎∎∎∎∎∎

Much of the Baltimore metropolitan area's drinking water is supplied by three reservoirs: Liberty, Loch Raven, and Prettyboy. These reservoirs, the dams that create them, and almost 19,000 acres of watershed land surrounding them are owned and operated by the City of Baltimore.

The sole purpose of watershed land is to maintain an ample supply of water of the highest quality for purification and distribution. The city recognizes that watershed lands are also a valuable recreational resource, and it permits certain kinds of use by the public, as long as that use does not interfere with the quality of the drinking water supply. Any activity with a negative effect on water quality is subject to regulation or prohibition.

There are a great many activities currently prohibited on watershed lands. These have been posted at most trailheads as the infamous "NO" signs familiar to hikers: no motor vehicles, no fires, no camping, no alcoholic beverages, no dumping, no cutting of vegetation, no swimming, no smoking, etc. Hunting of any sort is prohibited at Loch Raven, since the watershed property is surrounded by moderate density residential neighborhoods and because the trails are so heavily used. Hunting with bow and arrow in season with a permit is allowed at Liberty and Prettyboy.

Current regulations specifically permit some activities. Fishing from the bank is allowed, except in certain areas near the dams. Canoeing and boating with an electric motor are allowed on the reservoirs with an annual permit. Picnicking and hiking are allowed (although all trash must be removed). Horseback riding is allowed on fire roads only, as long as the footing is not wet or muddy.

The most controversial regulations in recent years concern the use of mountain bikes. During the preparation of this book, I found evidence of mountain bike use on every fire road in all three watersheds. Usage varies greatly; fire roads at Loch Raven are heavily traveled, while those at Prettyboy and Liberty are lightly ridden. What most mountain bikers do not know is that only a small subset of fire roads, perhaps 20 percent of the total, are officially open for mountain bike use. However, the city has done a poor job of conveying this information at trailheads and by other methods to mountain bikers. During the summer of 2000, signage went up at many (but not all) of the trailheads in the Loch Raven watershed indicating whether mountain bikes were permitted or not. No signs have been posted as of this writing at Prettyboy and Liberty watersheds, but they are likely to appear soon. Fire roads open for mountain bike use are indicated on a map accompanying each of the Loch Raven, Prettyboy, and Liberty sections of this book. Keep in mind that even "open" fire roads should not be ridden when the trail is muddy; in general, that means within forty-eight hours of rain.

Mountain bikers also use on a regular basis a number of footpaths (termed "single track" in mountain bike parlance) in the Loch Raven watershed. Both mountain bikes and horses are prohibited from such foottrails. Please ride responsibly and avoid all single track.

Hiking is allowed on footpaths in the three watersheds. Many of these narrow paths were established by fishermen or hikers years ago and are now eroding under heavy use. Avoid such trails in wet weather or when they are muddy. Remember, the purpose of the watershed lands is protection of the quality of our drinking water. The city will allow continued recreational use only if that quality is not threatened. Indeed, some similar watershed lands around the country have been completely closed to recreational use. None of us that use watershed lands would want that drastic step to be taken here. Therefore, hike only in a responsible and environmentally friendly fashion, obeying all regulations.

For more information, contact the Reservoir Natural Resources Office, Baltimore City Department of Public Works, 410-795-6151.

LIBERTY WATERSHED

Liberty Reservoir and its surrounding watershed lands are located in western Baltimore County and in eastern Carroll County. The dam and lands are owned by the City of Baltimore and operated by the Department of Public Works, Bureau of Water and Wastewater. Liberty Reservoir was formed in 1953 when Liberty Dam was completed, backing up the North Branch of the Patapsco River. It has a maximum capacity of 43 billion gallons, equal to the size of Prettyboy and Loch Raven Reservoirs together. This fact is surprising, because to a casual observer, Liberty seems like the smallest of the three reservoirs. This may be due, in part, to the fact that Liberty is rarely full, and there are often extensive gravel and mud flats visible. In fact, some coves near the north end have small trees growing below the crest elevation, so long has it been since the reservoir was last full. The drainage basin serving Liberty covers 164 square miles, compared to 303 square miles for the Gunpowder River drainage into Prettyboy and Loch Raven. Thus, inflow to Liberty is substantially reduced despite its larger capacity, contributing to the typical less-than-full condition.

Since water almost never overflows Liberty Dam, the North Branch of the Patapsco downstream is a river in name only. The only water in the riverbed is whatever seeps in from springs and side streams that enter below the dam. Fortunately, the North Branch merges with the South Branch only a few miles downstream of the reservoir, restoring a semblance of naturalness to the river in the rest of the valley. Land downstream of Liberty Dam is part of Patapsco Valley State Park, owned by the State of Maryland.

More than 9,200 acres of watershed lands surround Liberty Reservoir. Most of this land is heavily wooded. Nevertheless, the forest could best be characterized as "maturing" rather than "fully mature." Trees are tall, but usually of less than eighteen inches diameter; they will continue to grow in girth and, to a lesser extent, in height, during the coming century. The herbaceous flora of this forest floor is not as diverse as that in state parks like

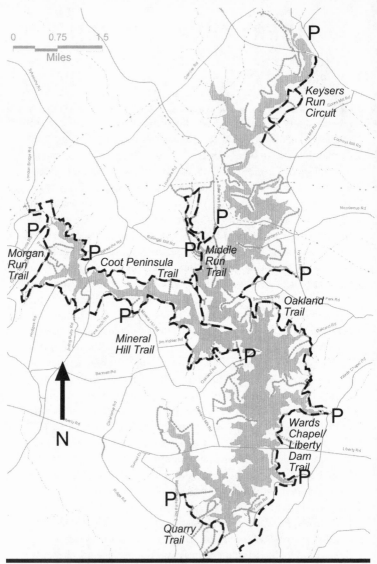

36. LIBERTY WATERSHED HIKING TRAILS

Patapsco and Gunpowder. This condition reflects the history of land use; before the land was bought for the reservoir in the 1940s and early 1950s, much of it was used as farmland or pasturage.

Beyond the watershed boundaries, both Baltimore and Carroll Counties are settled at a light to moderate density, with frequent woodlots separating scattered houses on large parcels of land. The rolling Piedmont landscape is pleasant to the eye and a joy to drive through. However, this may not continue much longer. Carroll County is developing rapidly, and controls on growth are at present ineffectual. Development can be expected to change the face of Carroll County in the next few decades, and this bodes ill for water quality in Liberty Reservoir.

Those hiking trails in the Liberty watershed described in this book are exclusively on fire roads (termed "woods roads" by the City of Baltimore). None is blazed or marked in any way as of this writing, so close attention to the map is necessary when hiking. Fire roads, in general, are wide enough to accommodate an emergency vehicle. However, maintenance of these roads is spotty. Occasional downed trees span the road, some steep spots are severely eroded, and lightly used trails have a knee-high growth of herbaceous vegetation by midsummer. Trail usage is light, consisting mostly of local residents out for a stroll and fishermen walking a direct route from a parking area to the reservoir's edge. Equestrians use a number of the fire roads to the same moderate extent as hikers. Mountain bikers are a rarity at present on many of Liberty's trails, even those designated as official mountain bike routes.

Seven different hikes are described on Liberty watershed lands. These routes were selected for their natural values, interesting terrain, suitable length, and ease of access. There are several other fire roads at Liberty not described here. Most are short out-and-back hikes that I felt did not merit inclusion. Two walks featured in an older guidebook, the Oklahoma Circuit and Ireland's Point, no longer have safe public access with nearby parking, and accordingly were not included.

Outside of local residents, the Liberty watershed trails are poorly known and lightly used. While they remain so, take advantage of this wonderful recreational resource by visiting soon!

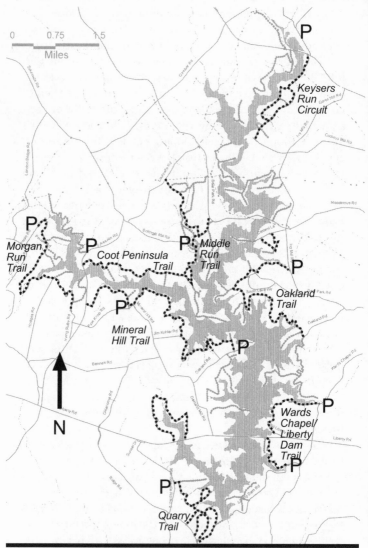

37. LIBERTY WATERSHED MOUNTAIN BIKE ROUTES

▼ **Wards Chapel / Liberty Dam Trail**

Distance: 5.9 miles one way; shorter hikes possible
Difficulty: Moderate

Directions: From the Baltimore Beltway (I-695), take I-70 west.
Exit right (north) at Marriottsville Road, exit 83. Go 4.8 miles,
past the entrance to the McKeldin Area of Patapsco Valley State
Park, to the unnamed gravel road that is the start of this hike.

As you stand at the base of a concrete plug like Liberty Dam, you
can't help but wonder: what did the river and its valley look like
before? Were there placid meanders through swampy grass flats
and past shady riparian forest? Or was there a series of rapids,
where the river plunged over steep falls and dashed among
house-sized boulders? Did whitetail deer step cautiously from the
forest to drink, disturbing the piscine meditations of a great blue
heron? Who in our grandparents' generation swam and splashed
in the river with the heedless abandon of youth in that more in-
nocent time? Imagination infuses the solid presence of a dam
with visions of an older reality.

  This trail of almost 6 miles connects Patapsco Valley State
Park with the complex of fire roads in the Liberty watershed.
There are three visually distinct sections. The southernmost portion is a narrow, usually wet foottrail adjacent to the waterless
bed of the North Branch of the Patapsco. The middle section,
from the dam spillway to the fire road origin, is a paved road
with wide grassy shoulders wandering across a rolling landscape.
The northernmost portion is a fire road typical of the watershed
property, a wide lane roughly paralleling the reservoir shoreline
through a maturing forest.

  There are several intermediate access points on this hike, so
it may easily be broken into smaller segments. The walk is described from south to north, but can just as easily be done in the
reverse direction.

  Begin your hike from the unnamed lane off Marriottsville
Road, a few paces east of where it crosses the North Branch Patapsco River into Baltimore County. There is plenty of parking along
the shoulders of this park road. Just before this gravel road bears
right and uphill onto posted private property, a foottrail enters
the forest, running parallel to the river. This path bears the seem-

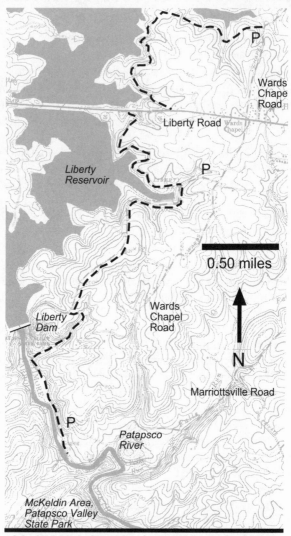

0.50 miles

N

Liberty Reservoir

Liberty Road

Wards Chape Road

P

Wards Chapel Road

Liberty Dam

P

Patapsco River

Marriottsville Road

McKeldin Area, Patapsco Valley State Park

38. WARDS CHAPEL / LIBERTY DAM TRAIL

ingly contradictory distinction of being both rocky and muddy; fortunately, the rocks provide islands of good footing among the general swampiness. The adjacent wetlands are a good place to look for amphibians in early spring, including wood frogs, spring peepers, American toads, and several kinds of salamanders.

The adjacent North Branch Patapsco River is a shadow of its former self. There are no water releases from Liberty Dam, and the reservoir spills over only during hurricanes or the wettest of winters, so only a few puddles dot the riverbed. Without reliable flowing water, the normal aquatic food chain cannot exist. There are some algae growing in wet areas, and a few insects arrive from the surrounding wetlands, but this is not a productive, attractive watercourse.

At mile 0.7, a trail branches off to the right up a side canyon. You may want to proceed straight a few hundred yards more to view the base of Liberty Dam, but this side trail is the only way to get to the top of the dam. It follows a small creek in a narrow valley shaded on one side by hemlock trees. Do not be dismayed by the sound of frequent gunfire; there is a ridge between you and the nearby rifle range. Rising steadily on a rocky footpath, the trail ends after another 0.5 miles at a paved road with wide grassy shoulders.

This paved road is the access road to Liberty Dam. Turn left and walk several hundred yards to view the dam and reservoir, or turn right to continue the hike northward. Traffic is very light on this road; it closes at 4 p.m., and is sometimes closed during the day as well. Ample mowed lawns on either side of the road make the walk very pleasant. At one point, there is an overlook with fine broad views of the reservoir. When the orange gate comes in sight at mile 2.5, walk downhill to the left on a grassy sward to the water. A fire road enters the forest here.

The fire road trends generally north along the shore of Liberty Reservoir, and often gives good views of the water. It is wide and frequently used, but not by fishermen; no fishing is allowed between the dam and Liberty Road. This busy highway is reached at mile 3.9.

Cross Liberty Road with care and walk uphill along the shoulder for 0.3 miles. Turn left onto an abandoned asphalt road in front of a fine old stone house. Within one hundred yards, the dirt fire road branches to the right.

This fire road also runs generally parallel to the water, and there are frequently good views. It is a bit hillier than the previous section but does not present any difficulties. There are plenty of ferns trailside, and the tulip poplars and white pines are quite tall. Mountain laurels dot the dry slopes, flowering beautifully in late May. At mile 5.8, just after crossing a small stream, another fire road branches to the left. This is the Oakland Trail, described below. Continue straight 0.2 miles to the northern trailhead at Wards Chapel Road.

▼ **Oakland Trail**

Distance: 6.8 miles one way
Difficulty: Moderate to strenuous

Directions: From the Baltimore Beltway (I-695), take exit 18, Liberty Road (Route 26) west. Go 7.1 miles and turn right on Wards Chapel Road. Go 0.6 miles and park on the road shoulder at the bottom of the hill.

Conservation biologists have recently established the ecological value of linking tracts of natural habitat with one another. In general, the larger the parcel of land, the more kinds of plants and animals that can be found there. In western Baltimore County, the Liberty watershed land owned by Baltimore City abuts both Patapsco Valley State Park and Soldiers Delight Natural Environment Area. Together, these thousands of acres constitute a very large region of woodland and fields. The Oakland Trail runs along the border between Soldiers Delight and the Liberty watershed and then continues northward on a narrower strip of watershed land. Like many of the trails around Liberty Reservoir, it is lightly used.

Begin your hike at the trail entrance on Wards Chapel Road 0.5 miles north of Route 26, Liberty Road. There is parking along the road shoulder for about a dozen vehicles. Use care here, because the parking is at the bottom of a hill, and cars pass at a high rate of speed. The trail entrance is marked by an orange cable stretched between two orange posts. (Such cables bar vehicular access to many watershed fire roads.) Do not block emergency vehicle access to this fire road. A private driveway is adjacent.

Walk 0.25 miles to a T-intersection on the fire road and turn

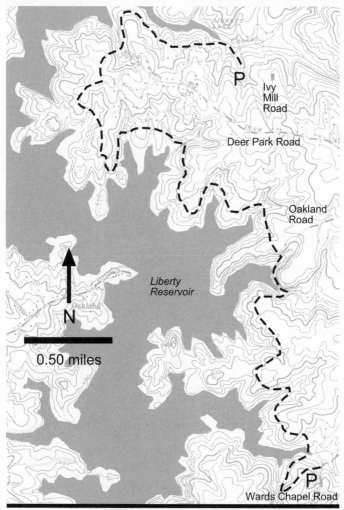

Ivy
Mill
Road

Deer Park Road

Oakland
Road

*Liberty
Reservoir*

N

0.50 miles

Wards Chapel Road

39. OAKLAND TRAIL

right. Within 100 yards, a footpath leads down to a narrow cove of Liberty Reservoir. Chimney Branch flows into the reservoir at this spot; cross the creek on steppingstones at the first riffle above the lake. An obscure footpath leads uphill, joining a fire road within 75 yards. Turn left.

The fire road roughly parallels the edge of the reservoir but

Periodical Cicadas

THERE ARE MORE KINDS OF INSECTS IN THE WORLD THAN THERE ARE OF ALL other known organisms together. In general, however, insects lead an anonymous existence—until they become a nuisance to us humans. Mosquitoes, termites, and ticks spring prominently to mind in this regard. And every seventeen years, another kind of insect enters our human sensibility: the periodical cicada, commonly but erroneously known as the seventeen-year locust.

Emerging synchronously over a period of just a few days in late spring, periodical cicadas flood the landscape in immense numbers. They seem to cover every vertical surface: tree trunks, telephone poles, fences, downspouts, and even humans who stand in one place too long. Weak fliers, periodical cicadas fill the air, bumping into you as you walk, sticking to your hair and clothing, emitting a loud, raspy call, and generally making outdoor life disconcerting.

Periodical cicadas are homopterans, a group of insects that feed by sucking plant juices with a beaklike mouthpart. Adults are robust, one to two inches in length, and have red bulging eyes and red wing veins. After mating, the female cicada will lay her eggs inside twigs and branches of trees using her powerful ovipositor. When the eggs hatch, the nymphs fall from the tree, burrow into the soil, and spend the next sixteen years attached to the roots of the tree, sucking tiny amounts of sap as necessary to sustain life. In the seventeenth year, the nymphs emerge from burrows, climb the nearest vertical surface, and molt into flying, sexually mature adults.

Typically, more than half the population emerges within a one-week period. While the first few that emerge are eagerly eaten by birds and some small mammals, there are soon so many cicadas that the predators are satiated. Because the adults emerge synchronously, the chances of any one insect being eaten are greatly reduced. Periodical cicadas keep track of time by sensing and counting the seasonal cycles of sap production in their host tree.

Periodical cicadas are the only animals that exhibit long year-periodicity. In the eastern United States, there are three species with a seventeen-year period and three others with a thirteen-year period. What's so special about these numbers? Why aren't there nine-year or twelve-year cicadas? The fact that both 13 and 17 are prime numbers has led scientists to hypothesize that these periods have evolved because predators cannot similarly synchronize their reproduction to take advantage of this periodical glut of food. For example, consider a bird or mammal that has young during the same year as a cicada emergence. The pulse of extra food (cicadas) will likely allow more offspring to survive in that year. But without any cicadas around the next year, fewer predators will survive. A bird or mammal that breeds only every second year or every third year or every fourth year will similarly not be breeding the next time there is a glut of cicadas; there is no way for the predator to synchronize its reproduction schedule to that of a creature whose reproduction period is a prime number of years.

For a simple insect with a very small brain, periodical cicadas are surprisingly complex and interesting animals. They have evolved a lifestyle and a reproduction schedule that are amazing and unique. And if you keep all this in mind during the next hatch of periodical cicadas, you just might find them more fascinating than creepy!

is set well back, so the views of the water are fairly distant and only visible when there are no leaves on the trees. The gradient is moderate, so walking is pleasant. The most scenic portion of the trail is reached at mile 2.9, where an unnamed creek flows into the reservoir. The trees are tall, the stream tumbles steeply among large rocks, and a rusting waterwheel recalls an older era when flowing water was put to work.

The trail joins a dirt road just beyond the stream; bear left. After a quarter-mile, this dirt road becomes the paved Oakland Road. However, there is no parking anywhere along Oakland Road, so it cannot be used as an access point. Continue on the fire road that bears left next to the Oakland Road gate. After a few fairly steep but short hills, the trail becomes less difficult. Because the reservoir buffer strip is narrow, houses are occasionally seen to the right. A few side trails are visible, but confusion regarding the route is easily avoided; side trails lead directly toward the reservoir, while the fire road runs parallel.

At mile 5.9, the fairly smooth dirt fire road becomes the heavily eroded remains of an abandoned paved road. In 100 yards, the gate at the end of Deer Park Road appears. Once again, there is no parking allowed, so Deer Park Road cannot be used as an access point. Instead, take the fire road to the left, marked with an orange cable. The route continues for another 0.9 miles, with a portion of the trail within view of the reservoir. The terminus of the Oakland Trail is at mile 6.8 on Ivy Mill Road. There is parking for several cars here.

■ ■

▼ Keysers Run Circuit

Distance: 5.0-mile circuit
Difficulty: Moderate

Directions: From the Baltimore Beltway (I-695), take I-795 toward Owings Mills. When the expressway ends, join Reisterstown Road (Route 140). Turn right on Glen Falls Road, which intersects Reisterstown Road just a few hundred yards before it crosses Liberty Reservoir.

We think of our publicly owned lands as being immune to development, a haven against the ever-increasing encroachment of housing projects, strip malls, and commercial development. And in many ways they are, preserved in perpetuity as open, natural space. But we sometimes fail to realize that if access is made difficult, recreational use of public land can become threatened. Such is the case with the Keysers Run Trail in the Liberty watershed. In 1970, this was a fairly popular hike, having the salutary characteristics of moderate distance, varied terrain, and proximity to a major road. Since then, parking has been prohibited at both ends of the trail, isolating it from convenient public access. Still, the dedicated hiker can reach the northern terminus of the Keysers Run Trail, albeit by risking life and limb in crossing Route 140, Reisterstown Road, at a blind curve.

Begin your hike by parking several hundred yards up Glen Falls Road north of Route 140. There is ample parking here well off the road, under shady sycamores. Walk to Route 140, wait patiently for a lull in the almost-constant high-speed traffic, and cross the road using great care. Walk downhill for 100 yards on the narrow shoulder, facing traffic, to what was once a small

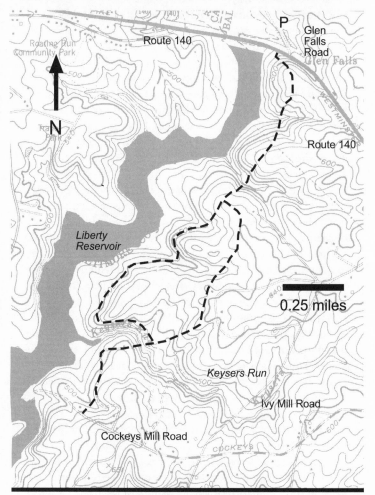

Route 140
Glen Falls Road
P
Roaring Run Community Park
N
Route 140
Liberty Reservoir
0.25 miles
Keysers Run
Ivy Mill Road
Cockeys Mill Road

40. KEYSERS RUN CIRCUIT

parking area, now heavily posted. At this point, the worst of the hike is behind you, and you can concentrate on enjoying the more natural aspects of this portion of the Liberty watershed.

The trailhead is marked by the usual orange cable stretched between orange posts. The trail leads uphill, at first parallel to Route 140, and then arcing south, passing through an area of heavy undergrowth and small trees. At mile 0.5, there are good views of the reservoir and its marshes at a power line cut. Beyond this point, the sound of traffic fades, replaced by birdsong and the whisper of the wind.

A fork in the trail is attained at mile 0.8. This central portion of the Keysers Run Trail is a loop, so either branch can be chosen. However, it is described here as a clockwise circuit, so bear left. The next mile of trail is unrelentingly hilly, passing through a forested landscape of maturing hardwoods interspersed with occasional stands of planted white pines. It is far from the edge of Liberty Reservoir, so there are no views of the water. The other end of the loop is reached at mile 1.6; bear left to go to the trail's end at Cockeys Mill Road.

This section of the trail descends gradually alongside Keysers Run. The presence of water enlivens any landscape, and Keysers Run is no exception. There is a marked increase in the diversity of plants, trees are larger, and more birds are likely to be both sighted and heard. As the trail crosses Keysers Run at mile 1.8, look for (in summer) a scattering of the bright red flowers of bee balm, one of our native mints. The showy, tubular flowers not only smell wonderful but attract hummingbirds.

Another 0.5 miles of hilly travel brings you to the remains of Cockeys Mill Road. Long closed, its asphalt is slowly cracking under the slow but inexorable force of tree roots, and herbaceous plants are gradually encroaching from the edges. Walk downhill to the reservoir's edge, where there are good views of the water; Liberty Reservoir is at its narrowest point here.

Cockeys Mill Road above the trail junction was once a popular access point, but it is now heavily posted with no parking signs for several hundred yards, as far as Ivy Mill Road.

Retrace your steps on the fire road and continue for 0.5 miles. Bear left at the fork to follow the other, western part of the loop on this, the return trip. This portion of the circuit is much less hilly, the trail running almost flat for most of its length. To the left, there are glimpses of the reservoir's waters between the boles of white pines, whose lower branches self-prune as they age. In winter, nuthatches, chickadees, and woodpeckers enjoy the shelter of these thick pine stands.

The circuit is complete at mile 4.2, as this trail merges with the eastern portion of the loop. Bear left, and reach Route 140 at mile 5.0. Recross Reisterstown Road, again with great care,

since the curvature of the road limits your view, and return to
your vehicle.

■ ■

▼ Middle Run Trail

Distance: 4.0-mile circuit
Difficulty: Easy to moderate

Directions: From the Baltimore Beltway (I-695), follow I-795
northwest. Take exit 7, Franklin Boulevard, west. Turn right on
Nicodemus Road. Continue for 3.4 miles to the Deer Park Road
bridge over Liberty Reservoir. The parking area is 1.0 miles west,
on the left, at a right turn in the road.

The typical trail around Liberty Reservoir is a fire road winding
through forested uplands with occasional views of the lake and
plenty of ups and downs. The Middle Run Trail is markedly different. Much of it lies in the shallow valley of Middle Run, a
pretty little stream complete with pocket wetlands, open meadows, and brushy coverts. It is fine habitat for birds and mammals.
And for us humans, the paths are broad and the few elevation
changes are gradual. All in all, this may be the best hike on the
Liberty watershed property.

Because it includes four stream crossings, this hike is not recommended in cold weather or after heavy rains.

There are three possible trailheads where parking is available, each shown on the map. The description below assumes
you begin from the parking lot at the first big curve in the road
1.0 miles west of the Deer Park Road bridge. There is ample parking here, and it is the most convenient trailhead for hikers arriving from Baltimore.

Unlike most of Liberty's trailheads, there is no bright orange
guardrail at the start. Look instead for the obvious foottrail behind the parking lot. Within a few yards, it is evident that the
trail was once a fire road, so do not take the narrow shortcut foottrails established by fishermen. The trail leads slightly downhill
and due south for a quarter-mile. At a four-way trail intersection,
turn right for the Middle Run Trail. The well-used trail continuing straight ahead leads to Piney Point.

The Middle Run Trail passes through a mixed forest of both

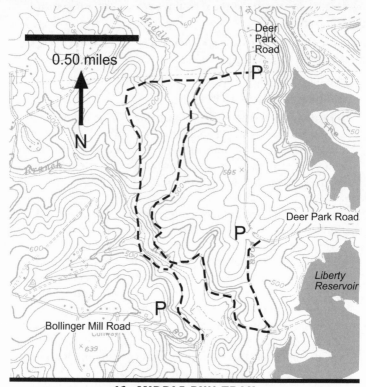

41. MIDDLE RUN TRAIL

hardwoods, like oak and tulip poplar, and a softwood, white pine. There is a nice understory of dogwood and mountain laurel and plenty of greenery on the forest floor. This diversity makes the forest pleasant to look at, and much birdsong enlivens it in the nesting season. The trail soon drops down into the floodplain of Middle Run. This is a fine place to do some birding; brushy areas hold sparrows, white-eyed vireos, and towhees, while the high trees host parula warblers, red-eyed vireos, various woodpeckers, and other forest songbirds.

At a T-intersection at mile 0.8, the left trail crosses Middle Run. Since this will be your return route, take a look at the stream crossing so that you'll be able to recognize it later. Then take the trail to the right at the T-intersection.

The trail soon leaves view of the creek, but the uphill grade is never severe. In places, the forest is very dark and shaggy; spruces have been planted so densely that no other plants can grow in the dim light. Most people can identify pines and hemlocks, but the differences between firs and spruces are less commonly known. It's simple, really; just "shake hands" with the tree. Spruce needles are sharp and sticky; those of firs are flat and friendly.

Just before the trail reaches a power line cut, at mile 1.9, turn sharply left. (Stay straight to reach the alternate trailhead on Deer Park Road; see the map.) This fire road soon reaches Middle Run and the first of four stream crossings in the next mile or so. In summer low water, this can be a pleasant fluvial interlude, but crossing at high water or when ice is present can be uncomfortable or even dangerous. Each crossing has been "improved" with flat slabs of concrete laid on the streambed. While making the crossing easier for emergency vehicles, this alteration has meant the removal of steppingstones for hikers.

On the west side of Middle Run, the trail ascends gently through a pine plantation to a T-intersection. Turn left. In a half-mile or so, the trail drops into the valley of Middle Run, crossing the creek twice in a hundred yards. This area is sunny and open, with a luxurious undergrowth of multiflora rose. The remainder of the trail parallels the stream; in late May, the far hillside is thick with flowering mountain laurel. At mile 3.1, a wide trail leads down to the final crossing of Middle Run, at the site you checked previously. Return uphill on the trail by which you entered the Middle Run Valley, reaching Deer Park Road after a hike of 4.0 miles.

▼ **Coot Peninsula Trail**

Distance: 8.9 miles as described; shorter distances possible
Difficulty: Moderate to strenuous

Directions: From the Baltimore Beltway (I-695), take I-70 to Route 32. Exit north and continue 9.8 miles, crossing Liberty Reservoir. Park on the north (right) side of the bridge, in a large dirt parking area.

When you look at a map of Liberty Reservoir, what stands out is the many isolated coves, shallow inlets, and convoluted chan-

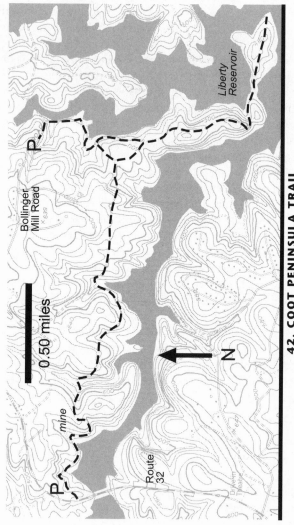

42. COOT PENINSULA TRAIL

nels possessed by this body of water. Conversely, dividing these waters are peninsulas of land, some of which are quite long and narrow. The best of these is Coot Peninsula, jutting more than a mile south and then east into the waters of Liberty Reservoir. Because it is more than a casual walk from the nearest road, Coot Peninsula has an isolated and remote feel to it. From the outermost tip of land, there are good views in three directions. Taken together, these factors make Coot Peninsula a fine destination for a long day hike, well worth the effort to get there.

Begin your hike from the dirt parking area just north of the Route 32 bridge over Liberty Reservoir. (This is also the parking area for the Morgan Run Trail.) The entrance to the Coot Peninsula Trail is at the south end of the parking area, marked by an orange cable strung between two orange posts.

For the first half-mile or so, there are very good views of the reservoir from the trail, which winds up and down several hills. A highlight of the Coot Peninsula Trail is reached at mile 0.7. An old chromite pit mine lies just to the left of the trail. It's an unimpressive sight, merely a shallow depression filled with rocks. In the nineteenth century, chromium was extracted from these rocks (and from similar ones at Soldiers Delight, a few miles away) for use in paint and steel. Richer ore deposits elsewhere supplanted Maryland chromite by 1900, but the mines were reopened during World War I when foreign supplies became unreliable.

Continue on the well-used fire road, avoiding the branch trail on the right that merely leads to a dead end. The next 1.7 miles are quite hilly, passing through areas that are either white pine plantations or a mix of native deciduous trees. At mile 2.4, a T-intersection is reached; turn right to go to Coot Peninsula. Within 100 yards, bear left at a fork, then right after another 0.1 miles. Stay right at the next fork too. If all of this sounds confusing, just consult the map.

The trail is now on Coot Peninsula proper. Nevertheless, the ridge is wide enough that there are only occasional views of the water. Beginning at mile 3.3, however, as the trail turns east, Liberty Reservoir is easily visible to both the left and right. The fire road ends at mile 3.8. Several footpaths lead 60 yards to water's edge.

Neither wildflowers nor birds are plentiful along the woodland portions of the Coot Peninsula Trail, but mound-building ants are especially abundant. These industrious, cooperative social insects create huge mounds of soil and fine woody debris, some of them three feet high and six feet across. Do your ant-watching from a distance, though, or you may find several dozen of them crawling up your leg.

The tip of Coot Peninsula is a good place to look for water birds on the reservoir. As the name implies, coots may be seen on occasion in winter. Coots are nondescript grayish birds about the size of a small duck. They are intensely sociable, found always in tight flocks, calling softly in a companionable way.

Returning up the peninsula, go 1.2 miles to the first major intersection. You may go left, retracing your steps exactly to the Route 32 trailhead for a hike of 7.6 miles; but to see some new and interesting trail, bear right. For the next 0.7 miles, the trail runs near the water, and there are always good views of an increasingly narrow and shallow arm of the reservoir. At a fork in a sunny glade, turn left and go uphill 100 yards to Bollinger Mill Road, or continue straight to the Middle Run trail system. If you have left a car at Bollinger Mill Road for a shuttle back to the trail's origin, the hike concludes here after 5.9 miles.

To return to Route 32 by trail, retrace your steps southward, near the water. After 0.5 miles, an old road filled with rocks branches steeply uphill. Judging by the depressions in the land nearby, rock was once mined here as well. The trail reaches the ridgetop in 0.1 miles. You'll recognize this trail intersection from the trip out; the rest of the hike back to Route 32 is on familiar trail. Total mileage for this route is 8.9.

▼ **Morgan Run Circuit**

Distance: 6.7-mile circuit
Difficulty: Moderate

Directions: From the Baltimore Beltway (I-695), take I-70 west to Route 32. Exit north and go 9.8 miles to the bridge over Liberty Reservoir. Park just beyond the bridge.

The Morgan Run Trail encircles the western arm of Liberty Reservoir, crossing the major tributary of Morgan Run. This stream valley is a beautiful place, split by a clear, cold trout stream, shaded by large trees, and filled with lush vegetation. The rest

Butterflies, Pesticides, and Genetic Engineering

EACH YEAR, AMERICAN FARMERS APPLY MORE THAN 100 MILLION KILO-grams of pesticides to crops in an effort to control insect damage. As a result, about 35 percent of supermarket foods contain detectable levels of these pesticides (although the amounts are considered tolerable in 97–99 percent of these foods). Agricultural pesticides have a variety of effects on nontarget organisms. For example, an estimated 70 million birds die each year in the United States due to pesticide poisoning. Overwintering populations of monarch butterflies declined by about 70 percent over two years in the mid-1990s, probably due to a combination of habitat loss and insecticide poisoning. Finally, the number of innocuous, or helpful, insects (pollinators and biological control organisms) killed by pesticides is unknown but is undoubtedly immense.

Against this backdrop of widespread nonspecific pesticide use, agricultural biotechnology companies are trying to use the techniques of molecular biology to engineer insecticides that reduce impacts on nontarget organisms. Perhaps the most promising line of research is inserting genes for Bt endotoxin into the germ line of corn. Bt endotoxin is a chemical made by a bacterium that interferes with molting of the larvae of lepidopterans (butterflies and moths). Corn seeds transformed with the Bt endotoxin gene grow into plants that make the endotoxin in every cell throughout the plant. Such corn plants kill corn rootworms and European corn borers as they feed inside the corn plant. Thus, not only is this insecticide effective, it never escapes into the environment to poison nontarget species of insects.

Or does it? Pollen released by transformed corn plants also contains the Bt endotoxin, and that pollen drifts several hundred feet in the breeze. In 1999, scientists noted the pollen coating the leaves of milkweed plants, which commonly grow along the edges of cornfields. They fed the pollen-dusted leaves to the caterpillars of monarch butterflies, and noted increased mortality and decreased feeding.

These results made headlines worldwide, because many people have concerns about genetically engineered organisms. However, a number of follow-up studies have shown little or no effect of Bt corn pollen on nontarget insects. For example, black swallowtail butterfly larvae were unaffected even by pollen concentrations far in excess of those found in nature. No studies so far have shown a clear-cut decline in butterfly larval survival or butterfly populations in the field.

Our society has to weigh the benefits of this new technology against the unknown potential costs. The use of Bt endotoxin food plants may cut the use of general-broadcast insecticides and their impacts on nontarget organisms, including humans. On the down side, increased use of Bt endotoxin plants will surely speed the evolution of resistant insects, leading to more-intractable pest control problems down the road. Although Bt endotoxin has no known effects on humans, an increased concentration in our food supply might at least become allergenic in sensitive individuals. Like all new technology, the implications of Bt endotoxin food plants are mostly unknown. We can only use our collective societal wisdom to discern the most effective, least harmful policy regarding its use.

of the circuit is pleasingly diverse. The northern portion of the trail has mostly gentle grades and good views of the reservoir, while the southern side is quite hilly, with some upland portions passing though pleasantly cool white pine plantations.

Begin your walk from the dirt parking area just to the north of the Route 32 bridge over Liberty Reservoir. There is ample parking here, safe from the speeding traffic on Route 32. Cross Route 32 with care and walk uphill along the road shoulder for 0.2 miles to the trailhead. As usual, it is marked with an orange cable strung between two orange posts. The noise of traffic is quickly left behind as the fire road descends to the edge of the water. For the next 1.6 miles, the trail generally follows the indentations of the reservoir, with only minor changes in elevation.

The delta of Morgan Run is soon visible. Silt eroded off the Morgan Run watershed has accumulated here, making a rich alluvial substrate perfect for the growth of reeds and grasses. The calls of red-winged blackbirds echo across this grassy expanse as early as March and through the late spring and summer breeding season.

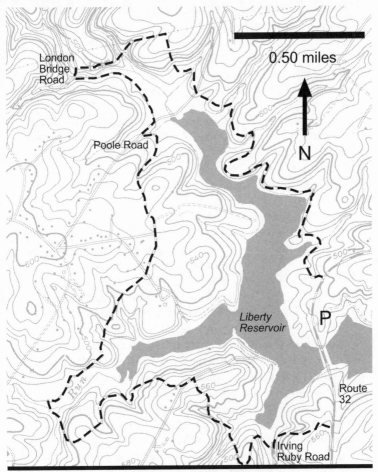

London
Bridge
Road

0.50 miles

N

Poole Road

Liberty
Reservoir

P

Route
32

Irving
Ruby Road

43. MORGAN RUN CIRCUIT

The trail rises steeply uphill to a set of power lines that crackle and pop, making your hair stand on end in dry weather. Turn left, following the steep trail under the power lines down into the valley of Morgan Run. At this point, the route becomes a narow footpath. Follow the trail upstream to London Bridge Road at mile 2.5. Cross Morgan Run on the road bridge and immediately turn downstream on a narrow fisherman's path. The trail winds past some laurel-studded rock outcrops and then through a floodplain forest of large trees. Birdsong abounds in this cool, sheltered valley, and many spring and summer wild-flowers line the trail. As the path enters a white pine plantation, a foottrail forks to the left. Rather than going that way, continue on the fire road 100 yards to Poole Road, at mile 3.0. There is parking here at the terminus of this lane, popular with people who fish nearby.

Another orange cable strung between orange posts indicates the entrance to the next segment of trail, south of Poole Road. The trail rises through a white pine plantation, and the bed of the fire road is cushioned by decades of accumulated pine needles. Al-though the hiking is pleasant, pure stands of closely planted ever-greens are virtual biological deserts, providing little food or com-plex habitat structure for most animals. At the top of the hill, several wide trails lead to the left, down to the reservoir, and are used mostly by fishermen. Continue straight, past the terminus of a country lane and a number of residential back yards.

The trail soon descends into the valley of Little Morgan Run, and all traces of civilization are left behind. Little Morgan Run is aptly named, a miniature version of its big brother a mile to the north. After crossing the creek, the trail traverses a series of steep but short hills, eventually arriving at the end of another residential road. Within 100 yards, the trail branches to the right; continuing straight will bring you to the edge of the reservoir. On the branch to the right, more steep hills ensue, and the trail passes within sight of the gate at the end of Irving Ruby Road at mile 5.8. Continue on the woods road for another 0.3 miles, where the traffic on Route 32 is both visible and audible. A trashy, eroded footpath leads to the road shoulder. Walk down-hill on the road shoulder, crossing the Liberty Reservoir and ar-riving at the parking area at mile 6.7.

■ ■

▼ Mineral Hill Trail

Distance: 5.7 miles one way
Difficulty: Easy to moderate

Directions: From the Baltimore Beltway (I-695), take I-70 west to Route 32. Exit north and go 9.0 miles to Pine Knob Road. Turn right and go 1.0 miles to the trailhead. To reach the Oakland Road trailhead from here, continue east on Pine Knob Road, which becomes Mineral Hill Road. After 2.0 miles, turn left on Oakland Road. The parking area is 1.1 miles farther, at the end of the road.

The Mineral Hill Trail runs along the south side of the Morgan Run arm of Liberty Reservoir. It has several endearing aspects: changes in elevation are minor compared to many other Liberty Reservoir trails, there are frequent views of the water, and the trail surface is wide and generally well-drained and soft underfoot. On the negative side, the watershed buffer is relatively thin in a neighborhood with many houses, trail usage is fairly heavy, and off-road vehicles use the trail, in violation of watershed regulations. Nevertheless, a hike here has far more positives than negatives and is a pleasant affair in all seasons.

Perhaps the most convenient point at which to access the trail is along Pine Knob Road one mile east of Route 32. There is ample road shoulder parking here in a woodsy setting. Other possible access points are at Route 32, where parking on the road shoulder of this busy highway is a poor choice, and at the end of Oakland Road, where a number of houses are visible within the first half-mile of this eastern terminus of the trail.

The linear nature of the Mineral Hill Trail dictates an out-and-back strategy for a hike, or use of a car shuttle. For a short walk, take the fire road west from Pine Knob Road to Route 32, 1.3 miles each way. A longer hike runs from Pine Knob Road eastward to Oakland Road, 4.4 miles each way. This latter, longer portion of the trail is definitely the more scenic.

Canada goose and goslings

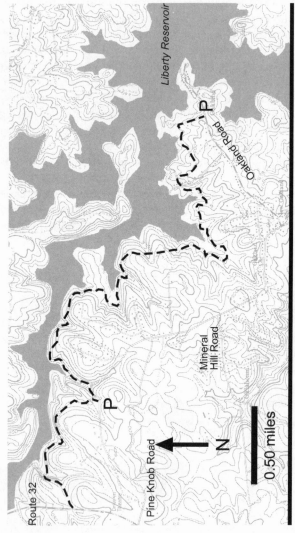

Liberty Reservoir

Oakland Road

Mineral
Hill Road

Route 32

Pine Knob Road

N

0.50 miles

P

P

P

At the Pine Knob Road trailhead, there are two gates, marked by orange cable strung between orange posts. Take the western fire road to go toward Route 32. This trail descends gradually for more than a half-mile, crosses a shallow stream, and then rises equally gradually to within sight of Route 32. The gate is set back from Route 32, so it may be difficult to see if you are cruising the highway looking for it. The gate is 0.4 miles north of Pine Knob Road.

To hike the longer trail, enter the fire road at the eastern gate. This well-graveled road heads directly downhill, arriving within sight of the reservoir at mile 0.3. For the next 3 miles, the trail is rarely out of sight of water. After a dry spell, the shallow water in the coves of Liberty is very clear, while deeper portions take on a beautiful green hue. Canada geese occupy most of these coves, raising their young in spring through early summer. Even ten years ago, most geese were migratory, and it was a rare sight to see goslings in summer. As of this writing, as many geese nest in Maryland as migrate in each fall, and this ratio is increasing rapidly. There may come a time when Canadas are as reviled as starlings; each goose produces a tremendous amount of waste, and that waste is unwelcome in the reservoirs that form Baltimore's drinking water supply.

Mineral Hill Trail is bordered by deciduous woods and a few white pine plantations. Where the trail drops into small stream valleys, the rich protected soils harbor some very tall tulip poplars and various oaks. Ovenbirds and wood thrushes call from the thick vegetation on the forest floor.

While a great many foottrails enter the fire road from private property uphill, there are very few forks. Only at mile 4.2 does one bear left, to the reservoir. Instead, continue on the main fire road another 0.2 miles to the trailhead at Oakland Road. The parking area is 0.3 miles down Oakland Road, toward the end of the peninsula.

▼ Quarry Trail

Distance: 2.2 miles one way
Difficulty: Moderate

Directions: From the Baltimore Beltway (I-695), take Liberty Road (Route 26) west. From the point where Liberty Road begins to cross Liberty Reservoir, proceed west 1.9 miles. Turn left on Old

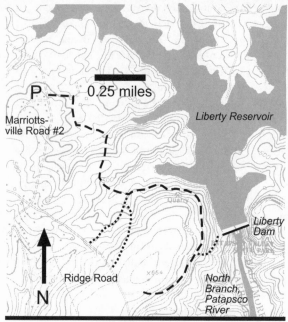

P - - ⌐ 0.25 miles

Marriotts-
ville Road #2   *Liberty Reservoir*

↑
N   Ridge Road   *North
                                    Branch,
                                    Patapsco
                                    River*

*Liberty
Dam*

45. QUARRY TRAIL

Liberty Road, and left again on Sunset Drive. Proceed 1.0 miles
to the trailhead (Sunset Drive becomes Marriottsville Road #2).

Baltimore, Howard, and Carroll Counties abut one another along
the Patapsco River near Liberty Dam, and this general area is
among the most geologically diverse in Maryland. Over the centuries, there has been a considerable amount of mining near here.
For example, chromium-bearing rock was quarried at Soldiers Delight through much of the nineteeth century. The little Baltimore
County community of Granite was named for the local rock.
Today, there are active flagstone quarries near Marriottsville. And
tucked away in an obscure corner of the Liberty watershed are the
remnants of a marble and quartz quarry, operated to supply rub-
ble fill during the construction of Liberty Dam in the early 1950s.
    The Quarry Trail is a cluster of fire roads leading to and
around this small open pit mine. It is isolated from the other fire
roads of the Liberty watershed and so is little known and lightly
used.

Begin your walk from the trailhead on Marriottsville Road #2, marked by the orange cable and orange posts. There is limited roadside parking here, but this is the only access point with any parking at all. The fire road drops downhill for less than 0.1 miles to an intersection. Trails to the left and straight ahead are fishing paths that lead to the reservoir's edge; turn right on the fire road. The trail crosses a small stream and then goes uphill through an oak woods. In midsummer and early fall, a misty rain will reveal the many webs of filmy dome spiders, each constructed horizontally between roots and rocks. Filmy dome spiders are major predators of insects and arthropods found in the soil and among the detritus of the forest floor. Few people realize how many spiders occupy the forest until their webs are made visible by rain or dew.

Between mile 0.6 and 0.9, the trail forks at least three times. Go right, left, and left, respectively; if in doubt, consult the map, and always take the widest, most heavily traveled path. Underfoot will be an increasing number of loose rocks, ranging from golf ball–size to soccer ball–size. The source of all these rocks soon becomes evident, when hillside pit quarries appear on the uphill side of the trail. The rocks are whitish in color, some pure quartz, some a quartz-marble mix. This is in marked contrast to the dark gray, crystalline rock so typical of the Patapsco Valley and which is found a bit farther along the trail, on the other side of the hill.

There are good winter views of Liberty Reservoir between mile 1.0 and mile 1.2, near the quarries. At mile 1.5, a side trail branches off downhill, arriving at the top of Liberty Dam. A concrete observation deck gives good views of both the reservoir upstream and the North Branch of the Patapsco River Valley downstream. Returning uphill, the fire road emerges from the trees atop one of the highest points in the area, where there is a microwave tower. Walk left down the driveway to Ridge Road at mile 2.2.

To return to the trailhead on Marriottsville Road #2, you may either retrace your steps, or choose one of the two fire roads that originate from Ridge Road in the next 0.2 miles. Neither is marked with orange cable, so they are difficult to notice. You will need to use care in locating them. These fire roads will return you to the original trail on the west side of the quarries.

LOCH RAVEN WATERSHED

Loch Raven Dam and Reservoir are located on the Big Gunpowder River just north of Baltimore. Loch Raven is the more downstream of the two city-owned reservoirs on this river and is the primary water-storage facility for the Baltimore metropolitan area's drinking water.

The Big Gunpowder River has been used for municipal drinking water since 1873. The first dam, a small rock and cement affair, was constructed near what is now Cromwell Bridge Road in 1881, and is still visible. By 1914, however, increased demand for clean, potable water necessitated the construction of a larger dam, sited farther upstream. In 1923, Loch Raven Dam was greatly enlarged, adding fifty-two feet to the original thirty-foot height. Concerns about the dam's safety in a major flood led to substantial reinforcement in 2001. Loch Raven Reservoir covers 2,400 acres when full and has 50 miles of shoreline.

The reservoir is kept at as high a level as possible without overflowing. If the volume of water in Loch Raven drops significantly, extra water is released from Prettyboy Reservoir, upstream, to restore levels in Loch Raven. Thus, Loch Raven has less of an unsightly "bathtub ring" than do most reservoirs. Typically, water flows over the Loch Raven dam only in winter and spring of wet years and during major floods, like those caused by hurricanes.

Approximately 8,000 acres of city-owned land surround Loch Raven. Almost all of this acreage is wooded, although some trees were selectively logged in the 1970s to supply the city with construction timbers. In general, however, this is a mature forest, with many trees that are a century old. Despite this lack of recent disturbance, displays of spring wildflowers are not nearly as good as in nearby state parks, indicating that sensitive plants require very long periods of time to recolonize after extirpation, which in this case was caused by farming and grazing.

The Loch Raven Reservoir area is an island of greenery in the midst of a long-developed suburbia. Except for a narrow riparian

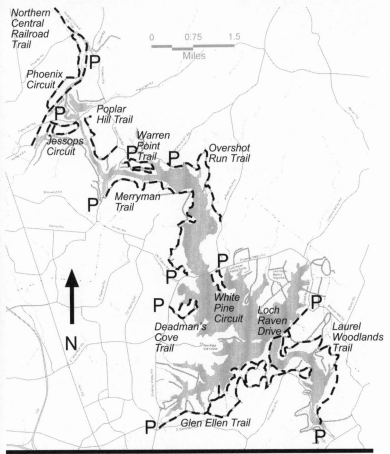

46. LOCH RAVEN WATERSHED HIKING TRAILS

corridor on the upstream and downstream ends, it is isolated from all other natural landscapes. Even so, Loch Raven may be the most scenic of the three city-owned reservoirs. Because of surrounding development, it is a haven for wildlife, especially birds. Although the Loch Raven watershed is heavily used, it seems little the worse for wear.

Eleven hikes are described on Loch Raven watershed lands. They differ greatly in difficulty, ranging from a paved road closed to vehicular traffic, to short, mostly level woodland paths, to long, hilly fire roads. There is certainly a trail to please every

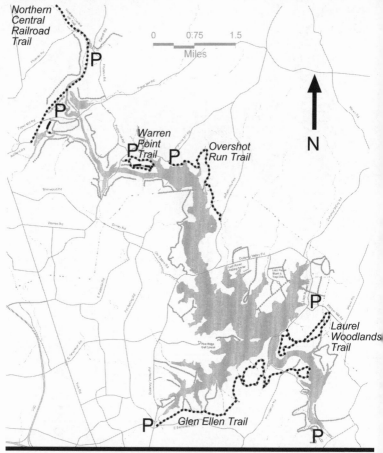

47. LOCH RAVEN WATERSHED MOUNTAIN BIKE ROUTES

hiker, regardless of age or conditioning. Although most of the mileage is on fire roads, there are a few sections of narrow footpaths incised into the landscape through years of common use. No trails are marked by blazes, but regular consultation of the maps should preclude getting lost.

Many of the trails in Loch Raven are used by mountain bikers; in fact, mountain bikers may often outnumber hikers. However, only four trails are officially open to mountain biking: Warren Point, Overshot Run, and portions of Glen Ellen and Laurel

Woodlands. In addition, Merryman is frequently used by mountain bikers even though it is officially off limits. Hikers looking for solitude would do well to avoid these trails. Mountain bikers who use this book should refer to the map of open trails and obey all regulations and trail closures.

Loch Raven watershed is a first-rate recreational resource that is both convenient and a joy to hike. Don't miss it!

■ ■

▼ Laurel Woodlands Trail

Distance: 6.8-mile circuit; shorter loops possible
Difficulty: Moderate

Directions: From the Baltimore Beltway (I-695), take exit 27 north, Dulaney Valley Road. Continue for 6.9 miles. There are two forks in this road that might confuse first-time visitors. First, just beyond the bridge over Loch Raven, Dulaney Valley Road bears right; do not take the larger Jarrettsville Pike, to the left and uphill. Second, at a large restaurant, continue straight rather than turning left. The road is now called Loch Raven Drive. Morgan Mill Road is reached at mile 6.9.

There is always parking available on Loch Raven Drive prior to Morgan Mill Road. Loch Raven Drive from Morgan Mill Road to Providence Road is closed to motor vehicles on weekends, 10 a.m. to 5 p.m. Parking is allowed along Morgan Mill Road during this time. On weekdays, when Loch Raven Drive is open to vehicles, there is parking along the curbs as designated by signs.

Mountain laurels are among the most beautiful members of Maryland's woody flora. In cold weather, their glossy evergreen leaves lend a cheery look to the drab winter forest. The twisted trunks provide variation from the architectural linearity of most trees, and the stringy bark is a rich mahogany in color. But the glory of mountain laurels is evident only in late spring, when the leaves are almost obscured by explosions of white-petaled flowers. Surely this woodland beauty is the reason so many places have the word laurel in their name.

The Laurel Woodlands Trail features a profusion of mountain laurels along its length. The trail is very popular, and with good reason. There is ample parking, and there are peaceful views of Loch Raven on the road to the trailhead. The trail is wide, well-

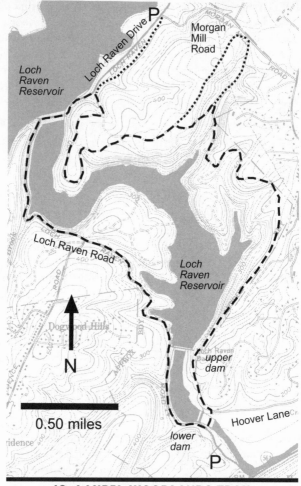

Loch Raven Drive

P

Morgan Mill Road

MORGAN

MILL

ROAD

Loch Raven Reservoir

400

Loch Raven Road

LOCH RAVEN

ROAD

400

300

Loch Raven Reservoir

N

Dogwood Hills

APPROX

400

BDY

Loch Raven upper dam

0.50 miles

idence

400

lower dam

P

Hoover Lane

56

48. LAUREL WOODLANDS TRAIL

used, and generally in good shape, with just a few mud wallows. Only at one location is the trail out-of-breath steep. The forest surrounding the trail is a mature one, containing large trees and many wildflowers and ferns, and offering fine birding. The only negative aspect of the Laurel Woodlands Trail is that there is much traffic on the trail, especially since the first portion of the hike described is a designated mountain bike trail. Even so, if everyone is courteous, heavy use does not necessarily degrade the outdoor experience.

The trail is described as a 6.8-mile circuit, the final 2.6 miles being along the shoulder of Loch Raven Drive. This last portion of the hike is not as bad as it might sound. Between the dam and Providence Road, the shoulders of Loch Raven Drive are generally wide and grassy, and there are frequent views of the reservoir. North of Providence Road, Loch Raven Drive is closed to vehicular traffic on weekends from 10 a.m. to 6 p.m.

Hikers with less energy may wish to shorten this walk to the route of the designated bike trail. The trail portion of this truncated route terminates at Morgan Mill Road after 2.0 miles, and it is but a short distance downhill along the road shoulder to the parking areas.

The trailhead for this hike is a bulletin board located about 150 yards west of the Loch Raven Drive bridge. If parking is not available near this trailhead (as on weekends), park on Morgan Mill Road and use a wide footpath running parallel to Loch Raven Drive between Morgan Mill Road and the bulletin board. Note that this path is not included in the trail mileage.

From the bulletin board, the trail leads uphill in a steep fashion to the first intersection, at mile 0.2. Turn right to follow a footpath that circumscribes a broad peninsula. In winter, there are good views of the reservoir from this fairly level footpath. At mile 1.2, another trail intersection is reached. Turn right. The trail now runs along the ridge, through a forest of oaks. At the

mountain laurel

next fork, mile 1.4, bear right, downhill. (Going left here will bring you to Morgan Mill Road.)

The trail descends into a very pretty stream valley, with large trees that harbor forest songbirds like warblers and vireos. Wildflowers like trout lily, rue anemone, jack-in-the-pulpit, and sweet cicely are common, scattered among the many Christmas ferns. The trail eventually crosses this unnamed stream and then bears steeply uphill.

At the top of the hill, bear left at a fork; the right fork leads to the reservoir. The next fork, at mile 2.3, is within sight of power lines; bear right, away from them. The trail now runs along the border of watershed property, along a level, narrow ridge, with residences within sight on the left. This delightful segment of the Laurel Woodlands Trail is no longer fire road but a narrow footpath through an open woods. The trail eventually drops downhill in an increasingly steep fashion, to emerge on the floodplain at mile 3.8.

The Big Gunpowder River is visible to the right. Although this point on the river is downstream of the large dam and main reservoir, the calm water visible here is a pool backed up by a smaller, older dam. Once past the old dam at mile 4.1, look for a deeply eroded trail that leads to the water's edge.

During most of an average year, it is possible to cross the river on a series of steppingstone rocks, because water flows through this portion of the Big Gunpowder's riverbed only when the Loch Raven Reservoir overflows. Typically, this occurs only in winter and spring of wet years. Indeed, in the last several decades, the river has been only puddles for as much as three years at a time.

This dewatering has had major consequences for the ecology of the Big Gunpowder in the ten miles of the river between the base of Loch Raven Dam and tidewater. Aquatic life exists here but cannot flourish during these dry spells. Especially affected is the bottom of the food chain, detritus that normally arrives from upstream, like single-celled algae, bacteria, protozoa, and other tiny aquatic animals. The valley looks pretty, but the river does not support the full spectrum of living things and does not recycle nutrients or participate in the hydrologic cycle in a normal way.

After crossing the river, walk uphill to Loch Raven Road. In the event that high water prevents you from using the stepping-stone rocks, it would be wise to retrace your steps. It is possible to continue on the footpath downstream to Hoover Lane. Then turn right on Glen Arm Road, cross the bridge, and turn right on Cromwell Bridge Road. At Loch Raven Road, turn right once more. This detour of several miles unfortunately is very dangerous, as Cromwell Bridge Road is heavily traveled and has no shoulders whatsoever.

On Loch Raven Road, walk upstream on the wide grassy road shoulders. At the upper dam, the shoulders disappear, so use care in this area. Once past this point, there is easy, safe walking to Providence Road. From Providence Road to the trailhead, there are again no shoulders, but this section of road is closed to vehicles on weekends, and traffic is light on weekdays except at rush hour. The circuit is complete after a walk of 6.8 miles.

▬▬▬▬▬▬▬▬▬▬▬▬▬▬▬▬▬▬▬▬▬▬▬▬▬▬▬▬

▼ Glen Ellen Trail

Distance: 10.1 miles; shorter loops possible
Difficulty: Moderate to strenuous

Directions: From the Baltimore Beltway (I-695), take exit 27 north, Dulaney Valley Road. After 0.8 miles, turn left on Seminary Avenue and park on the road shoulder.

The Glen Ellen Trail is one of the more popular trails in the Loch Raven Reservoir property, especially among mountain bikers. Although hilly, much of the rolling terrain near the west end is relatively gentle, so this portion of the trail attracts many novice riders. Unfortunately, unethical mountain bikers have opened a number of narrow side trails ("single track" in mountain bike parlance) during the 1990s, to such an extent that the area seems a maze of intersecting paths. Pursuant to an agreement between the City of Baltimore and MAMBO (Maryland Association of Mountain Bike Operators), only designated fire roads are open for mountain biking. Please ride accordingly.

Hikers have more options than just the fire roads. Hiking is permitted on watershed property except where specifically prohibited by signs. Nevertheless, hikers should use discretion and avoid using trails that are merely shortcuts.

Begin your walk at the intersection of Dulaney Valley Road

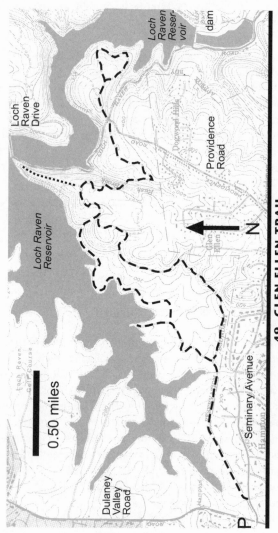

Loch Raven Drive

Loch Raven Reservoir

Loch Raven Reservoir

Loch Raven Golf Course

Dulaney Valley Road

Seminary Avenue

Hampton

Dogwood Hills

Providence Road

Glen Ellen

dam

0.50 miles

N

49. GLEN ELLEN TRAIL

and Seminary Avenue, where there is limited roadside parking on Seminary Avenue west of the intersection. The Church of Jesus Christ of Latter Day Saints, also located at this intersection, has kindly allowed parking in their lot except during services; take care to not abuse the privilege. Cross busy Dulaney Valley Road at the light and walk 100 yards east on Seminary Avenue to the fire road, which is marked by an orange cable strung between orange posts.

The first mile of this trail is moderately flat, passing through a pleasant forest of mixed pines and hardwoods. Suburban backyards are frequently visible, since the fire road borders private property. After crossing a pretty stream, bear left at a fork. The road eventually reaches a sheltered cove of Loch Raven, where mergansers and several kinds of ducks are frequently seen in winter. Return up the hill, and after about 200 yards, turn left on a narrow foottrail. For the next mile and half, this trail runs along the edge of Loch Raven, giving scenic views of the reservoir in all seasons. Although this trail is not a fire road, it is so popular with mountain bikers that it may never be successfully closed to them. Hence, beware of mountain bikes as you walk. A well-known landmark along this trail is Sam's Grave, the scenic final resting place of a faithful dog, whose leash and toys decorate the gravesite.

At mile 3.5, the trail bears away from the water's edge and runs steeply uphill alongside a small stream. Spring wildflowers seem more abundant here than in most of the upland areas of the watershed property. At the top of the hill, the trail joins the fire road. Turn right to return to Seminary Avenue, or left to continue the hike. The trail soon drops rather steeply into the valley of Rush Brook, a pretty little woodland stream. After rising to the surrounding uplands, the fire road eventually reaches Loch Raven Road at the point where it intersects Providence Road at mile 5.1.

To extend this hike, cross Loch Raven Road into a small grassy field. Another fire road rises steeply uphill from this point, forming a circuit with good views of the reservoir. At the top of the hill, bear right at a fork; the trail to the left leads steeply downhill to the water. Continue on the fire road as it loops around this peninsula, returning to Loch Raven Road at mile 6.2.

Cross Loch Raven Road and reenter the Glen Ellen Trail.

A Novel Zoonotic: West Nile Virus

IT'S A NASTY WORLD OUT THERE. FROM EQUINE ENCEPHALITIS AND GIAR-
dia to Lyme disease and rabies, there are some devastating diseases that can be passed to humans from other animals. Called
zoonotics, such diseases are becoming more numerous and more
common every year. The most recent arrival in Maryland is West
Nile virus.

West Nile virus first appeared in the United States in 1999
in Queens, New York. At least sixty-two people became severely
sick, and seven died. The victims who died were all elderly and
had already-weakened immune systems. In healthy individuals,
West Nile virus is a mild disease with flu-like symptoms; no
doubt most people who become infected never realize what they
have. In 2000, there were only seventeen known cases, all fairly
mild, and one death. This emerging pattern is consistent with
data from Israel, where West Nile outbreaks occur about once
every ten years.

The virus is most commonly found in birds, especially
crows. It is transmitted via female mosquitoes. If the mosquito
obtains a blood meal from an infected crow, she may then pass
it on to the next animal she bites. West Nile virus is not partic-
ularly host-specific; in addition to humans and birds, horses,
bats, raccoons, and rabbits have all been infected. There are
dozens of species of mosquitoes in the United States, but the
West Nile virus has so far been confined to *Culex pipiens*. Public
health officials worry that the virus may enter populations of
Asian tiger mosquitoes. These recent arrivals have plagued Baltimoreans recently, biting voraciously in the daytime.

West Nile virus entered the consciousness of Marylanders in
late summer and fall of 2000, when a number of infected crows
were found dead or dying. Since intensive testing discovered no
mosquitoes with West Nile virus, it seems likely that the infected
birds were migrants from the New York area. No humans tested
positive for West Nile in Maryland, but if the virus becomes established in the local mosquito population, a human victim
seems only a matter of time.

Public health officials responded promptly and perhaps ex-
travagantly to the first reports of dead crows. A synthetic contact
insecticide, permethrin, was sprayed at night through the neigh-

borhood where each infected crow had been found, in an effort to kill any mosquitoes that might have picked up the virus. Although permethrin is generally safe, exposure to skin and lungs should be minimized, and a tiny percentage of any population will be hypersensitive to such xenobiotic chemicals. Given that no mosquitoes have been found with the virus, this insecticide spraying campaign may have been an unwarranted response.

It seems likely that West Nile virus will be with us for the foreseeable future. The lessons of ecology tell us that a disease, once established, is impossible to eradicate and that insecticide spraying will be increasingly less effective over time. The wisest action Baltimoreans can take is to eliminate puddles of standing water where mosquito larvae develop. If the mosquito population can be reduced, transmission of the disease will be correspondingly lessened. And besides, who among us would bemoan a reduction in the mosquito population during a muggy Baltimore summer?

Take the fire road all the way back to Seminary Avenue rather than retracing your steps on the footpath described previously. This hilly route runs through upland forest with a few small stream crossings and gives different scenery than did the outbound trail along the reservoir. Seminary Avenue is reached after a hike of 10.1 miles.

▼ **Deadman's Cove Trail**

Distance: 1.5-mile circuit
Difficulty: Easy

Directions: From the Baltimore Beltway (I-695), take Dulaney Valley Road, exit 27, north. Go 3.0 miles and observe the wide spot in the road shoulder in the opposite, southbound lane. This location is 0.3 miles north of the well-marked entrance road for Stella Maris. Continue north until you find a safe place to turn around (this will likely be on the far side of the bridge over Loch Raven). Return to the tiny road shoulder parking area and park well off the road.

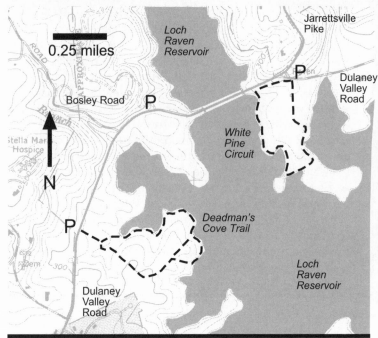

50. DEADMAN'S COVE TRAIL / WHITE PINE CIRCUIT

What an intriguing name! Unfortunately, the reason this obscure cove is so named has been lost. However, a walk on the Dead-man's Cove Trail reveals a tiny bay with a narrow, shallow mouth that would clearly be difficult to locate from the water; a body here could go a long time before it was found. We can only hope that this place was named for a less grisly event.

The Deadman's Cove Trail is a short, pleasant, mostly level walk. At least half of the mileage is on a footpath adjacent to Loch Raven's shoreline, so there are many views across the water. The trail is narrow, however, and rather overgrown in summer, so the going is unexpectedly difficult. The lack of sufficient, safe parking keeps the Deadman's Cove trail lightly used.

Begin your walk from the fire road marked by the orange cable strung between two orange posts and located 0.3 miles north of the Stella Maris entrance drive on Dulaney Valley Road. There is parking for a maximum of four vehicles on the south-bound side of the road. This is the only legal parking anywhere near this trailhead; if the authorities ever prohibit parking here, as they have done along most of Dulaney Valley Road, this trail will no longer be accessible. Use extreme caution in crossing Dulaney Valley Road to get to the trailhead; the road is narrow, the traffic heavy and the vehicular speeds frightening.

Once on the trail, the worst aspects of this walk are behind you. The fire road runs gradually downhill, crosses a tiny stream, and then bears left uphill. Much spicebush borders the trail. A small tree rarely more than ten feet high, spicebush puts out yellow flowers in spring that lend a lemony blush to the still-gray forest, and in fall produces bright red berries that are a favorite of migrating robins. At mile 0.3, the fire road bears left, running through a brushy area that was open fields thirty years ago.

A fork in the fire road is reached at mile 0.6, at the remains of an old and very small house. Turn right and follow the trail to the water's edge, where there is a grove of red cedars, a small tree that frequently grows in abandoned fields until it is shaded out by larger, deciduous trees. Here, the dry soil may allow the cedars to persist for a longer period of time than they otherwise would. The berries are popular with a variety of songbirds.

Follow a narrow and obscure trail to the left along the edge of Loch Raven. If you feel you have lost the trail, merely keep going; it runs within ten feet of the water in all places, and you will soon recognize the trail where it becomes more distinct. To the right are some of the longest views over open water from any trail in the Loch Raven watershed.

Pass the terminus of the other fork of the fire road at mile 0.9 and continue on the footpath near the water. It soon turns to the west into Deadman's Cove. This intimate, sheltered embayment is a fine place to look for ducks in winter, great blue herons in late summer, and kingfishers year-round.

At the head of the cove, the trail enters a wetland that is quite soggy in winter and spring but merely damp in summer and fall. Rather than continuing along the shore of the cove, turn left to follow a tiny rivulet upstream. Although a shoreline path is visible, it soon disappears, and further progress is an unpleasant bushwhack. The trail upstream is tiny, but it soon brings you to the fire road that forms the first part of the Deadman's Cove Trail. Turn right, taking the fire road to Dulaney Valley Road and completing the 1.5-mile loop.

▼ **White Pine Circuit**

Distance: 1.0-mile circuit, with an additional spur trail
Difficulty: Easy

Directions: From the Baltimore Beltway (I-695), take exit 27, Dulaney Valley Road, north for 4.1 miles. Just beyond the bridge over Loch Raven, bear right at the fork. Park on the road shoulder near the guardrail about a hundred yards from the fork.

Many of the trails in the Loch Raven watershed traverse steep, hilly terrain. One exception is the White Pine Circuit, which is almost level. It is therefore suitable for children and hikers who are just starting to get into shape. The trail encircles a narrow peninsula, running within view of the water for a majority of its short length. The White Pine Circuit is unusual also because it is not a fire road but is instead a narrow footpath.

Begin your walk from the trailhead, on Dulaney Valley Road west of the bridge over Loch Raven and about 100 yards downhill from the traffic light. There is ample parking on a wide road shoulder, and there are often vehicles parked here by fishermen using the bridge. Enter the inconspicuous trail at the point where the double guardrail becomes a single one.

The footpath leads straight into a white pine plantation, now approaching maturity. White pines are exceptionally grace-

*white pine needles
and cones*

ful and beautiful trees when allowed to grow to old age and given enough space to fully spread their boughs. These trees, however, were planted in rows, forty to fifty years ago, with the expectation that they would be harvested for a nice profit in the future. Times have changed, however, and the public will no longer accept logging on watershed lands when the sole purpose of those lands is protection of the drinking water supply. Not having been harvested, the pines are now too closely spaced for appreciable sideward growth to occur. Instead, they grow upward only, competing with each other for available sunlight. Lower branches, unable to gather enough light to photosynthesize, are without value to the tree and gradually die back. Although the impressive columns of their trunks are reminiscent of cathedral pillars, white pines in a plantation are a pale imitation of their free-range kin.

For a short, easy trail so close to Baltimore that one would expect heavy use, the White Pine Circuit is surprisingly obscure, and in places it can be difficult to follow. Be sure to follow the path that appears most heavily traveled.

The White Pine Circuit reaches the water's edge at mile 0.2, and then follows the shoreline for a short distance. At a fork, bear right to follow the White Pine Circuit as it crosses the peninsula to a southward view over Loch Raven. You may also choose to take the left fork to follow an optional out-and-back branch trail to the end of the peninsula. In summer, this trail fades away entirely before reaching land's end; if the reservoir is low, a walk on the exposed shoreline is preferable to fighting the spider webs and low-hanging vegetation inland.

After arriving at the water's edge on the peninsula's far side, the remainder of the White Pine Circuit is easy to follow, as the trail is always within a few feet of the reservoir. Bear right along a sheltered cove that sometimes harbors ducks in cold weather. The trail then crosses the base of yet another short peninsula. A side trip of a hundred yards or so to the tip of this spit of land gives more fine views.

The trail continues in a northerly direction toward the Dulaney Valley Road bridge. Only the noise from this busy artery disturbs the peace of this beautiful forest of mixed hardwoods and evergreens. In winter, this is a productive site for birding, featuring chickadees, woodpeckers, nuthatches, and tufted titmice, who like the southern exposure and diverse cover.

At the causeway built to support the Dulaney Valley Road bridge, the trail turns uphill, paralleling the road but far enough below it so that road noise is not objectionable. Parts of the trail here merely run alongside or even in a drainage ditch, so the footing is uncertain. The trailhead where the White Pine Circuit originated is reached after a walk of 1.0 miles.

▼ Merryman Trail

Distance: 5.0 miles one way
Difficulty: Moderate

Directions: From the Baltimore Beltway (I-695), take exit 27 north, Dulaney Valley Road, for 3.6 miles. Park in the small lot on the west side of the road. In the event that these parking spots are all filled, continue north on Dulaney Valley Road, crossing the reservoir. On the far side, bear right at the fork and park on the wide road shoulder. Hike 0.5 miles back across the bridge on a separate pedestrian walkway to reach the trailhead.

To reach the Warren Road trailhead, take I-83 north from the Baltimore Beltway. Take exit 18 east, Warren Road. From where Warren Road crosses York Road (Route 45), continue east for 1.8 miles to the trailhead. There are small parking areas on both sides of the road.

There are numerous beautiful trails in the Loch Raven watershed, but the Merryman Trail is exceptionally so. There are almost continuous views of the open waters of the reservoir, bosky dells riven by clear-flowing streams, and rich forest soils shaded by towering mature trees. Wildflowers are abundant in many places. Birding is excellent, especially during spring migration; in addition to good woodland habitat, the trail often runs along a high bench, such that the upper reaches of downslope trees are at eye level.

Start your hike from the small parking lot along Dulaney Valley Road just short of the long bridge over Loch Raven Reservoir. There is very limited parking here, for about a dozen cars, and it is in high demand. Use care near Dulaney Valley Road, as cars pass at a very high rate of speed. In the event this lot is full, there is always parking available at the other end of the trail, Warren Road. It is also possible to park on the road shoulder of

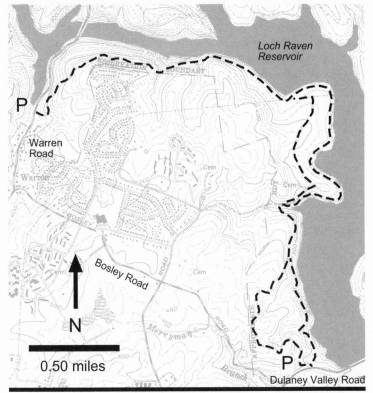

Loch Raven
Reservoir

P

Warren
Road

Warren

BOSLEY

Bosley Road

ROAD

Cem

Cem

N

Merryman

460'

ROAD

APPLE

0.50 miles

P

Branch

Dulaney Valley Road

51. MERRYMAN TRAIL

Dulaney Valley Road, on the eastern side of the bridge. The walk back to the Merryman trailhead is 0.5 miles one way.

Two trails depart from the little grassy sward behind the Dulaney Valley Road parking area. The narrow foottrail, nearer to the reservoir, is the most scenic path, and is recommended for hikers, birders, botanizers, and families with children. It is very narrow and subject to erosion, however, so be careful that your passage does not contribute to this problem.

The footpath enters the forest through a dense shrub layer of spicebush. It soon narrows even more, a mere trace carved into the hillside by constant use. There are lots of spring wildflowers to be seen over the next mile, including may apple, toothwort, bloodroot, windflower, hepatica, star chickweed, jack-in-the-pulpit, wild geranium, and Virginia waterleaf. In a few places, New York fern excludes all other plant life, creating gardens of delicate upright filigree. Tulip poplars dominate the canopy on these slopes. These tall, fast-growing trees with arrow-straight trunks unbroken for many feet by branches, produce large, cup-shaped flowers in early May. Squirrels often clip them off to get at the drop of nectar deep inside, so spent flowers sometimes litter the trail and forest floor.

Woodland birding is good along this trail as well. Winter residents like chickadees, tufted titmice, and various woodpeckers abound. During spring migration, the calls of orioles, vireos, and assorted warblers echo through the forest. These canopy birds can sometimes be seen more easily by looking toward the reservoir, where treetops farther down the slope are now nearly at eye level. This sideslope birding is the only known cure for "warbler neck"!

After 0.8 miles of fairly level travel, the foottrail joins the fire road. A short circuit hike of 2.1 miles can be created by turning left on the fire road, returning to Dulaney Valley Road. Such a hike would be perfect for families with small children or hikers with limited time.

There is still plenty of interesting terrain and miles of good trail ahead, so hikers should continue downhill on the fire road from this intersection. The trail crosses a very scenic little un-named creek. Within ten feet, take an obscure foottrail that branches off to the right. If you miss this path, you'll arrive at a T-intersection of fire roads within twenty yards. The road to the left goes out to Pot Spring Road via private property. The right-hand road eventually rejoins the described trail, but it is much less scenic. Therefore, go back to the stream and look carefully for the foottrail.

This narrow path follows the edge of Loch Raven, often within a few feet of the water. Once again, this is "birdy" habitat, but of a different sort. Trees near the water are shorter and the underbrush thicker. Cardinals, towhees, bluebirds, and blue-gray gnatcatchers are common. In winter, look for various gulls, ducks, and other water birds on Loch Raven.

Just beyond a power line crossing is Merryman Point. There are excellent views across the water in two directions from here. Unfortunately, the scenery degrades rapidly just beyond this. By some quirk of wind, the shallow cove on the west side of Merryman Point accumulates all sorts of trash. Amazingly, carp breed amongst the flotsam, roiling the waters noisily in May. Large turtles frequently haul out onto pieces of wood to sun themselves. Ironically, what is an eyesore to us humans is habitat to other species!

At this point, the foottrail rejoins the fire road. The rocky trail bed rises gradually up the hillside, but the reservoir is frequently in view. At mile 4.0, the trail stops abruptly at private property. When a house was built here in 1999, trail users created an informal path around the private property. Unfortunately, this reroute is on a very steep slope, and substantial trail work needs to be done to prevent erosion. After about a hundred yards, the trail rejoins a fire road; houses are visible to the left. The fire road continues steadily downhill for another mile to Warren Road.

■ ■

▼ Warren Point Circuit

Distance: 1.5-mile circuit
Difficulty: Moderate

Directions: From the Baltimore Beltway (I-695), get on I-83 north. Take exit 18, Warren Road. Cross York Road (Route 45) and continue for 2.8 miles. Park on either side of the road near the intersection with Poplar Hill Road.

The Warren Point Circuit is yet another of the network of fire roads that twine through Loch Raven Reservoir property, giving hikers and bikers access to a close-in recreational resource. And close-in it is; development crowds Loch Raven on several sides. Nevertheless, Warren Point is a triangular peninsula flanked by the northwest arm of the reservoir on one side and the flooded valley of Royston Branch on the other, with busy Merrymans Mill Road forming the short base. The Warren Point trail seems more isolated than it really is, and that makes it a pleasant destination for a short hike.

Park on the wide shoulder of Poplar Hill Road where it intersects Merrymans Mill Road. The trail begins on the far side of Merrymans Mill Road where a section of orange guardrail blocks vehicular access to the fire road. The first portion of the trail is wide and flat. Notable are the many old logs, downed snags, and

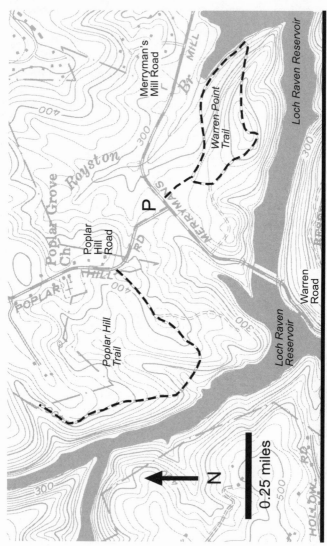

N

0.25 miles

52. WARREN POINT CIRCUIT / POPLAR HILL TRAIL

other woody debris that cover the forest floor. Even more obvious is the understory: acres and acres of almost nothing but spicebush, a small shrub or tree six to eight feet high. Spicebush has oval leaves that turn yellow in autumn, and when the leaves fall, bright red fruits are revealed on every branch. It's a very pretty plant with good food value to birds and other wildlife.

After a hundred yards or so, turn right on a fire road that leads uphill. At the top, bear left; the right fork merely returns you to Merrymans Mill Road at the Warren Road bridge. The forest here is almost all tulip poplar, tall trees with unbranched trunks that lend a cathedral-like appearance to any woods. Continue on this hilly fire road, bearing right at every fork so as to remain within sight of the reservoir. After about a mile of walking, you emerge onto a narrow ridge where the waters of Loch Raven are visible on both sides. Abandon the fire road and walk down this spiny ridge on a faint foottrail. You will see beautiful rock outcrops that glisten as the sun strikes flecks of mica. Continue downhill to reservoir level, where there is a scenic picnic spot looking east across the length of Loch Raven. Be sure to carry out your trash, as there is already a significant litter problem along the reservoir's shoreline.

Depart on the north side of the peninsula; the trail soon becomes a fire road again. Note the many Christmas ferns on the adjacent shady, north-facing slope. The fire road runs directly back to Merrymans Mill Road, completing the loop. Hikers with small children who want to sample the best of the Warren Point trail without the rigors of its several hill climbs may hike the fire road on the north side out to the point and return the same way.

▼ **Poplar Hill Trail**

Distance: 1.5 miles one way
Difficulty: Moderate

Directions: From the Baltimore Beltway (I-695), get on I-83 north. Take exit 18, Warren Road. Cross York Road (Route 45) and continue on Warren Road for 2.8 miles. Poplar Hill Road is the first left turn, several hundred yards beyond the bridge over Loch Raven Reservoir. Park along the road shoulder on Poplar Hill Road near Warren Road (at this point called Merrymans Mill Road). To reach the trailhead, walk 0.3 miles up Poplar Hill Road.

Frequently, it's hard to fathom how a geographical area got its name. Witness Soldiers Delight, Spook Hill, Mingo Forks, and Deadman's Cove, all hiking venues in this book. But for the Poplar Hill Trail, the source of its name is both fitting and obvious. Much of the uplands traversed by this trail is dominated by tulip poplar trees. Growing arrow-straight and branchless for dozens of feet, tulip poplars are among our most graceful of trees. They lend a cathedral-like sense to the forest, and in autumn their falling leaves form a golden blizzard.

This hike is a short, moderately difficult out-and-back walk, with fine birding and, in winter, good views of Loch Raven. Until 1999, the Poplar Hill Trail was a circuit, including a small portion on a public road. However, several hundred yards of the northern end of the trail are now a private driveway, so hikers must return by their incoming route. Even so, the beauty of this very lightly used trail makes it worthwhile. Mountain bikes are prohibited.

The trail entrance is about 300 yards from the intersection of Poplar Hill Road and Merrymans Mill Road. There is plenty of roadside parking at this intersection. Walk uphill on Poplar Hill Road, using care, since there are no shoulders. Enter the trail at the orange guardrail.

Almost immediately, the big tulip poplars loom far overhead. There is also a dense understory of spicebush and a varied herbaceous layer of wildflowers and woodland grasses. This structural complexity, as ecologists term it, is the best evidence of a woodland that harbors a wide variety of nesting birds. Although many birds nest in trees, other species set up housekeeping in shrubs or even on the ground. For example, ovenbirds make concealed nests on the forest floor, while wood thrushes and hooded warblers use small trees and shrubs as homes. If these low plant features are reduced or absent, as in a beech forest, birds with such requirements will not be present. In recent years, large increases in the deer population have denuded many area woodlands up to a height of about five feet from the ground. This "browse line" is often evident.

But not, however, along the Poplar Hill Trail. Ovenbirds, pewees, wood thrushes, and hooded warblers all nest here, their distinctive calls echoing through the May forest. The Poplar Hill Trail is a rewarding venue for spring birding.

After 0.4 miles, the trail descends slightly, and views of the

Hooded Warblers, Cuckoldry, and Evolutionary Advantage

EACH SPRING, OUR FORESTS FILL WITH SONGBIRDS THAT HAVE WINTERED IN Central and South America. They come to nest and raise their young amidst the plenty of a Maryland summer. Among the most appealing, if not common, of these migrants are hooded warblers. The loud and distinctive song of males alerts birders to their presence, although actually seeing them is frustratingly difficult. Scientists have been unraveling the natural history of hooded warblers for decades, but only recently have the invention of molecular biology and DNA-sequencing techniques revealed secrets heretofore unsuspected.

Hooded warblers are small songbirds that dwell in mature forests and have a yellow face and chest and a distinctive black hood. A mated pair builds a nest in thick undergrowth a few feet off the ground, preferring ravines and floodplains. Each pair has a territory, delineated by song and defended aggressively by the male. In suitable habitat, territories abut one another. The pair bond seems strong, and both birds cooperate in feeding nestlings.

Studies on a population of hooded warblers in northwestern Pennsylvania yielded surprising results. Blood samples of adults and nestlings were taken and the DNA sequence of several genes determined. The results showed unequivocally that about 30 percent of the young were fathered by a male different from the one defending the nest! The data allowed determination of parentage, and in any given brood, there were often two or even three fathers. Careful observation revealed that not only were nearby males sneaking onto other territories, but females were leaving their own territories for dalliances elsewhere! Cuckoldry appears much more frequent among hooded warblers than was ever suspected, and in fact may be common in a great number of other bird species as well.

For such a mating system to develop, it must have had evolutionary advantages. Mate fidelity ensures a strong pair bond. Pair bonding ensures that the nest will be actively defended against predators and that young will be fed and cared for until fledging. Although a female chooses her mate according to his perceived fitness, not every male is equally fit. Cuckoldry likely bestows upon a brood of young a more diverse genetic heritage than would be possible with only one father. This genetic diversity may be advantageous in a variable and uncertain environment. In effect, female hooded warblers are hedging their evolutionary bets, attaining the advantages of both a dedicated mate for raising young and a diverse genetic heritage for those same offspring.

reservoir appear ahead. The trail bears right and runs parallel to the shoreline and far above it. The habitat changes on this side-slope; the soil is drier and the understory more open. Oaks become the dominant tree species. There is mountain laurel along the edge of the fire road and wildflowers like bluet and hawkweed in the roadbed itself.

Over the next mile the trail descends into two shallow stream valleys, but otherwise it generally runs on an even grade. Where the Paper Mill Road bridge comes into sight (in winter) or earshot (in summer), the trail bears right. Within a hundred yards or so, the fire road enters private land; a large house becomes visible through the forest. Turn around at this point, 1.5 miles, and retrace your steps to the trailhead.

male and female
hooded warblers

▼ **Jessops Circuit**

Distance: 1.3-mile circuit with a 0.3-mile (one way) spur
Difficulty: Moderate

Directions: From the Baltimore Beltway (I-695), take I-83 north to exit 20, Shawan Road. Exit right, to the east, continuing to the end of Shawan Road. Turn right, south, on York Road (Route 45). Go approximately 0.2 miles and turn left on Ashland Road. Go 1.1 miles to where the road (now called Paper Mill Road) crosses the Northern Central Railroad Trail. Continue for another 0.2 miles to the Jessops Trail entrance.

Good things come in small packages, it's been said, and this circuit hike of almost 2 miles total hiking distance certainly supports the adage. The Jessops Circuit has dramatic views from the higher portions of the footpath, excellent wildlife habitat in the river bottom wetlands, and a variety of spring wildflowers throughout. The entrance to the Jessops Circuit is just a short stroll from the Northern Central Railroad Trail and makes a nice leg-stretching walk after a bike ride on the NCRT. Bicycles are not allowed on the Jessops Trail.

Begin your hike from the trailhead on Paper Mill Road, 150 yards east of the Northern Central Railroad Trail crossing. There is always ample parking along the shoulders of Paper Mill Road, but watch for unwary hikers and bicyclists as you drive and for unheeding motorists when you walk. This is the most popular access point for the heavily used Northern Central Railroad Trail, so it is always congested. However, all those people seem to walk or ride right past the Jessops Trail; it is lightly traveled.

The usual orange posts connected by an orange cable mark the trail entrance. Now owned by the City of Baltimore as part of the Loch Raven watershed, this peninsula was owned by the Jessops family in the eighteenth century and early nineteenth century. The family cemetery is just across Paper Mill Road from the trailhead.

After 50 yards or so on what little remains of an old macadam road, the fire road bears left. (The continuation of the road, to the right, is the spur described below.) A steady uphill climb through a forest of pines and hardwoods reveals a few sheltered areas with such spring wildflowers as toothwort, spring

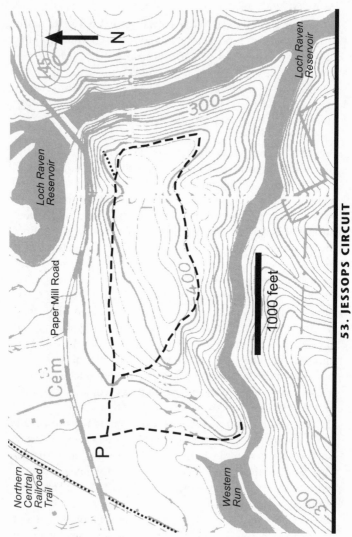

N

Loch Raven Reservoir

300

Loch Raven Reservoir

400

Paper Mill Road

Cem

Northern Central Railroad Trail

P

Western Run

300

1000 feet

53. JESSOPS CIRCUIT

beauty, star chickweed, and even a few Dutchman's breeches. At the point where the reservoir and the Paper Mill Road bridge can be glimpsed through the trees, look for a small footpath bearing left. It leads to a rocky outcrop with dramatic views almost straight down to the water.

These rocks are covered by a variey of lichens. A lichen is a symbiotic association of a fungus and an alga, and frequently grows directly on bare rock. The most obvious lichen here is rock tripe, a dry, leaflike structure clinging precariously to the cliffs. Old stories abound of a soup or gruel made from rock tripe, but it was clearly starvation fare, to be eaten when absolutely nothing else was available. There are also small blueberry bushes growing here. Look for berries in midsummer, but they will be small and fairly dry unless it is a wet year.

Continue along the Jessops Trail as it stays near the top of the ridge without much change in elevation. Once it trends eastward, there are very good views of the steep hillsides sloping downward toward Western Run. The southern exposure of this hillside makes the soil fairly dry; look for wildflowers that prefer such soils, including bluet, hawkweed, and wild pink. After 1.0 miles, the trail descends the hillside to complete the circuit. Turn left to get to the trailhead.

One short spur trail off the Jessops Circuit is well worth a visit. As you return to Paper Mill Road, a fire road on the left just off the macadam driveway beckons. Initially, there is heavy brush that makes good habitat for birds like sparrows, cardinals, and towhees. Soon, however, the shade deepens and large trees cover the trail as it runs along the edge of a nontidal wetland. Look for wood ducks and mallards on the water, shorebirds on the mud flats during spring and fall migration, and great blue herons among the vegetation. Various songbirds frequent the willows and other trees in the swamp. The trail ends at the flowing portion of Western Run; return by the same route. Families with small children can easily manage a stroll on this level but scenic spur trail, 0.3 miles each way.

▼ **Phoenix Circuit**

Distance: 4.2-mile circuit
Difficulty: Moderate to strenuous

Directions: From the Baltimore Beltway (I-695), take I-83 north to exit 20, Shawan Road. Exit right, to the east, continuing to the end of Shawan Road. Turn right, south, onto York Road (Route 45). Go 200 yards. Turn left onto Ashland Road and go 1.1 miles to where the road (now called Paper Mill Road) crosses the Northern Central Railroad Trail.

About half of the Phoenix Circuit follows a section of the heavily used Northern Central Railroad Trail (NCRT). The NCRT is an incredible recreational and natural resource, but it is a linear trail on which you pass the same scenery on both the outward and returning trip. The other half of the circuit is on a fire road on Loch Raven watershed property where you will be unlikely to meet anyone else. The contrast with the NCRT is marked, and not just in terms of quiet and isolation; the two pass through quite different habitats as well.

This hike is described as a clockwise circuit and should be hiked that way. In the counterclockwise direction, finding the obscure footpath that leads to the NCRT from the fire road is almost impossible. The steep nature of the trail and the potential for severe erosion of a section of the Phoenix Circuit precludes mountain bikes.

Access the Phoenix Circuit from Paper Mill Road where it crosses the Northern Central Railroad Trail. Park in the large lot adjacent to the trail. Additional parking may be found along Paper Mill Road east of this lot. Walk northward on the NCRT.

The old railbed of the NCRT is crushed limestone, pleasant to walk on and easy to ride upon. Keep to the right so as to avoid blocking passage of the many bikes that use the trail. The NCRT is lined by heavy vegetation that forms a visual buffer against the adjacent townhome community. The most common floral species is multiflora rose, an invasive alien shrub that outcompetes native species. Multiflora rose is not without benefit or charm: it provides shelter and food for birds and other wildlife, and the perfume of its May flowers is glorious. Other wildflowers are visible along the trail margins, the varieties changing with the seasons.

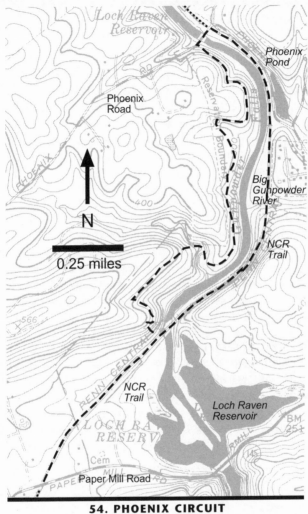

54. PHOENIX CIRCUIT

A few feet before the trail crosses the Big Gunpowder River, look for a single picnic table on the left. Behind the table, a very faint foottrail leads straight up a steep hill. You'll have to use your hands to scramble up this obscure path. About sixty feet above the NCRT, the trail levels out, bears right, passes a springhead, and then continues steeply uphill. After another hundred yards, the path crosses a fire road. Turn right.

Lifestyles of the Moist and Fossorial: Salamanders

THE FIRST WARM, WET NIGHT OF EARLY SPRING: A GROUND FOG RISES wraithlike from the still-cool land, while overhead a gibbous moon gutters through the scudding clouds. The thin, pale light reveals movement across the packed leaves of the forest floor; first one, then another, and in a short while, dozens of animals scurry downhill toward the floodplain ponds. These are spotted salamanders, and they can still be found in the Baltimore area—if you know when and where to look.

Spotted salamanders are chocolate brown in color, with a row of yellow spots along each side of the spine. Unlike many salamanders, they are robust animals, up to nine inches long, with thick, muscular bodies. Spotted salamanders are fossorial, meaning that they dig, spending most of the year underground. In fact, the only time you're likely to see one is during the breeding season, when they congregate around temporary pools of water to mate and lay eggs. Upon arrival at a suitable breeding pond, males and females pair off, perform a courtship ritual, and the male deposits a gelatinous, slightly irridescent spermatophore on a leaf, twig, or patch of gravel. The female picks it up with her cloaca, storing the sperm package until she lays her eggs. The fertilized eggs are small but are surrounded by a gelatinous coating that may be almost half an inch in diameter. The eggs are laid in clumps, and these masses are frequently softball-sized or larger. Algae may colonize the interstices between jelly coats; they may help camouflage the otherwise obvious egg masses. The sala-

red-backed salamander
and eggs

mander embryos develop over a period of time, the length of which depends greatly on temperature. Upon hatching, the juveniles stay in the water, breathing through gills. After some months, if they have not been eaten and if the pond has not dried up, they transform into small adults and disperse into the surrounding forest. For small, slow-moving animals, spotted salamanders may travel quite a distance; one or two are found annually in a rock-walled Baltimore County basement, about a quarter-mile from and 150 feet in elevation above the nearest breeding pond.

The most common salamander in Maryland, and perhaps in North America, is the red-backed salamander. Red-backs are very thin animals, typically four to five inches long, with the tail making up almost half that length. As their name implies, a wide stripe varying in color from brick red to a creamy yellow runs down the back and onto the tail. Red-backed salamanders lack lungs; they breathe by exchanging gas through moist skin. However, of all the salamanders, they are the least dependent on standing water; eggs are laid in damp, rotting wood and are often defended by the mother until hatching. The juveniles do not have a larval stage but are miniature versions of the adults.

While spotted salamanders are uncommon, red-backed salamanders are exceedingly plentiful creatures of the forest. In fact, salamanders are often the most abundant vertebrate in forested ecosystems, and their biomass exceeds that of birds and small mammals. Red-backs are nocturnal, territorial, and do not migrate. They forage along and through the leaf layer, eating insects and other small invertebrates. In dry weather, they adapt by moving farther underground, occupying the spaces in damp logs, under rocks, and even in old animal burrows.

Woodland salamanders, including red-backs, are very sensitive to logging practices. Clear-cutting, a method in which all the trees in a given plot are harvested, is devastating to salamanders, who cannot live in the hot and dry habitat that results. Perhaps surprisingly, however, salamander diversity and numbers do not fully recover from logging for more than 100 years, long after the site has become forested again. For this reason, salamanders are sensitive indicators of environmental quality; they remind us that a forest is more than merely a collection of trees.

This fire road at first runs flat, about halfway between the river and the ridgetop. It soon descends into a narrow unnamed stream valley, a very shady defile filled with birdlife. The trail continues in a surprisingly hilly fashion, with the Big Gunpowder River just visible through the trees in winter. The fire road reaches Phoenix Road at mile 1.9.

Turn right and cross the river on the road bridge. There is no pedestrian lane, but traffic is generally light. On the far side, Phoenix Road bears right, running parallel to the NCRT. There are wide grassy shoulders to walk on, allowing hikers to avoid any conflict with traffic. Within 200 yards, the road passes between Phoenix Pond and the NCRT.

Phoenix Pond is an excellent spot for nature study. Among the amphibians using the pond, wood frogs and spring peepers start the seasonal chorus, followed by the trilling of American toads and gray tree frogs. By summer, green frogs and bullfrogs have joined the choir. Birds abound here throughout the year. It is one of the most reliable places in the metropolitan area to see the namesake of one of Maryland's favorite sports teams, Maryland's official state bird, the Baltimore oriole.

Rejoin the Northern Central Railroad Trail at the Phoenix Pond parking lot, mile 2.5. Another 1.7 miles of walking returns you to the trailhead at Paper Mill Road.

▼ Overshot Run Trail

Distance: 3.5 miles one way
Difficulty: Moderate

Directions: From the Baltimore Beltway (I-695), get on I-83 north. Take exit 18, Warren Road. Cross York Road (Route 45) and continue on Warren Road, crossing Loch Raven on the old iron bridge. The road's name changes to Merrymans Mill Road. Continue 1.0 miles beyond the bridge to a parking area at the crest of a small hill at a curve in the road.

The Overshot Run Trail is a beautiful, easy walk to a forest glen enlivened by the sound of water music. Where the trail crosses Overshot Run, birds and wildflowers abound. A side trail leads down to a beautiful water-level view of Loch Raven and the surrounding hills. The remainder of the trail is more difficult but

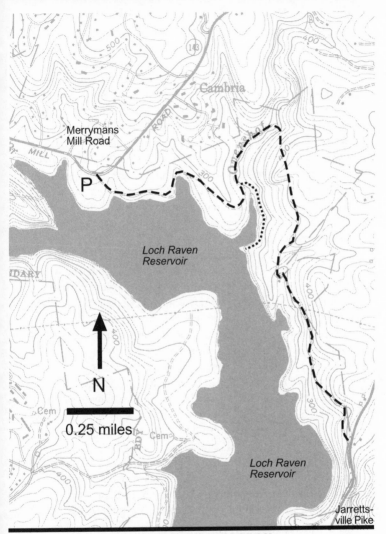

Merrymans
Mill Road

P

*Loch Raven
Reservoir*

N

0.25 miles

Cem

Cem

*Loch Raven
Reservoir*

Jarretts-
ville Pike

55. OVERSHOT RUN TRAIL

still worthwhile, dipping into two more stream valleys from its usual upland course.

Begin your walk at a small gravel pullout on Merrymans Mill Road. Use caution in pulling into and out of this parking area, as it is located on a blind curve in the road, and traffic seems to take the curve faster than might be wise. Because no parking is available at the terminus of this trail, on Jarrettsville Pike, it must be walked as an out-and-back hike.

The first part of the Overshot Run Trail is slightly downhill on an eroded fire road. In winter there are views of Loch Raven to the south, but the trail is far enough from the water that these views are only occasional when the trees are leafed out. After almost a mile of walking, Overshot Run is reached. This is a very pretty little valley with a good flow of water dancing and sparkling over rocks and boulders. The far slope has lots of beech and tulip poplar trees, which lend an open feel to the forest. In spring and early summer, listen for the calls of forest songbirds as they go about their daily activities associated with nesting. Wildflowers include spring beauty, jack-in-the-pulpit, several kinds of violet, and daisy fleabane.

As the fire road first reaches Overshot Run, take a detour on a 0.4-mile side trail that leads to the banks of Loch Raven. Cross Overshot Run on a series of steppingstone rocks; on the far side, a narrow foottrail bears right, paralleling the creek and leading down to a sheltered cove. Along here are found the ruins of a large, old stone house, its chimney and few remaining foundation stones having gathered lichens and moss over the long years. Continue on a narrow foottrail for a hundred yards or so until you emerge in a shaded meadow at water's edge. This is as pretty a picnic spot as you're likely to find anywhere; there are long views down Loch Raven in both directions. If you stop here, you might carry out any trash that may have accumulated, so as to keep this little point of land pristine.

Retrace your steps to the Overshot Run Trail, cross back to the west side, and continue on the fire road in a northerly direction. Since the fire road parallels Overshot Run for several hundred yards, there is ample opportunity to enjoy nature in this forest setting. Listen for red-eyed vireos, wood thrushes, and parula warblers, and watch for a kingfisher patroling the creek.

The fire road drops to Overshot Run in another 0.4 miles. Cross on a line of rocks; a hiking staff is useful to aid in balance at such crossings. The trail now runs directly uphill, rising more than 100 feet over the course of a hundred yards. Continue over hill and dale for another 1.5 miles to Jarrettsville Pike. Since there is no parking along Jarrettsville Pike, return the same way you came.

■ ■

▼ Loch Raven Drive

Distance: 1.7 miles one way
Difficulty: Easy

Directions: From the Baltimore Beltway (I-695), take Dulaney Valley Road, exit 27, north for 4.1 miles. At the fork just beyond the bridge over Loch Raven, bear right; this is still Dulaney Valley Road. Continue for another 2.8 miles, going straight onto Loch Raven Drive at a large restaurant, to the intersection with Morgan Mill Road. Park wherever it is convenient and legal.

When the city of Washington, D.C., closed Rock Creek Drive to vehicular traffic on weekends, recreationalists rejoiced. Over the years, this urban artery surrounded by parkland has become a beloved destination for citizens of the nation's capital. A few years later, the City of Baltimore, in cooperation with Baltimore County, did the same thing with a short section of Loch Raven Drive in the watershed of the same name. This closure too has proven very popular, especially with families.

Loch Raven Drive between Morgan Mill Road and Providence Road is closed to vehicles on weekends and holidays from 10 a.m. to 5 p.m. This 1.7-mile stretch is mostly level, although the final third of a mile rises at a steady rate to Providence Road. There are extensive views of the reservoir, and the surrounding forests are beautiful, composed of large, mature trees. It is an ideal and idyllic place to take small children. Toddlers who have just learned to walk will appreciate the smooth surface. Pre-K kids enjoy riding tricycles and bicycles with training wheels. Older children who have moved on to in-line skates find this a wonderful, safe place to roll. The nearby slopes are perfect for a picnic afterward.

Begin your walk on Loch Raven Drive from the northern "trailhead" at Morgan Mill Road. There is no parking within at least a half-mile of the Providence Road end of the trail, so Morgan Mill Road is the only option. There is usually ample parking along the curb lane of Loch Raven Drive and on the shoulder of

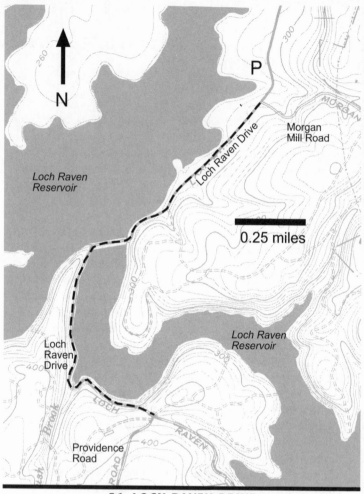

56. LOCH RAVEN DRIVE

Morgan Mill Road, but be sure to obey the signs that prohibit parking in certain places. Only on beautiful spring days does demand exceed parking space supply.

Mornings find Loch Raven Drive in cool shade from the wooded hillside to the east. Most of the trees adjacent to the road are white pines, planted years ago and now grown to a stately maturity. To the west, clumps of trees are interspersed with

The Problem of Whitetail Deer

FOR BALTIMORE-AREA HIKERS, A GOOD LOOK AT A WHITETAIL DEER IS STILL the most memorable part of any ramble in the forest. These appealing animals, the region's largest wild mammal, have become increasingly common over the last half-century. Indeed, an hour's walk in Patapsco Valley or Gunpowder Falls State Parks will invariably turn up one or more whitetails. Hunted almost to the point of extirpation by 1900, deer populations have rebounded with a vengeance, to the point where their numbers pose a real threat to vegetable gardens and automobiles throughout the Baltimore metropolitan area.

As homeowners and drivers are beginning to complain about "too many deer," naturalists and conservation biologists are also beginning to realize that whitetails have a significant and largely undocumented negative effect on the ecology and biodiversity of our forested lands. In areas of high deer populations, foresters have long noted a "browse line," a five-foot-high demarcation below which everything green has disappeared. Only recently, however, has it become clear that seedlings of oaks and other hardwoods are not recruiting into the sapling stage in locations with heavy deer populations. Thus, when a large tree falls and creates a light gap in the forest, there are no smaller trees ready to grow into the breach. Instead, non-native plants and less desirable trees that are not favored by deer colonize the light gap.

High densities of deer also affect the herbaceous flora of forests. Annuals may never become mature enough to set seeds. Perennials like trillium respond to repeated browsings by becoming shorter and producing fewer seeds. Wildflowers in the lily and orchid families are especially sensitive to deer browsing. It has been shown that the herbaceous flora of eastern forests may require more than a century to become reestablished after logging or agricultural abandonment; heavy deer browsing can only lengthen this timeline. Exclosures—large fenced areas that keep deer out—always show increased plant growth, floral diversity, and vegetational structure on the inside.

This change in vegetational structure due to deer browsing has a negative effect on forest songbirds, especially those that nest on the forest floor or in low shrubs. These include some of our best-loved species: ovenbirds, wood thrushes, and several warblers. A study in Shenandoah National Park demonstrated that the abundances of these species correlated positively with vegetational structure, which in turn was dictated by deer density.

Our society continues to be ambivalent about deer and deer management. Many suburbanites object to recreational hunting of deer, citing both safety and ethical concerns. Hunters respond that their sport is the only cost-effective way to keep deer populations in check. But hunting regulations have more to do with appeasing recreational demands than with scientific management for the full spectrum of biological diversity. Only as research reveals the negative effects of high deer populations on forest ecology might both sides be able to reach common ground.

mowed lawns that slope down to the reservoir's edge. The resulting scene is so attractive that painters are often seen here with their easels and brushes. In winter, ducks and other waterbirds frequent the calm waters. Canada geese and several kinds of gulls are visible year-round. On land, woodpeckers, chickadees, cardinals, and nuthatches are the most commonly seen birds.

The bridge over Loch Raven divides this walk roughly in half, with the Providence Road portion being slightly longer. This southern part of Loch Raven Drive borders a narrower arm of the reservoir, which is seen sporadically through a screen of trees. A rocky slope rises on the uphill side, home to a variety of wildflowers in spring. At mile 1.4, the road begins a steady rise uphill that children on bikes and skates will probably want to stay away from. Providence Road marks the top of the hill, at mile 1.7.

Strollers on Loch Raven Drive who are curious to find out what lies up the trail in the nearby forest have two options. The Laurel Woodlands trailhead is marked by a bulletin board just a hundred yards north of the bridge. The Glen Ellen Trail is located at the Providence Road gate. Both trailheads open up an extensive system of backcountry trails that are used by hikers and mountain bikers, and both are described elsewhere in this book.

PRETTYBOY WATERSHED

■ ■

Prettyboy Dam and Prettyboy Reservoir are located in northern Baltimore County on the Big Gunpowder River. The dam is about 20 miles upstream of the upper edge of Loch Raven reservoir, and all water released from Prettyboy is captured by Loch Raven. In fact, no water is drawn from Prettyboy via pipe; the reservoir exists exclusively to keep the Loch Raven pool at optimal levels.

The Big Gunpowder River above Prettyboy Dam drains a fairly small basin that extends into Carroll County and extreme southern Pennsylvania. This area is sparsely populated, with extensive tracts of privately owned farmlands and forests. The streams that drain into Prettyboy have excellent water quality, with high concentrations of oxygen and high biological diversity. As a result, there is little algal growth in the reservoir, and visibility down to twelve feet is routine.

Accordingly, the water released from Prettyboy is of such high quality that it supports a blue-ribbon trout fishery in the Big Gunpowder River. In fact, the river may have the best fishing in the eastern United States that is within an hour's drive of a major metropolitan area. In order to maintain this fishery, Prettyboy continuously releases a minimum amount of water into the river.

Prettyboy reservoir has a capacity of 20 billion gallons, the smallest among the city's three major reservoirs. The reservoir covers 1,500 acres when full and has 46 miles of shoreline.

Baltimore City owns 7,380 acres of land surrounding Prettyboy reservoir. It is virtually all wooded, although several tracts on mostly level uplands were clear-cut about 1990. When gypsy moths arrived in Maryland in the late 1980s, the oak woodlands around Prettyboy were especially hard hit. The areas logged consisted almost entirely of dead trees, killed by gypsy moths.

Eight trails in the Prettyboy watershed are described in this book. All but two are primarily fire roads. These roads are wide enough to drive an emergency vehicle on, but there are occasional trees that have fallen across the trail. Annual vegetation,

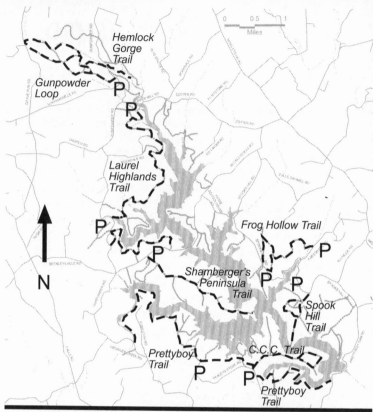

57. PRETTYBOY WATERSHED HIKING TRAILS

like grasses and asters, grows in the bed of many of the fire roads, since foot traffic is light. A number of these trails are quite remote, and it is unusual to see anyone else in the course of a hike.

Most trails at Prettyboy feature lots of up-and-down hiking over fairly steep hills. There are exceptions: the C.C.C. Trail and Shamberger's Peninsula Trail are surprisingly level in a region of dissected topography.

Mountain bike usage of Prettyboy trails is light at present. Riding is permitted on the C.C.C. Trail and parts of the Spook Hill, Laurel Highlands, and Gunpowder Loop Trails. Consult the map for the locations of these trail sections.

For Baltimore hikers, a visit to the Prettyboy watershed is an occasion. Even the closest trail is more than a thirty-minute drive

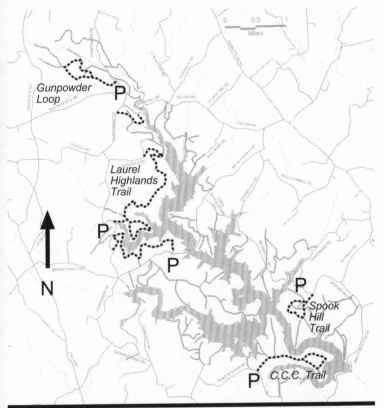

Gunpowder
Loop

Laurel
Highlands
Trail

N

Spook
Hill
Trail

C.C.C. Trail

58. PRETTYBOY WATERSHED MOUNTAIN BIKE ROUTES

north of the Baltimore Beltway. The rural landscape lends a feeling of wildness and solitude that the other two city watersheds do not have. In an ever more crowded metropolitan area, this is an increasingly valuable characteristic. Visit soon!

▼ Prettyboy Trail

Distance: Less than 10 miles

Difficulty: Recommended for experienced, determined hikers only

Directions: From the Baltimore Beltway (I-695), take I-83 north to exit 31, Mt. Carmel Road. Go west on Mt. Carmel Road for 4.0 miles. Turn right on Prettyboy Dam Road. Go 1.0 miles and turn left onto Tracey's Store Road. Proceed 1.2 miles to the trailhead parking lot, at a sharp turn in the road. This trail shares a trailhead with the C.C.C. Trail.

Time is the healer of all things, it's been said, and that seems to include the marks humans leave on the landscape. The Prettyboy Trail is a narrow footpath that is slowly disappearing due to lack of use. Each year, vegetation encroaches a bit more, trees and branches fall across the trail, and heavy rains erode the path. As of this writing, the outermost sections of the Prettyboy Trail are impassable during the growing season, May through October. That's a shame, because much of this trail runs within a few feet of the reservoir shoreline, making it a very attractive place to hike. Only the center section is passable, due in large measure to its location near the more heavily traveled C.C.C. Trail.

The Prettyboy Trail is theoretically about 10.5 miles in length, running from Beckleysville Road on the west to Prettyboy Dam Road on the east. Prettyboy Trail is mostly a footpath, rather than a fire road, and is marked not by blazes but by metal jar lids nailed to trees and painted a light blue.

During the preparation of this book, I found large sections of the Prettyboy Trail so obscure that I cannot recommend it as a hiking destination. Nevertheless, a description of the trail's status is given below, as a general guide for the truly dedicated hiker who finds such paths a challenge. Good luck!

The section of the Prettyboy Trail from Beckleysville Road south to George's Creek Road no longer exists, in part because the George's Creek Road terminus, on the west side of George's Creek, is posted private property. A faint trail is visible on the east side of George's Creek and runs along the water's edge for several miles. Mountain laurel is common and has so overgrown the path that forward progress is difficult. This obscure footpath eventually meets a well-used fire road that ascends to Tracey's Store Road. From Tracey's Store Road east to the C.C.C. Trail parking area, the trail is narrow but marginally passable.

East of the C.C.C. Trail parking area, the Prettyboy Trail is at first pleasant, as it is used by fishermen. But once the trail reaches the edge of the reservoir, it becomes increasingly obscure. Once again, it is mountain laurel "hells" that make hiking difficult. The final mile eastward toward Prettyboy Dam Road has virtually

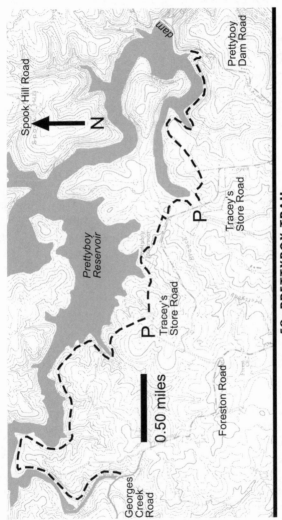

59. PRETTYBOY TRAIL

disappeared. In large measure, this is because there is no access to the east end of the trail; parking is not allowed anywhere along Prettyboy Dam Road.

■■

▼ C.C.C. Trail

Distance: 2.5-mile circuit
Difficulty: Easy

Directions: From the Baltimore Beltway (I-695), take I-83 north to exit 27, Mt. Carmel Road. Go west on Mt. Carmel Road for 4.0 miles. Turn right on Prettyboy Dam Road. Go 1.0 miles and turn left onto Tracey's Store Road. Proceed 1.2 miles to the trailhead parking lot, at a sharp turn in the road.

Among all the federally sponsored work programs that have existed over the years, perhaps none is more fondly remembered than the Civilian Conservation Corps, the C.C.C., instituted during the Depression in the 1930s. Young men were housed in barracks or tent camps and labored to improve parks and other public facilities. Participants built trails, campgrounds, picnic shelters, and rustic park buildings. The fruits of these labors are still visible today in many places.

The C.C.C. Trail on the Prettyboy watershed property is one such remnant of this constructive program. It is short and easy, on a wide roadbed with little elevation change. It is a pleasant stroll through the woods, suitable even for families with small children. In summer, wildflowers line the trail, delighting both the botanist and the casual flower lover.

The trailhead is a large gravel parking area on Tracey's Store Road, located at a sharp left turn in the road. This is a very rural area; only forest and cornfields are visible in every direction. The trail entrance is marked by an orange cable strung between two orange posts.

The trail passes through a fairly young and diverse forest and is wide enough to admit sunlight, which dapples the path at midday. Spur trails branch off to the left (north) at mile 0.5 and 0.6. These trails are pleasant, leading to favorite local fishing spots, and are worth a stroll on the return trip if you still want to do more walking. Continuing on the C.C.C. Trail eastward, a fork is reached at mile 0.8. You may go either way, as this is merely a

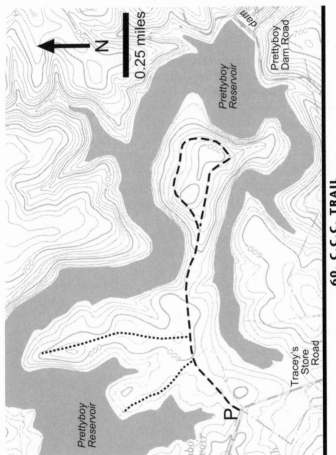

Herbivory and the Chemistry of Green Plants

"BETTER LIVING THROUGH CHEMISTRY," A COMMERCIAL SLOGAN WIDELY adopted in the United States during the past fifty years, reflects our optimism for the brighter future we can create with new and useful chemical compounds. By comparison with green plants, however, we humans are merely children tinkering blindly at the kitchen table with a basic chemistry set. Plants produce a wondrous array of phytochemicals, some of them so complex that they cannot yet be synthesized in a laboratory.

Plants make these exotic chemical compounds for three basic purposes: to deter herbivory by insects, to ward off microbial and fungal infections, and to attract pollinators. Of these three, the broadest spectrum of chemicals is made to discourage insects from feeding.

Among the best-known examples of this group are the cardiac glycosides produced by milkweed plants. This family of related chemicals affects the heart and circulatory system of mammals. While a few kinds of insects, like milkweed bugs and monarch butterfly larvae, have adapted to cardiac glycosides, the presence of these toxins clearly reduces the damage to milkweed leaves by herbivory. Another cardiac glycoside is digitoxin, which has been isolated from foxglove plants and is used in treating human heart disease.

A second well-known naturally occurring phytochemical is nicotine. Nicotine is an extremely effective feeding deterrent for insects; in fact, nicotine sprays are efficacious insecticides. Nicotine is an alkaloid; other alkaloids from plants include caffeine, morphine, codeine, and cocaine. The classes of phytochemicals produced to deter herbivory and used for a variety of purposes by people include tannins, which are used as dyes; saponins, which act as detergents; and coumarins, which inhibit blood clotting.

For centuries, humans have used plant extracts for medicinal purposes. Even today, several major pharmaceutical companies regularly collect vegetation samples from remote corners of the globe and screen the extracts for activity in a variety of assays. Ethnobotanists visit isolated tribal societies to learn traditional medical uses of local plants. About one-third of the drugs in the modern pharmacopeia are derived from plants.

Most of us view plants as sometimes pretty but otherwise rather common and uninteresting members of our planet's biota. Surely, the lives of plants pale in comparison to the endless activity and fascinating behaviors of animals. And yet, plants are in many ways as complex as animals, and certainly so in terms of the chemical compounds they produce. Our lives would be both shorter and less healthy if not for the feeding deterrents plants make to protect themselves from insects and other insults of a harsh and competitive world.

loop that will eventually return you to this point. The route is described, however, as a clockwise circuit.

After bearing left at the fork, the trail passes through a forest with a rich understory of sassafrass, tupelo, and dogwood trees. By late August, the tupelo leaves turn a bright red; it is the first tree in the region to show fall color. The forest canopy is dominated by chestnut oak, the typical tree of ridgetops. These are not yet fully grown. In places, the uncommon wildflower trailing arbutus grows directly in the trail. Arbutus is one of the earliest-blooming wildflowers, putting out modest but sweet-smelling flowers in late March and early April.

As the trail approaches the end of the peninsula, there are glimpses of the reservoir through the trees to the left. However, this is the only view of the water on the C.C.C. Trail, and to reach the level of the reservoir requires a bushwhack through thick brush.

The trail soon begins to curve, eventually returning up the peninsula. The path is less heavily traveled here at its most distant point, and diverse summer wildflowers grow in and along the path. The common names of these plants are a delight: yarrow, Deptford pink, Venus's looking glass, whorled loosestrife, blue-eyed grass, beardtongue, oxeye daisy. Those who gave common names to wildflowers had imaginations as active as the ancients who named the constellations!

At mile 1.7, the loop is complete. Return to the parking area on the first portion of the C.C.C. Trail, arriving after 2.5 miles of walking.

▼ **Shamberger's Peninsula Trail**

Distance: 2.1 miles one way
Difficulty: Easy

Directions: From the Baltimore Beltway (I-695), take I-83 north. Take exit 31, Middletown Road, going in a northwesterly direction. After 4.6 miles on Middletown Road, turn left onto Beckleysville Road. Go 3.0 miles, cross the bridge over the reservoir, and continue another 0.7 miles to the trailhead.

There are very few easy trails on the Prettyboy reservoir watershed. The rolling nature of the landscape here in the central Piedmont ensures that any trail will have a number of changes in elevation. Trails typically drop into a stream-dissected valley, then rise to an upland ridge, only to lead downhill again. Shamberger's Peninsula Trail is one of the two exceptions. This pleasant, shady trail runs straight down the shallow ridge of a low peninsula, gently descending to water level. It is very suitable for families with small children who desire a pleasant stroll through the forest.

Park on the wide shoulder of Beckleysville Road 0.7 miles west of the bridge over Prettyboy. The trail is marked not only by the usual orange posts but also by an old stone plinth. The trail is an old roadbed that once led to Shamberger's grist mill (the remains of which are now submerged under the reservoir). Note how decades of use and erosion have incised the road into the

milkweed seed pods and associated insects

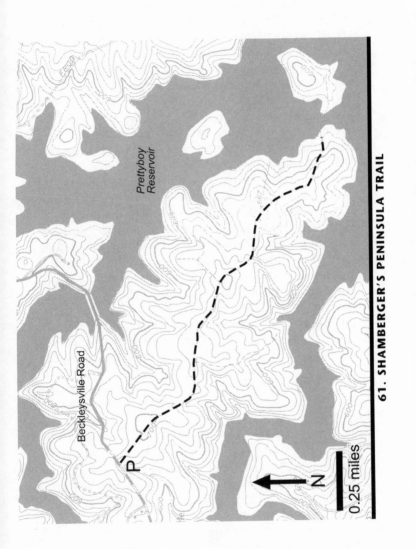

0.25 miles

N

Beckleysville Road

Prettyboy
Reservoir

P

61. SHAMBERGER'S PENINSULA TRAIL

landscape; in places, the surrounding forest is several feet above the level of the roadbed.

The trail runs almost straight, down the spine of the peninsula. Several trails branch off, leading to favorite fishing spots, but all dead end. You may extend your walk by exploring any of these.

The forest surrounding the Shamberger's Peninsula Trail is of mixed age and composition. There are a few exceedingly large trees, purposely left behind during the last cycle of logging to broadcast their seeds and renew the forest. Younger but still large trees include both deciduous hardwoods and evergreens. A few areas feature densely packed red maple saplings. These trees are so close together that no light reaches the forest floor. Competition has not yet thinned this stand of maples, but it soon will; only the largest, those most able to reach sunlight, will persist.

Gaps in the forest border the trail. Look for milkweeds growing in these disturbed places. In late summer, the seedpods break open, releasing to the wind flat, brown seeds borne aloft by white, silken plumes. The stem and leaves of the milkweed plant contain a sticky whitish liquid that discourages grazing insects. Nevertheless, several kinds of insects, including monarch butterfly larvae and milkweed bugs, have adapted to this usually toxic sap. Monarch butterflies accumulate these toxins within their bodies. Predators, like blue jays, who feed on monarchs will get sick and vomit up the insect, and they will thereafter avoid anything that resembles a monarch.

In shady areas along the trail there are dense collections of ferns. The dark green foliage of Christmas fern is evergreen, the only common fern to brighten the forest in winter. The large, lacy ferns are hay-scented fern, perhaps our most common summer fern. Hay-scented fern is deciduous, turning a pale yellow in early autumn and disappearing by Thanksgiving. Ferns are not flowering plants; they disperse spores to the wind each summer. In both species, look for brownish spore-containing sori on the underside of the leaflet tips.

The trail eventually descends modestly to the shores of Prettyboy Reservoir. There are pleasant views to the east, but the vista is not extensive. Return to your car by the same route.

▼ **Laurel Highlands Trail**

Distance: 6.4 miles one way; shorter segments possible
Difficulty: Moderate to strenuous

Directions: From the Baltimore Beltway (I-695), take I-83 north. Take exit 31, Middletown Road, going in a northwesterly direction. After 4.6 miles on Middletown Road, turn left onto Beck-leysville Road. Go 4.4 miles, passing over the reservoir and by the southern terminus of the Laurel Highlands Trail. Turn right onto Gunpowder Road and continue 3.3 miles. Turn right onto Clipper Mill Road, and park by the bridge.

The Laurel Highlands Trail is a hilly and lightly used fire road trail on the west side of Prettyboy Reservoir. It is an excellent trail for hikers looking for a physical challenge. There are occasional views of the reservoir, but the majority of the trail is in a forested setting. Despite its name, there are relatively few mountain laurels along this trail. When these hills are viewed from the waters of Pretty-boy, however, the display of laurel in June is truly breathtaking.

Although the Laurel Highlands Trail can be hiked in either direction, it is described here from north to south.

Parking is available on the west side of the Clipper Mill Road bridge. The trail begins on the south side of the road, marked by the usual orange posts. After rising gradually for 0.4 miles, a T-intersection is reached. Go left; the right fork leads out to Gun-powder Road. At mile 1.0 there are good views of Prettyboy Reservoir, which is very narrow and steep-sided here. Soon, how-ever, the trail turns back into the forest for good. Take care to avoid the well-posted private property at mile 1.3.

The trail continues in a winding fashion, passing a few sunny openings that are now growing up in shrubs, vines, and small trees. Cross Poplar Run at mile 3.5. At the top of the hill another fire road crosses the trail, leading from Gunpowder Road out to a peninsula that juts into the reservoir. Continuing straight, the Laurel Highlands Trail drops downhill, running alongside the marshy delta of Grave Run. In spring this is a good place to listen for the vocalizations of several species of frogs.

Gunpowder Road is reached at mile 4.0. Walk uphill for 0.4 miles on the road shoulder to the next trailhead, marked by an orange guardrail. Upon entering the forest, the roadbed soon be-

N

Clipper Mill Road

0.50 miles

Gun-
powder
Road

Rockdale Road

Gunpowder Road

Pretty-
boy
Reser-
voir

Beckleysville Road

62. LAUREL HIGHLANDS TRAIL

comes covered with a carpet of pine needles. The white pines here have been planted farther apart than is typical on watershed property; more light reaches the forest floor, so there is a well-developed understory. The trail continues over a series of hills for the next 2.0 miles. At the halfway point, Beckleysville Road is visible just 100 yards up a side trail. Various species of ferns line

Poisonous Snakes

IN THE FAST-DEVELOPING REGIONS JUST OUTSIDE METROPOLITAN BALTI-more, poisonous snakes are rarely thought of and almost never encountered. And yet, our rural areas harbor two such species, the copperhead and the timber rattlesnake. Both are shy, reclusive, and uncommon, but nevertheless an interesting part of our native fauna.

Both species are pit vipers, a highly advanced group of snakes that uses heat sensing pits between the eyes and nostrils to sense prey. Both have triangular heads, the shape being created by venom storage sacs in the cheek area. They are the only local snakes with elliptical eye pupils; the pupils narrow to vertical slits in bright sunlight (our nonpoisonous snakes have round pupils). These two features are the best way to distinguish copperheads from the very common and similarly patterned northern water snake.

Copperheads (*Agkistrodon contortrix*) are stout-bodied snakes two to four feet long with a bold, hourglass-shaped crossbanding pattern. They are generally brown to copper to dark brick-red in color. Copperheads are typically found on wooded hillsides with rock outcrops near a stream or pond. Stone walls, piles of old lumber and barns are typical habitats for copperheads in rural areas. In winter, they congregate, sometimes along with rat snakes and timber rattlesnakes, in rocky underground dens that often have an eastern or southern exposure. The same den is used year after year; some have been known for more than a century. Females bear live young in August through early October. The seven-to-ten-inch young snakes are born with fangs and venom, and are soon ready to hunt.

Timber rattlesnakes (*Crotalus horridus*) are exceedingly rare in Baltimore County. Only one den site, near Prettyboy Reservoir, is known, and this is the only place you might encounter a rattler. In addition to the triangular head and elliptical pupils, the hornlike rattles on the tail distinguish the timber rattler. One "button" is added to the rattle each time the snake sheds its skin, about twice a year. However, snakes cannot be aged by the number of rattles, since the endmost ones wear off over time. Timber rattlers are often lighter in color than copperheads, with a pattern that ranges from yellow to brown and gray to black bands.

They may be longer than copperheads, typically averaging three to six feet, and can be quite chunky in the middle. Like the copperhead, rattlers bear live young in late summer to early fall and overwinter in communal den sites. A female takes four to five years to mature, and may live thirty years, at least in captivity.

These two species of pit vipers eat primarily rodents, but they may take lizards, frogs, and large insects. The snake waits along a game trail or runway and strikes, delivering venom through the fangs. The venom paralyzes the prey, which is then eaten whole. The fangs are retracted while eating, but a row of tiny, backward-curving teeth in the jaw aids in grasping the prey.

Both copperheads and rattlesnakes are exceedingly unaggressive toward humans. They will strike only when stongly provoked and will try to back away if they can do so safely. Should you ever encounter one of these handsome creatures, admire them from a distance, but leave them alone to continue their serpentine lives.

this entire portion of the Laurel Highlands trail; they include Christmas, hay-scented, and interrupted ferns. The trail terminates at Beckleysville Road after 6.4 miles. Walk downhill along the road shoulder to the bridge, where there is a large parking area.

▼ Gunpowder Loop

Distance: 3.7-mile circuit
Difficulty: Moderate to strenuous

Directions: From the Baltimore Beltway (I-695), take I-83 north. Take exit 31, Middletown Road, to the west. Go 4.8 miles and turn left onto Beckleysville Road. After 0.3 miles, Beckleysville Road bears left; stay straight, on Cotter Road (presently lacking a road sign). Cotter Road eventually becomes Clipper Mill Road and crosses the Prettyboy Reservoir. Make the first right, onto Gunpowder Road. Go 0.5 miles and park on the wide road shoulder just beyond the Hoffmanville Cemetery.

It seems that the best trails, as a general rule, run alongside streams. Certainly, the increased soil moisture along the riparian buffer encourages a lusher and more diverse flora. And flowing

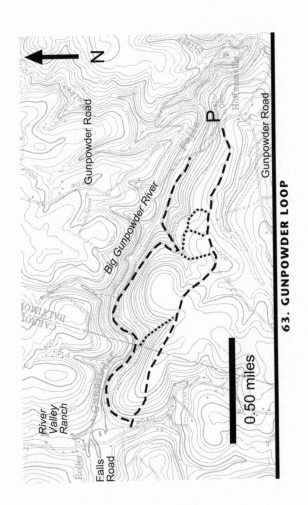

63. GUNPOWDER LOOP

water is nature's air conditioner, cooling every narrow water-course in both summer and winter. Finally, most streams are incised into the terrain, so that surrounding hillsides cast a shade into the valley morning and evening.

The Gunpowder Loop confirms this hypothesis. The outward half runs along a ridge, and is pleasant but unexceptional. In contrast, the return trail runs along the upper reaches of the Big Gunpowder River and is a memorable place to visit. The river is narrow and lively, first dashing over and around small rocks then pooling up into slow stretches. Rocky outcrops lend an Appalachian feel to parts of the trail. Finally, there is a deeply shady section where huge hemlock trees tower over the river.

Begin your hike at the trailhead along Gunpowder Road just a few yards downhill of the Hoffmanville Cemetery. An orange-painted guardrail marks the trail entrance, an old fire road. There is parking for several cars on the wide road shoulder, and more at the bottom of the hill. This first part of the Gunpowder Loop runs along a ridge for 1.5 miles, so elevation changes are minimal. Most of the land it traverses is forested, although in a few places there are views across privately owned agricultural fields.

The upland forest here has some older, larger trees, but there are many with diameters of less than eight inches, indicating that the area was selectively logged within the past 40 years. Interestingly, a few young chestnut trees are found scattered throughout this forest. Until seventy years ago, chestnuts were a dominant species in eastern forests. However, a fungal disease, chestnut blight, decimated the species in the 1930s. Young saplings continue to sprout from old roots and stumps, but the fungus lives on in the old roots, and new growth will be killed by the blight within about twenty years of sprouting.

In this first 1.5 miles, several trails and fire roads branch to the right. All lead downhill to the river, so avoid them and stick to the ridgetop. The fire road eventually ends, and a foottrail leads steeply downhill for about 300 yards to what maps identify as Grave Run Road but which is marked with a sign as Falls Road. The return portion of the Gunpowder Loop begins a few yards before the trail reaches the road. However, you may want to walk a short distance down Grave Run Road / Falls Road to visit River Valley Ranch. A youth camp dressed up as a western town, River Valley Ranch is an interesting and nostalgic attraction.

Return to the trail, enter the forest from the road, and bear left, downhill. The first 0.1 mile is narrow, rocky, and well churned by the hooves of horses from the ranch, but the footing improves when the trail reaches the fire road paralleling the Big Gunpowder River. Here, in the sheltered valley, the trees are large and the vegetation lush. There is a good assortment of spring and summer wildflowers; among the most common are cranesbill and jewelweed. There are plenty of Christmas and hay-scented ferns here as well.

At mile 2.4, the fire road begins to ascend a long hill to the ridgetop. Adventurous hikers, however, should take the obscure foottrail that runs along the river. Because this trail is very lightly used by hikers, and not at all by equestrians, it is very overgrown. There are dozens of trees down across the trail, flourishing gardens of poison ivy, exuberant growths of thorned shrubs like multiflora rose and various berries, and plenty of mud. There is even a deep stream to cross, just narrow enough to invite a vigorous, long jump but just wide enough to make success unlikely. The reward for all this hardship comes in some beautiful rock cliffs and outcrops, very good views of the river, and plenty of bird life. The impression is one of some obscure stream in West Virginia, not the Piedmont of rural Baltimore County.

After 0.3 miles of this sort of masochistic fun, the dry ground of another fire road is attained. Leaving the river, the trail ascends gradually to a point about halfway up to the ridgetop. At each of two trail intersections, bear left; the goal is to descend to river level. This trail soon drops downhill along a hemlock-shaded stream. When the Gunpowder River comes into sight, the trail bears right to parallel the river. Gunpowder Road is reached after a walk of 3.7 miles. Walk uphill along the road shoulder to your car.

If you are hiking in this area, be sure to visit Hemlock Gorge (described next), the trailhead of which is only a hundred yards from the terminus of the Gunpowder Loop Trail. The foottrail to Hemlock Gorge is on the opposite, downstream side of the Gunpowder Road bridge.

▼ **Hemlock Gorge Trail**

Distance: Approximately 0.5 miles one way
Difficulty: Easy to moderate

Directions: From the Baltimore Beltway (I-695), take I-83 north. Take exit 31, Middletown Road, to the west. Go 4.8 miles and turn left onto Beckleysville Road. After 0.3 miles, Beckleysville Road bears left; stay straight, on Cotter Road (presently lacking a road sign). Cotter Road eventually becomes Clipper Mill Road and crosses the Prettyboy Reservoir. Make the first right, onto Gunpowder Road. Go 0.7 miles and park on the wide road shoulder just beyond the bridge over the Gunpowder River.

The forest primeval: shafts of sunlight slant through the branches of giant hemlocks, illuminating the swirling mists above the river. The water slips over rocks with hardly a sound, carrying the crimson leaf of a maple toward the sea. The morning quiet is broken only by the rattle of a kingfisher sweeping up the river, a small fish clasped tightly in her bill. There is no evidence of humankind, and the scene is at once peaceful and timeless. Every hiker wants to find such a special place, where beauty and solitude promote contemplation and serenity.

Such a place exists, even in Baltimore County. Hemlock Gorge, on the Big Gunpowder River upstream of Prettyboy Reservoir, is a tiny slice of Appalachia far from the mountains. Deeply incised into the surrounding landscape, the rocky gorge of the Gunpowder is lined by the trail's namesake hemlock trees, some of which are hundreds of years old. Given the scenic beauty of this trail, it is surprising how lightly it is used. When you visit such a pristine surrounding, be sure to haul out any trash you create; and if others have not been as respectful, you might take their debris as well. Minimize your impact on the fragile soils by staying on the trail and avoiding slopes where erosion is likely. The greatest threat to beautiful places like Hemlock Gorge is that they will be loved to death by too many of us.

After parking along the shoulder of Gunpowder Road just beyond the bridge, walk down the wide grassy shoulder onto the floodplain. Within a few yards of the river, turn left, downstream, on a narrow footpath. For about 100 yards, this level path traverses a thick growth of riparian vegetation. There is a wide diversity of wildflowers in spring and again in late summer, and butterflies feed on the blossoms of tickseed sunflower and Joe Pye weed. Especially common is a small tree, witch hazel, from which a popular liniment is extracted. Witch hazels are unique, because

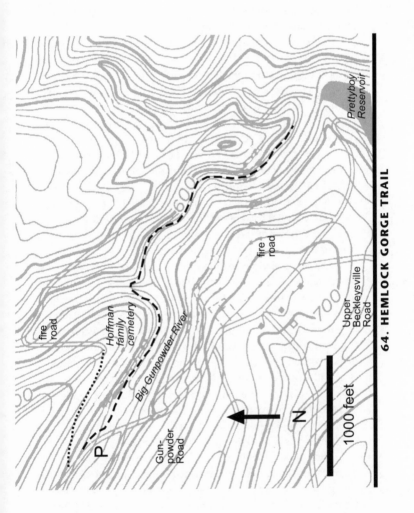

N

1000 feet

Prettyboy
Reservoir

fire
road

Upper
Beckleysville
Road

fire
road

Hoffman
family
cemetery

Big Gunpowder River

Gun-
powder
Road

P

they flower in the fall, and their stringy yellow petals brighten the November forest after all the leaves have dropped.

The landscape and vegetation soon change. As the valley walls steepen and draw close to the water, hemlock trees begin to dominate, and they soon form a monoculture. Their dense shade precludes anything else from growing on the forest floor, so it is possible to see a long way through the forest. In addition, hemlocks self-prune, because the lower branches are shaded by upper ones, dropping their needles to enrich the duff on the forest floor. Indeed, the thick, spongy soil here is well-drained but holds in the underlying moisture, much as a mulch does. Soil compaction by heavy use affects soil structure and function, which is one reason walking off the trail can have a negative impact.

A few of the hemlocks are very large, with diameters of more than four feet. These giants are probably more than 300 years old. There are also hemlocks of lesser stature, and many thin young trees. Lumbering probably took place long ago in Hemlock Gorge, but at least not every tree was taken. Uphill from the trail, there are faint traces of several old wagon roads, probably used to haul out the trees or in mining.

The other obvious feature of the landscape is the many exposed rock outcrops. Although the rock itself is not green in color, it could easily be called greenstone, because mosses and lichens grow on every surface. These simple and commonplace plants are important to the ecology of any landscape. They secrete acids that, over time, slowly dissolve the rock into its constituent minerals, eventually creating soil for the growth of higher plants.

Within another hundred yards, the trail crosses a side stream. Beyond this point, the path becomes more difficult to walk, as you clamber over rocks and through a slalom course of trees. The river is now much lower than the trail, and the high perspective gives great views of the photogenic valley.

After about a half-mile of travel, the valley widens just enough to create a small alluvial floodplain, and the slopes become less steep. The floodplain is often overgrown with vegetation, and most hikers turn around at this point and retrace their steps.

Upon your return to Gunpowder Road, there is another short walk in the immediate area that is well worth the time and effort. Adjacent to the road shoulder parking area is a fire road marked by orange posts. It leads steadily uphill for more than a quarter-mile to a ridge above Hemlock Gorge. Atop this narrow, stony ridge is the Hoffman family cemetery, with headstones dating back to the 1700s. William Hoffman, a German immigrant, settled this area near the start of the Revolutionary War and constructed Maryland's first paper mill on the Gunpowder just downstream of Hemlock Gorge. The little cemetery is a peaceful place, but digging graves in the rocky soil must have been quite a task!

▼ **Frog Hollow Trail**

Distance: 1.8 miles one way; a shorter loop possible
Difficulty: Easy to moderate

Directions: From the Baltimore Beltway (I-695), take I-83 north to exit 31, Middletown Road. Go west on Middletown Road for 0.6 miles and turn left onto Molesworth Road. After 0.7 miles, turn right onto Armacost Road. Go 0.6 miles to the end and turn right onto Spook Hill Road. Proceed 3.0 miles and park at the second trailhead on the right. (Spook Hill Road becomes Frog Hollow Road.)

Frog Hollow: the name conjures up some of our fondest memories from childhood. How many of us spent happy days getting muddy and wet chasing after elusive amphibians in some nearby swamp. It seems like every locale has its own "frog hollow," and the Prettyboy watershed is no exception. A narrow cove of the reservoir gives way in its upstream end to a shallow marsh, fed by a small stream with wet, swampy edges. Each spring, as early as March, wood frogs, spring peepers, and American toads make their way from nearby hillside estivation sites to the marsh. There, the males set up territories and call to attract females. The resulting cacophony can be deafening on warm, rainy spring nights.

The amphibian breeding season is short, spanning no more than two months of intensive activity, but the Frog Hollow Trail is suitable for a pleasant hike year-round. Despite its name, almost all of this trail is on upland, forested paths; only the final few yards traverse Frog Hollow. For those with very limited time or small children, a 1.1-mile loop trail that has only minor changes in elevation can be chosen.

Begin either walk from the trailhead on Frog Hollow Road.

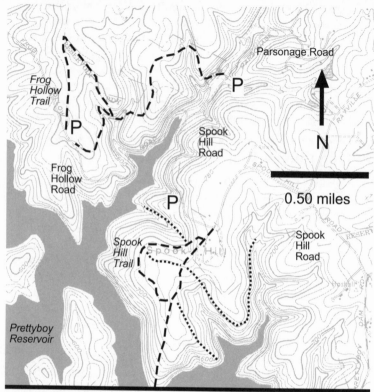

Parsonage Road

Frog
Hollow
Trail

P

Spook
Hill
Road

N

Frog
Hollow
Road

0.50 miles

P

Spook
Hill
Road

Spook
Hill
Trail

Prettyboy
Reservoir

65. FROG HOLLOW TRAIL / SPOOK HILL TRAIL

As you drive northwest on this road out of the low point of Frog Hollow, the trailhead described is the second set of orange posts on the right, just beyond the crest of the hill.

The fire road is initially level and straight for a quarter-mile. At a trail intersection, turn right; going straight eventually reaches a dead end at private property. This portion of the trail, along a dry ridgetop, is shaded by large oaks with an open forest floor. As the trail heads downhill, the forest becomes more lush with vegetation. At mile 0.6, next to a small stream, another trail intersection is reached. Turning right and crossing the stream will return you to Frog Hollow Road at the first set of orange posts after a circuit of 1.1 miles. This is the good alternative walk for families with small children.

The Frog Hollow Trail continues straight from this intersection, downhill. Another small creek is crossed at mile 0.8. As the trail rises steeply up the far slope, notice that the appearance of the forest has changed. This portion of the watershed was logged about thirty years ago, so the trees are less than thirty feet in height, only a few inches in diameter, and are tightly packed. Another fifty years of growth will thin out the less competitive trees, and the forest will assume a more familiar appearance, like that on the near side of the creek.

Another quarter-mile of uphill walking achieves the crest. A spur trail to the right merely goes out to a dead end, so continue straight on the main fire road. The trail soon begins a long descent into Frog Hollow, which is reached at mile 1.8. Cross the small creek, which is lined by willows, jewelweed, and other water-loving plant species. Parsonage Road is just beyond the far side of the creek. There is a gravel pullout here with parking for six to eight cars. You can return to your vehicle by retracing your steps on the Frog Hollow Trail, by walking the road shoulder for 1.4 miles, or you can have left a shuttle vehicle at Parsonage Road.

▼ **Spook Hill Trail**

Distance: 3.1-mile circuit, with several spur trails
Difficulty: Easy to moderate

Directions: From the Baltimore Beltway (I-695), take I-83 north to exit 31, Middletown Road. Go west on Middletown Road for 0.6 miles and turn left onto Molesworth Road. Drive 0.7 miles and turn right onto Armacost Road. Go 0.6 miles to the end and turn right onto Spook Hill Road. Continue for 1.6 miles and park at a large gravel pullout part way down the hill.

Northern Baltimore County is sparsely populated in places, and some spots can be isolated, but ghosts? Sorry, there's nothing really spooky about the Spook Hill Trail. The area is supposed to have been named for a number of oddly shaped trees in the vicinity and for the weird night noises emanating from the hollows. The eerie sounds at night were merely the calls of breeding frogs and toads, and the crooked trees are no longer obvious, but the unusual place name has stuck.

This trail is a fairly short circuit near the ridgetop, with several spur trails leading downhill to Prettyboy Reservoir. There are several open meadows where wildflowers abound and summer butterflies feed on their nectar. A walk here is a pleasant, but never spooky, affair.

The nearest and most convenient parking is a half-mile from the trailhead on Spook Hill Road, but do not be discouraged if that seems far away. Most of the walk to watershed property is on a quiet country road in a forested setting and is quite pleasant. Park at a wide, graveled pullout part way down a long hill. Walk uphill for 0.35 miles, passing a fire road gate that merely leads directly to the reservoir. Turn right on an unpaved driveway, walking past four houses, to the trailhead, marked by an orange cable strung between two orange posts.

This trail is described as a clockwise circuit, so walk past the fire road that comes in from the right after only 50 yards of walking. The trail continues straight and soon reaches the top of Spook Hill, at mile 0.65. A large meadow, about 100 yards in diameter, crowns the hill. By late summer, a wide variety of wildflowers grow waist-high. Goldenrods are everywhere, and Queen Anne's lace is common. One of our prettiest wildflowers, rose pink, can be found here. It has pink petals with yellow eyes and conspicuous yellow stamens. Two members of the mint family can also be seen: mountain mint, perhaps the most fragrant mint, and self-heals-and-heals-all, a small but very common purple-flowered mint.

Why are all these meadow wildflowers here? A look at the surrounding trees gives a clue. Most of them are less than thirty feet in height, and they are packed to a density that precludes light from the forest floor. The absence of any large trees and the uniform age of those present indicate that Spook Hill was logged by clear-cutting about thirty years ago. Indeed, the stumps of large trees can still be seen. Since then, whatever plant seeds remained in the soil, or were transported here by wind or animal, have germinated and grown. Fast-growing herbaceous plants dominate a clear-cut during the first five years or so, but when slower-growing shrubs and small trees get large enough, they shade out the annuals and ruderals. Eventually trees that grow tall enough fast enough will shade out those that do not, and the density of trees becomes reduced as the size of individual trees increases. The trees on Spook Hill are growing, but the grove has not yet been thinned by competition. Areas like meadows that have no trees are due to occasional mowing.

Black Bears in Baltimore County

HERE IN MARYLAND, WE ASSOCIATE BLACK BEARS, MORE THAN ANY OTHER animal, with wild landscapes. The species was almost extirpated in Maryland by about 1960; fewer than a dozen survived at that time, all in the most remote areas of Garrett County. Since then, however, the population has rebounded, due to immigration from Pennsylvania and West Virginia and a high rate of reproduction among breeding females. Habitat continues to improve as well; protected forests are becoming more mature, providing greater mast production and a wider diversity of food plants. In 2001, there are probably several hundred black bears in Maryland. Most of these animals reside in the mountains of Garrett and Allegany Counties; most of the remainder live along the forested ridges of the Catoctin and Blue Ridge mountains.

Once every few years, there are reports of a black bear's being sighted in Baltimore County. These are almost always wandering juveniles in search of suitable territory. Black bear cubs are born in the winter and stay with their mother for more than a year. Eventually, however, the mother will drive off the yearling so that she can breed again. If nearby territories are all occupied by adult bears, the juvenile will have to travel great distances to find his or her own territory, and may wander into human-dominated landscapes like those in Baltimore County.

black bear

Most of these juvenile bears don't last long. Some are killed in collisions with motor vehicles, and others may die of starvation or disease. If the habitat is of marginal quality, they may linger briefly, then continue on, never to be seen again. The Owings Mills bear of 1999 and the Arundel Mills bear of 2000 were sighted frequently for a few weeks, and then disappeared.

An exception to this pattern occurred beginning in 2000. A large adult black bear has been sighted near Spook Hill on the Prettyboy Reservoir watershed property. This is no inexperienced juvenile, lost and confused, but a prime male in peak form. The rugged terrain and sparsely settled landscape provide a suitable refuge from constant human encounters, while the surrounding cornfields and bird feeders supplement the bear's normal diet of wild foods. The Prettyboy bear seems likely to stay. If a female happens to wander by during breeding season, these two may found a population of Baltimore County bears. Our landscape would be the richer if its largest mammal were restored, and hiking would be all the more exciting!

Although you will be continuing straight on the main fire road, two others branch off. The left fire road goes for 1.0 miles into a stream valley, but then dead ends. The fire road to the right merely short-circuits the loop. Therefore, continue straight. At mile 0.8, in a second small meadow, two spur fire roads lead downhill, while the loop bears sharply right. The right spur is well worth a visit. It drops steadily but not steeply downhill for 0.5 miles to the edge of the reservoir at a large rock outcrop. There are good views in three directions over the narrow waters of Prettyboy. The water of the reservoir is crystal clear, and rocks on the bottom fifteen feet down are easily seen. This is a good place for the esoteric sport of fishwatching. In May, the many mountain laurels in bloom on the far hillside make a fine display.

Return 0.5 miles uphill to the main loop, and turn left, west. The trail is less well used at this point; it continues with little change in elevation around Spook Hill. Several side trails appear, the remains of old logging roads; stick to what looks like the widest and most used trail. The fire road eventually reaches a T-intersection at mile 2.6. To the left, the orange cable of the trailhead is visible. Return to your car, after 3.1 miles of walking.

INDEX